TO CATCH A SPY

THE ART OF COUNTERINTELLIGENCE

JAMES M. OLSON

Former Chief
of CIA Counterintelligence

GEORGETOWN UNIVERSITY PRESS / WASHINGTON, DC

Library of Congress Cataloging-in-Publication Data
Names: Olson, James M., 1941- author.
Title: To catch a spy : the art of counterintelligence / James M. Olson.
Description: Washington, DC : Georgetown University Press, 2019. | Includes bibliographical references and index.
Identifiers: LCCN 2018043578 (print) | LCCN 2018046471 (ebook) | ISBN 9781626166806 (hardcover : alk. paper) | ISBN 9781626166813 (ebook)
Subjects: LCSH: Intelligence service—United States. | Espionage—United States. | Spies—United States. | Intelligence service—China. | Espionage, Chinese—United States. | Intelligence service—Russia (Federation) | Espionage, Russian—United States. | Intelligence service—Cuba. | Espionage, Cuban—United States.
Classification: LCC UB271.U5 (ebook) | LCC UB271.U5 O47 2019 (print) | DDC 327.1273—dc23
LC record available at https://lccn.loc.gov/2018043578

♾ This book is printed on acid-free paper meeting the requirements of the American National Standard for Permanence in Paper for Printed Library Materials.

20 19 9 8 7 6 5 4 3 2 First printing

Printed in the United States of America.

Jacket design by Faceout Studio, Tim Green. Cover image by tunart / iStock by Getty Images.

To my students at the Bush School of Government and Public Service
of Texas A&M University who inspire me every day
with their dedication and commitment to serving our country.

CONTENTS

ACKNOWLEDGMENTS

My sincerest thanks go first to the Central Intelligence Agency (CIA) for assigning me to the brand new Bush School of Government and Public Service at Texas A&M University in 1998 to assist in developing a graduate program in intelligence studies. I was part of the CIA's Officer in Residence program, which had for its purpose to send experienced CIA officers to various universities at their request to promote the teaching of intelligence as an academic discipline. My assignment was for two years, after which I was expected to return to Washington for a new job in clandestine operations. It did not work out that way. My wife, Meredith, and I quickly grew to love the Bush School, Texas A&M, the students, the faculty, the community, and our many new friends. When the time came for us to return to Washington, we were deeply conflicted. I was being offered a nice job in the Directorate of Operations at headquarters, but I had by then discovered that I had a passion for teaching. Meredith, who had also worked at the CIA, was in nursing school and was looking forward to launching her second career here. I felt guilty about not going back, but Meredith finally convinced me that I could do more good for our country by staying here and preparing the next generation of national security public servants than I could by sitting at a desk in Washington.

I owe a deep debt of gratitude also to the faculty and staff of the Bush School, who accepted this non-PhD "practitioner" spy guy into their school and patiently taught him the ropes of academia. I would be remiss in not singling out for special thanks the first dean of the Bush School, Dr. Charles Hermann, who took me under his wing and gave me his full support. He is still on the faculty of the Bush School. Chuck and his wife, Lorraine, are Meredith's and my closest friends here, and we will be forever grateful to them for their many kindnesses to us.

The manuscript for this book was reviewed and approved by the

Publications Review Board (PRB) of the CIA before anyone else, including the publisher, could see it. I am favorably impressed by the fairness and professionalism of the CIA's review process. The PRB ensures that nothing I write reveals classified information or puts past, present, or future operations in jeopardy. All CIA officers sign a legally binding lifetime secrecy agreement when they enter on duty. This book is a summation of my many years in counterintelligence, specifically my recommendations on how US counterintelligence can be improved and how the costly mistakes of the past can be avoided. I do not speak for the CIA or any other government agency; my views are strictly personal and should be regarded as such.

My agent, Sam Dorrance, guided me through each stage of the editing, negotiating, and publishing process, thereby freeing me to concentrate on my writing. Sam is a real pro, and I feel very fortunate to have had the chance to work with him. Thank you, Sam.

I would also like to acknowledge the invaluable contributions of my students Andrew Domel, Jessica Koloini, Cassidy Dobbins, Sean Danielson, and Adreanna Scribner, who did intensive counterintelligence study under my direction and allowed me to use their research in the writing of this book. They saved me countless hours and unearthed details I would have missed without their help. I hope my students know how proud I am of them. Fine things are in store for all of them.

Finally, I could not have done what I did in my spying and teaching careers without the constant love and support of my wife, Meredith; my sons, Jeremy and Joshua; and my daughter, Hillary. I love them more than words can express. And on top of everything else, our three children have given Meredith and me *eleven* grandchildren: Simeon, Ruby, Stuart, Amelia, Bridget, Benjamin, Patrick, Gideon, Chiri, Jasper, and Josephine. They are the joy of our life.

INTRODUCTION

Treachery! Seek it out.

—William Shakespeare, *Hamlet*

Few Americans realize the extent to which foreign intelligence services are stealing our most important secrets, right here at home, right under our noses. America is hemorrhaging its vital secrets and sensitive technology, and we are not doing nearly enough to stop it. How many more traitors like Clyde Lee Conrad, Jonathan Pollard, Chi Mak, Edward Lee Howard, and Ana Montes do we need before we begin to take betrayal from within more seriously? How can we sit idly by and watch the US Office of Personnel Management database be breached, almost certainly by China, and not do more to hold those responsible accountable and to prevent future attacks?

Counterintelligence (CI) consists of all the measures a nation takes to protect its citizens, secrets, and technology from foreign spies. It is axiomatic in CI that there are friendly countries, but there are no friendly intelligence services. With only a handful of exceptions, everyone spies on everyone else, friends and foes alike. Over eighty foreign countries—that we know of—either have successfully spied against the United States or have attempted to spy against us. That list, of course, includes countries that are at least nominally considered our friends. Even our good friends the Israelis risked our special relationship by running the American spy Jonathan Pollard against us in 1984 and 1985. We Americans, however, should not express our outrage too vehemently or try to take the high moral ground, because the Israeli military intelligence officer Yosi Amit was convicted of spying against Israel on behalf of the US Central Intelligence Agency (CIA) in 1987. The fact that everybody does it should not make it acceptable, since our concern is the harm being done to *us*. We are losing the espionage wars, and it is time for us to tighten our counterintelligence.

The three most aggressive and damaging culprits currently undermining US national security are China, Russia, and Cuba. I will be singling them out for separate discussion and analysis in later chapters. What these three countries are doing in terms of espionage and covert action inside the United States is outrageous and must be stopped. At no time in my career have I considered the challenges for US counterintelligence greater than they are right now. I wish I could personally reenter the battle, but short of that I derive great satisfaction in teaching courses on intelligence and counterintelligence at the Bush School of Government and Public Service at Texas A&M University to the next generation of intelligence professionals. Nothing brightens my day more than to hear back from former students about the exciting and important work they are doing in keeping our country safer. Perhaps the best example of that was when one of my former students, now a Federal Bureau of Investigation (FBI) special agent doing foreign counterintelligence work, sent me this message: "Professor Olson, I thought you might be interested in knowing that I was the lead FBI investigator for the Kendall and Gwendolyn Myers case. And there's more, Mr. Olson. I personally put the cuffs on them!"[1] Way to go!

Several years ago, I wrote an article for the CIA's professional journal *Studies in Intelligence* titled "The Ten Commandments of Counterintelligence."[2] I consider these guidelines for counterintelligence professionals as valid today as when I wrote them, but in light of subsequent events, I believe they need expansion. I propose to reexamine each of these ten commandments and to add some corollaries that have surfaced in several recent counterintelligence cases. My hope is that this review of counterintelligence principles and methodologies will be of value not only to professionals in the field but also to any US government official or classified contractor responsible for safeguarding our country's sensitive secrets and technology. Finally, I believe that a better informed and alert public can play a valuable role in spotting anomalous behaviors that have counterintelligence implications and in notifying the appropriate authorities.

A certain amount of theory and doctrine is good, but the crux of counterintelligence is in the specifics. It may be a by-product of my legal education that I have become a strong proponent of the case study method of teaching.[3] In my intelligence classes, I rely heavily on actual espionage cases to teach the principles, tradecraft, and ethics of intelligence. I have found this to be a particularly effective technique in teaching counterintelligence. In my book *Fair Play: The Moral Dilemmas of Spying*, I used fifty morally questionable "scenarios" from the world of spying to highlight the murky ethical landscape of modern intelligence operations.[4] I will do something similar here. By examining the specifics of several different spy cases, I believe the reader can appreciate better the complexities and nuances of contemporary spy catching. It is not an easy task, because counterintelligence is extremely hard to do. I sometimes refer to it in my classes as "playing eight-dimensional chess against the best minds of other countries' intelligence services." James Jesus Angleton, the legendary chief of counterintelligence at the CIA from 1954 to 1974, described counterintelligence as "a wilderness of mirrors" that produces "an ever-fluid landscape where fact and illusion merge." He was right.

Counterintelligence can be an excruciatingly frustrating profession. You lose when you win. You feel good about uncovering spies in our midst, but you are then inevitably hit with the cutting follow-up questions: How could you let that happen? Wasn't it your job to prevent things like that? What took you so long? It is perfectly understandable to me that when Robert Hanssen, the arrogant FBI spy for the Russians, was arrested by the FBI on February 18, 2001, he chose to deliver to his arresting team what he thought would be the ultimate CI insult: "What took you so long?"

So why do we do it? First, counterintelligence is the most demanding of all the intelligence disciplines, and many of our brightest men and women in national security careers welcome such a challenge. Counterintelligence never fails to stimulate the mind. It appeals to people who love solving puzzles, unraveling knots, and navigating labyrinths. There is also an inherent beauty in dedicating one's life to catching American spies and traitors and to foiling the machinations of our devious adversaries. I had the honor of spending much of my CIA career as a spy catcher and can state categorically that nothing in intelligence work compares to the ecstasy one feels in breaking a big CI case.

That brings me to a not inconsequential benefit of being a counterintelligence professional: you join a very special club. I worked with many fine people in my lengthy intelligence career, and I have tremendous respect and admiration for them. But CI professionals are a breed apart. We feel a natural affinity for one another. We know how frustrating and thankless our chosen profession is and how dangerous a steady diet of conspiracy and doublethink can be to our mental health. Still, we buckle up and march on. We get the job done. My best friends in the intelligence community were my CI colleagues. It made no difference to me if they were CIA, FBI, military, or any of the other constituent members of the director of national intelligence (DNI) community. We are the same people. We are brothers and sisters.

I salute the fine men and women who are in CI careers now—and I encourage those of you out there now who aspire to join us one day to follow your dream. As a practitioner and teacher of intelligence, I have had the luxury of studying and reflecting on what constitutes good counterintelligence. I believe we can do it a lot better than we are now. We need reinforcements. Come join us. This book, for what it is worth, is my modest effort to contribute to the dialogue by offering my thoughts and recommendations on how to improve the art of counterintelligence. I do not pretend to have a monopoly on CI wisdom, but I hope my many years in the business will translate into some useful observations.

ONE
China

> We have not yet begun to consider Red China espionage as a serious menace to our security in the U.S., though in the years to come it may well become a formidable instrument for spying and subversion.
>
> —Allen Dulles, *The Craft of Intelligence*, 1965

If I were to start my CIA career all over again, I would try to get into our China program, learn Mandarin, and become a Chinese counterintelligence specialist. China is without question the number one counterintelligence threat facing the United States. I do not know a single counterintelligence expert anywhere who will say anything different. The Chinese are mounting a massive espionage, cyber, and covert action assault on the United States. Their goal is to catch up with the United States technologically, militarily, and economically as quickly as possible. If the American people fully understood the audacity and effectiveness of this campaign, they would be outraged and would demand action. Our top priority in US counterintelligence today—and into the future—must be to stop or to drastically curtail China's spying.

The Chinese have always been adept at espionage. In the early years of Chinese communism, the Russians provided intelligence training and material support to their struggling comrades. The Sino-Soviet split put an end to this cooperation, so beginning in the 1960s, Chinese intelligence has been on its own. By the 1970s China had emerged as a world-class intelligence power and had decided that spying, especially commercial and industrial spying, was the fastest and cheapest way to build economic and military strength.

The vast Chinese intelligence apparatus was restructured in 2015 and 2016. The principal Chinese external intelligence service is the Ministry of State Security (MSS), which is responsible for overseas espionage operations. The Ministry of Public Security (MPS) concentrates on domestic activities but also occasionally runs agents abroad. The MSS and MPS were relatively unaffected by the recent organizational changes in the Chinese intelligence community. The major impact has been on the People's Liberation Army (PLA), which since the 1950s has been heavily engaged in intelligence operations. While in theory the PLA has concentrated on *military* intelligence, it has defined its role broadly and has competed with the MSS in a wide range of economic, political, and technological intelligence collection operations overseas, in addition to its more traditional military targeting. The PLA has been responsible for the bulk of China's cyber spying, but there are indications that the MSS has been assigned an expanded role in this area as well. Oversight of the PLA's technical intelligence capabilities (including cyber, signals, and imagery intelligence) resides with the new Strategic Support Force under the Central Military Commission. The PLA's human intelligence (HUMINT) operations are managed by the new Joint Staff Department, which likewise comes under the Central Military Commission. The previous breakdown of the PLA into intelligence departments, familiar to a whole generation of American intelligence officers, has been eliminated. There is no longer a 2PLA responsible for human intelligence, a 3PLA responsible for cyber operations and signals intelligence, or a 4PLA responsible for electronic warfare. These functions remain but have been rolled into the new structure.

The MSS and PLA make regular use of diplomatic, commercial, journalistic, and student covers for their operations in the United States. They aggressively use Chinese travelers to the US, especially business representatives, academics, scientists, students, and tourists, to supplement their intelligence collection. US intelligence experts have been amazed at how voracious the Chinese have been in their collection activity. They take a vacuum cleaner approach and scoop up literally any kind of data they can get their hands on.

The question of Chinese students in the US is especially pertinent. According to Statista, in 2016–17 there were 350,755 Chinese nationals studying at US colleges and universities, accounting for approximately one-third of the total of international students in our country. A large majority of the Chinese students are studying science or engineering, fields that have direct relevance to China's industrial and military aspirations.

Many Chinese students are encouraged by Chinese intelligence to remain in the US, to obtain employment, and to acquire lawful permanent resident status. Lawful permanent residents can apply for US citizenship after five years of residence, three years if they are married to a US citizen. Naturalized US citizens are eligible for US government security clearances after five years of citizenship. This length of time is a trade-off between our need for certain skills—particularly technical skills—and security. Any intelligence service worthy of the name would jump at the chance to infiltrate its officers or co-optees into the government agencies, national laboratories, and high technology firms of a priority target country.[1] We have no numbers, of course, but it is inconceivable to me that the MSS and PLA would have overlooked this enticing and easily exploitable path to access.

The enormity of the Chinese espionage effort is staggering. And it is getting worse. The FBI announced in 2015 that it had seen a 53 percent increase in economic espionage against US companies over the previous year, most of it from China. The FBI does a fine job of briefing US high technology firms on the nature of the threat, but it admits that Chinese spying is so pervasive and relentless that US companies remain extremely vulnerable.

The MSS and PLA primarily play the ethnic card in their recruitment operations. They target the large numbers of ethnic Chinese—the so-called overseas Chinese—who live in the United States and virtually every other country in the world. The number of ethnic Chinese in the United States is approximately four million, and many of them are only a generation or less from the mainland. Large numbers of them still have relatives in Communist China, and lots of them, quite understandably, feel pride and sympathy for the culture and accomplishments of China, particularly the great achievements and buildup of economic and military strength under Mao and his successors. The common tactic is to play on loyalty to Mother China and to exert pressure via relatives still living in China. A Chinese American working in the US government or in a high-tech firm would usually be approached on that basis. Not to be discounted, however, is that venality and greed can also play a large role in any recruitment of a spy. All Americans who visit China, but particularly Chinese Americans, are assessed as potential recruitment targets—and those who have access and show susceptibility are singled out for aggressive development.

Does it work? You bet it does. We can assume that many of these approaches are rebuffed, but here is just a quick partial listing of Chinese Americans who have fallen into this trap:

- *Lt. Cdr. Edward C. Lin*, US Navy, a signals intelligence specialist on the navy's Lockheed Martin P-3E reconnaissance aircraft, was accused of giving classified US military information to China; he was sentenced to six years in prison.
- *Szuhsiung Ho*, a nuclear engineer at the Tennessee Valley Authority, was accused of recruiting at least six other American engineers to pass sensitive US nuclear technology to China; he was sentenced to two years in prison and fined $20,000.
- *Peter Lee*, a physicist at Los Alamos National Laboratory and TRW, was accused of passing microwave submarine-detection technology and other classified defense information to China; he was sentenced to one year in a halfway house.
- *Chi Mak*, an engineer working for Power Paragon in California, was accused of passing to China highly classified information on US Navy surface ships and submarines; he was sentenced to twenty-four years in prison.[2]
- *Fe Yei*, a Silicon Valley engineer, was accused of stealing computer microprocessor technology on behalf of China; he was sentenced to one year in prison.
- *Walter Lian-Heen Liew*, owner and president of USA Performance Technology Inc. of Oakland, California, was accused of passing chloride-route titanium dioxide production technology to China; he was sentenced to fifteen years in prison.
- *Greg Chung*, an engineer at Boeing, was accused of passing proprietary information on the US space program to China; he was sentenced to fifteen years in prison.

Katrina Leung was a different kind of spy. Her objective was not to steal US technology but to infiltrate US counterintelligence—and she succeeded brilliantly. Leung was born in China in 1954. She immigrated to the US as a teenager in 1970 and graduated from a New York City high school in 1972. Obviously very bright, she graduated from Cornell University in 1976 and then earned an MBA degree from the University of Chicago. In 1980 Leung and her husband moved to Los Angeles, where they found success working at an export-import company and a business consulting firm. They had a lavish lifestyle and cultivated influential friends in California business and politics. Leung was active in the local Chinese American community and bragged that she had excellent contacts in China, including prominent political leaders. In fact, when high-ranking

Chinese visitors came to California, Leung often served as their guide, interpreter, and host.

Leung's activities did not escape the FBI's attention, and in 1982 she was recruited by the bureau to report on Chinese government officials. Her recruiter and handler was FBI special agent James J. Smith, who was Leung's case agent for eighteen years until his retirement from the FBI in 2000. At FBI direction, Leung traveled frequently to China to ingratiate herself with her current contacts and to seek new ones. The FBI was delighted to learn that some of Leung's contacts were MSS officers. In a short time, Leung, code-named Parlor Maid, became one of the best informants on Chinese intelligence personnel and activities that the FBI had. Smith urged Leung to dangle herself to the MSS in the hope that she could become a double agent (DA). The ploy worked, and Leung was recruited by the MSS in 1984, the same year she became a US citizen.

Leung was a productive source for the FBI for twenty years. Her reporting went to the highest levels of the US government. Smith's trust of her was so complete that he overlooked strong indicators as early as 1991 that she was not being truthful and, moreover, had unauthorized and unreported contacts with MSS officers. Smith shared classified information with Leung to assist her in her DA role. The FBI paid Leung $1.7 million in salary and expenses. When Smith retired in 2000, he was awarded the Intelligence Medal of Achievement for his work with Parlor Maid.

One reason that Smith was so protective of Leung and deflected all CI suspicion of her was that he had been having an affair with her since the early 1980s. Not only that, but Leung was also sleeping with another FBI counterintelligence special agent, William Cleveland, who worked out of the FBI's San Francisco office. Smith was so careless that he carried top-secret documents in his briefcase when he had trysts with Leung at her Los Angeles home, giving her the opportunity to copy the documents when he was asleep or in another room. Leung had been working for the MSS all along.

The duplicity began to unravel in 2000. The FBI put Leung under surveillance and made a surreptitious search of her home. There agents found a stash of FBI documents. Leung and Smith were arrested in 2003. The FBI did not welcome parading its dirty laundry in public or revealing sensitive sources and methods. Furthermore, the elements of espionage are extremely difficult to prove in court. So the case was settled with plea agreements. Smith pleaded guilty in 2004 to a reduced charge of lying to the FBI about his affair with Leung and was fined $10,000. Leung pleaded guilty in 2005 to filing fraudulent tax returns and lying to the FBI. She was sentenced to three years' probation, a hundred hours of community service, and a $10,000 fine. Cleveland was never charged, and after he left the FBI, he became chief of security at Lawrence Livermore National Laboratory.

This list is certainly incomplete and does not include Chinese citizens who have permanent resident alien status in the United States or who travel frequently to the US on business. Not listed as well are some US citizens who are not Chinese Americans who have been caught spying for China. Although they are relatively few in number because of the strong Chinese propensity to recruit Chinese Americans, some of them have done serious damage. One recent example is the hapless Benjamin Bishop, a former US Army lieutenant colonel working at US Pacific Command in Hawaii who was sentenced in 2014 to seven years in prison for passing classified defense information to his Chinese girlfriend. The twenty-seven-year-old woman entered a romantic relationship with the then-fifty-nine-year-old Bishop while she was a graduate student in the US on a J-1 exchange visitor visa.

On March 28, 2017, Candace Claiborne, a sixty-year-old US State Department administrative officer, was arrested by the FBI and charged with "obstructing an official proceeding" and lying to the bureau about her contacts with Chinese intelligence officials. Claiborne is alleged to have had unauthorized dealings with the Chinese from 2011 to 2016 and to have received benefits for herself and relatives amounting to tens of thousands of dollars. There is no indication that ethnicity was a factor. Claiborne began working for the State Department in 1999 and had a top-secret clearance. She had several overseas assignments, including in Shanghai and Beijing. It has not yet been made public what Claiborne passed to the Chinese, how and where she was recruited, or how she was handled. It is known, however, that her cooperation with Chinese intelligence continued after her departure from Beijing in 2012 and her reassignment to State Department headquarters in Washington, DC.

Another example of a nonethnic recruitment of Americans by the Chinese is Glenn Duffie Shriver. Shriver was a nineteen-year-old college student from Michigan studying Chinese language and international relations. He went to China for a summer study program in 2001. He was so taken with Chinese language and culture that he went back to China in 2002 for a junior year abroad. After his graduation from Grand Valley State University in 2004, he returned to China to perfect his Mandarin and to immerse himself in all things Chinese. He soon fell prey to a classic intelligence spotting mechanism; he answered an ad seeking a volunteer to write an article on US-China relations. He wrote the article, was of course praised by the article's sponsor, and received a fee of $120. The MSS now had a hot prospect and was off and running.

Shriver soon realized that he was in contact with Chinese intelligence officers, but that did not faze him. He accepted a payment of $10,000 from the MSS to take the US Foreign Service exam, which he did in 2005. He did not pass. For another payment of $20,000, Shriver retook the exam in 2006, but again failed. Next, he was instructed by his MSS handler to return to the United States to apply to the CIA's clandestine service, which he did in 2007. As a now-fluent Mandarin speaker, Shriver was an attractive candidate for the CIA. His processing was suspended, however, when he returned to China (to meet with his MSS handler) and then continued to South Korea to teach English. During Shriver's China stopover, he was paid $40,000 by the MSS to encourage him to press forward with his CIA application. The MSS thought it was closing in on an eagerly sought penetration of the CIA's clandestine service. Shriver traveled to Washington, DC, in May 2010 for what he believed was his final processing. In reality, the CIA and FBI, for reasons never publicly disclosed, were already on to him. Shriver was arrested by the FBI on June 22, 2010, and charged with making false statements in his CIA application and conspiring to provide US national defense information to China. In a plea bargain, he confessed to one count of conspiracy and was sentenced to four years in prison. He was released in 2013.

There are approximately 14,000 Americans studying in China. The MSS has an elaborate spotting program to identify those students who show political or cultural sympathy for China, who are potential candidates for US government jobs, and who show themselves to be money hungry. Shriver fell into that trap. In April 2014 the FBI released a twenty-eight-minute video called *Game of Pawns*, based on the Shriver case, to warn American students who go to China of potential pitfalls.

China has stolen sensitive US technology for nuclear weapons, missiles, submarines, computers, phased-array radars, military guidance systems, satellite communications, thermal imaging cameras, microwave amplifiers, night-vision goggles, and on and on. The new Chinese unmanned aerial vehicle unveiled at China's big airshow in 2012 is the spitting image of the US MQ-1 Predator. US military experts have said that there is no significant Chinese weapons system that is not based on stolen US technology. A senior FBI counterintelligence official may have been overdramatic—but maybe not—when he told a counterintelligence conference at the Bush School that his greatest fear was that his children or grandchildren would one day go to war against China and be killed by weapons based on stolen US technology.

That's not all. The Chinese have been trying to influence US political campaigns through illegal contributions since at least the 1990s. There was a huge brouhaha in 1996 when the *Washington Post* reported that the Department of Justice was investigating possible illegal Chinese contributions to the Democratic National Committee (DNC) in an effort to influence both the presidential and congressional elections that year. Chinese businessman Johnny Chung funneled over $300,000 in illegal contributions to the DNC; he eventually pleaded guilty to violating US election laws. Another Chinese businessman, John Huang, arranged for Vice President Al Gore to attend a fund-raiser at a Buddhist temple in California, where illegal contributions of roughly $170,000 were made to the DNC. China, of course, has denied any involvement in influence buying, but covert activity of this kind would have to have official sponsorship. The FBI determined that the 1996 illegal funding operation was coordinated from the Chinese embassy in Washington, DC. The late senator Fred Thompson, the chairman of the 1997 Senate Governmental Affairs Committee, said, "High-level Chinese government officials crafted a plan to increase China's influence over the U.S. political process." The issues at stake for the Chinese government are not difficult to divine: US support to Taiwan, intellectual property laws, trade policies, the environment, human rights, and Asian security.

Candidates of both political parties have been targeted for influence buying. Chinese hackers have been detected in the campaign websites of both candidates in every presidential election since 2000, another indication that the threat of Chinese election tampering has not gone away. In 2016 Virginia governor Terry McAuliffe was notified by the US Department of Justice that he was a target of investigation for allegedly accepting a questionable campaign contribution of $120,000 from Chinese businessman Wenliang Wang. McAuliffe has not been charged with any crime. There has been considerable controversy lately about alleged *Russian* tampering in the US presidential election of 2016. That allegation must be investigated thoroughly, of course, but it should be kept in mind that the Chinese have been doing this kind of thing for twenty years.

Cyberattacks from China are nothing new. The first major attack was discovered in 2005, but it was quickly determined that infiltrations of US government computer networks had been going on since at least 2003. The 2003 operation, called Titan Rain, was a coordinated attack by Chinese cyber spies to download sensitive data from networks at the US Departments of Defense, State, Energy, and Homeland Security, as well as a host of American defense contractors. In just one day, the hackers stole reams of sensitive aerospace documents with schematics of propulsion systems, solar paneling, and fuel tanks for NASA's Mars Reconnaissance Orbiter. Other targeted locations included the US Army Information Engineering Command, the Naval Ocean Systems Center, the Missile Defense Agency, and US national laboratories. Cyberattacks like Titan Rain present a unique challenge in terms of attribution. Are the perpetrators government spies, individual hackers, or an organized criminal enterprise? In the case of Titan Rain, however, it is not credible to conclude that a multifaceted and sophisticated operation of this magnitude could be anything other than a Chinese government–sponsored activity. Official Chinese cyber spying was, for many years, the domain of the Third Department of the People's Liberation Army (3PLA), the rough equivalent of the US National Security Agency (NSA). As we have seen, however, since 2016 it has been the primary responsibility of the PLA Strategic Support Force.

In 2010 Google announced that the company had "detected a highly sophisticated and targeted attack on [its] corporate infrastructure originating from China that resulted in the theft of intellectual property from Google." While China's involvement in cyberattacks was by no means surprising, Google's decision to publicize the breach was unusual. Typically, companies are wary of publicizing such leaks for fear that perceptions of insecurity could negatively affect their business. The explanation may lie in the fact that Google executives, who had continually met resistance from the Chinese government regarding censorship since the company had entered the Chinese market in 2006, finally decided enough was enough.

Google first learned of the attack from Chinese human rights activists in the US who reported that their Gmail accounts had been accessed by unknown users. As details of Operation Aurora, as it was known, emerged, it became clear that the attack was highly tailored and complex. The cyber spies exploited a flaw in Internet Explorer 6.0 to gain access to targeted computers. Once the vulnerability was identified, the hackers determined which officials at various companies had access to sensitive information. Emails that, once opened, installed malware on the target computers were then sent from servers in Taiwan to the chosen company officials. The hackers from then on had unfettered access to the officials' computers and could steal any information they deemed valuable.

Google was not the only American company targeted by the Aurora cyber spies. In fact, no fewer than thirty-four companies, including Yahoo, Symantec, Adobe, Northrop Grumman, and Dow Chemical, were victimized. According to the *Washington Times*, "Each of the companies was targeted differently, using software developed from the attackers' knowledge of the individual networks and information storage devices, operating systems, the location of targeted data, how it was protected, and who had access to it."[3] Cybersecurity experts in the US government state categorically that attacks of this precision and sophistication can be achieved only with substantial support from the Chinese government. PLA strikes again.

Perhaps the most egregious of all the attacks on US computer systems became public in June 2015, when the US Office of Personnel Management (OPM) announced that its database had been breached by unknown persons. The personal records of 21.5 million US government employees, past and present—including Social Security numbers, biographical information, and the results of security background investigations—were stolen. In the wrong hands, this information could clearly be used to the great disadvantage of the persons concerned. Particularly troubling to me was that several of my students at the Bush School who applied for government jobs and were at the beginning of their public service careers had their sensitive personal information compromised.

The US intelligence community has placed blame for the attack squarely on China. The Chinese government denied any official responsibility for the breach and, in fact, announced in December 2015 that it had arrested a small group of nongovernment hackers for having committed the crime. No information was provided on the hackers' identities, place of employment, or sentencing. Skeptics suspected a convenient cover-up to ease tensions with the US before the scheduled state visit of President Jinping Xi. The only Chinese entity, state-sponsored or otherwise, that I can think of that would have a motive for stealing all the OPM data is the MSS. This information would be a gold mine for any intelligence service seeking to spot, assess, and develop US government employees for future recruitment.

The United States and China signed a bilateral agreement in September 2015 pledging that neither side would use cyberattacks to steal intellectual property for commercial purposes. Director of Intelligence James Clapper told the Senate Armed Services Committee the same month that in his opinion the agreement would not stop cyber spying by China. In fact, a US cybersecurity company documented a Chinese cyberattack on a US company the day after the agreement was signed. Within three weeks, there were at least seven more attacks from China against US high-tech companies. In follow-up testimony to the Senate in December 2016, Clapper provided an update on the threat: "China continues to have success in cyber espionage against the U.S. government, our allies, and U.S. companies." Mike McConnell, the former director of national intelligence and director of the National Security Agency, put it even more bluntly: "The Chinese have penetrated every major corporation of any consequence in the United States and taken information. We've never, ever not found Chinese malware."

What is China's next cyber target in the US? Clapper and Adm. Mike Rogers, then director of the NSA, warned Congress about the vulnerability of the US power grid. Clapper said that China's cyber capabilities are so good that it could conceivably bring down the entire power grid. He did not rule out a "massive Armageddon-like attack against our infrastructure." Rogers's testimony to the House Intelligence Committee in November 2014 included the following: "Once you're into the system . . . it enables you to do things like, if I want to tell power turbines to go offline and stop generating power, you can do that. It enables you to shut down very segmented, very tailored parts of our infrastructure that forestall the ability to provide those services to our citizens."

Our best hope of discovering what the Chinese intelligence services are doing to us is to penetrate them. That is hard—but not impossible—to do in a closed society with effective counterintelligence. And we were making progress. But then the *New York Times* reported on May 20, 2017, that eighteen to twenty of the CIA's best spies inside China had been imprisoned or executed. The *Times* based its information on "ten current and former American officials" who chose not to be identified. The losses reportedly occurred between 2010 and 2012 and effectively wiped out the CIA's excellent stable of assets inside the Chinese government.

If true, this disaster is eerily reminiscent of the decimation of the CIA's Soviet agent program in 1985. From 1975 to 1985, the CIA built up a remarkable inventory of well-placed agents inside the Soviet Union—only to see them disappear, one by one, because of the perfidy of Edward Lee Howard and Aldrich Ames. According to the *Times* report, the CIA's counterintelligence theories about what went wrong in China have mirrored the avenues we explored after 1985. Could our compromises have been the result of sloppy tradecraft? Were we being beaten on the street? Were our secret communications being intercepted? Or did we have a mole?

Arrests in rapid succession in a compressed period usually point to a mole. In fact, a former CIA case officer, Jerry Chun Shing Lee, was arrested by the FBI in January 2018 and charged with espionage. After Lee left the CIA in 2007, he moved to Asia with his family and was doing business there. In 2010 he was allegedly approached by Chinese intelligence officers. If, as alleged, Lee gave up the identities of CIA spies in China, he either took notes with him when he left the agency in 2007 or remembered who they were. As part of its investigation, the FBI is looking closely at unexplained deposits made to Lee's bank account. It took nine years to catch Ames. I hope it will not take that long to figure out what happened in China and, if the problem is in fact human, to bring the traitor to justice.

There are spies, and then there are Chinese spies. China is in a class by itself in terms of its espionage, covert action, and cyber capabilities. It is also in a class by itself because of its absolute obsession with stealing America's secrets. We must do everything we can to make it harder for the Chinese to do that. We are not doing enough now.

TWO
Russia

> Both Russia and China probably have more clandestine intelligence operatives inside the United States now, in the second decade of the twenty-first century, than at the height of the Cold War.
>
> —Henry A. Crumpton, *The Art of Intelligence*

In second place, albeit a distant second place, as a counterintelligence threat to the United States is Russia. The Russians seem not to have gotten the message that the Cold War is over. US counterintelligence experts have said that the level of Russian espionage in the United States today is as high or higher than it was at the height of the Cold War. The Russians rate only second place because the considerable resources they commit to the US target are still dwarfed by the massive espionage onslaught from China. When the Soviet Union collapsed in 1991, my first reaction was to take it personally: "How can they do this to me? This is my career. I'm a Russian specialist!" I need not have worried. As I frequently tell my students at the Bush School, "Those pesky Russians have not gone away." Despite the democratic posturing and economic liberalization of the new Russia, the Russian security services have not changed their colors. When I was on active duty in the CIA in the 1970s, 1980s, and 1990s, I had no illusions about the nature of our main counterintelligence adversary. The KGB (which translates as "Committee for State Security") was a ruthless and vicious organization that oppressed its own people, crushed religion, sent political dissidents to gulags or psychiatric hospitals, and killed its enemies.[1]

I remember a conversation I had with former KGB general Oleg Kalugin in Washington, DC, in 1997.[2] We were discussing our respective careers and reminiscing about how my organization, the CIA, and his, the KGB, had gone head-to-head in Moscow and elsewhere. The tone of the meeting was cordial and mutually respectful. At one point, though, I thought Kalugin was getting too "chummy." I stopped him and said, "Oleg, I respect you as an intelligence professional and as someone who served his country with honor. But let's be clear. We will never be friends—because I can never forgive you for your role in the murders of Nicholas Shadrin and Georgi Markov."[3] Kalugin said he understood but countered with this: "Yes, Jim, we killed those people, but how was that any different from the many Russian boys you in the CIA killed in Afghanistan through your covert support of the mujahideen?" He had a point.

Intelligence was reorganized in Russia in 1991 after the demise of the Soviet Union. The monolithic KGB was divided into two new agencies: the FSB (Federal Security Service) and the SVR (Foreign Intelligence Service).[4] Unlike in the former satellite countries (e.g., Poland, Bulgaria, Czechoslovakia, East Germany, Romania, Hungary, Latvia, Lithuania, Estonia), where the intelligence services of the new democratic regimes purged the old communist apparatchiks, many of the KGB's old and young guard stayed on and simply moved into new offices at Yasenovo (SVR) or Lubyanka (FSB). The Russians did not consider it professionally disqualifying for someone to have served previously in the repressive and undemocratic KGB.

The FSB is responsible for internal security in Russia, specifically counterintelligence, counterterrorism, domestic unrest, state crimes, and border security. The SVR is responsible for external intelligence collection and covert action. With this structure Russia has aligned itself more closely to the US and UK models, in that the FSB is the rough equivalent of the FBI or the British Security Service (popularly referred to as MI5) and the SVR corresponds to the CIA or the British Security Intelligence Service (or MI6).[5] Russian military intelligence is the responsibility of the GRU (Main Intelligence Directorate) and has operated under this name since World War II.[6] Both the SVR and the GRU conduct aggressive intelligence operations against US personnel and installations worldwide.

The Russians today are using the same types of cover for their intelligence personnel in the United States that they have always used: diplomats, trade representatives, journalists, students, and illegals. The Russian embassy, the Russian mission to the United Nations, Russian trade offices, and Russian consulates are filled with SVR and GRU officers under cover. Their targets are US politicians, military personnel, the CIA, the FBI, US technology, and US public opinion. Like the Chinese, the Russians have an insatiable appetite for US high technology, particularly technologies with military applications. There is no doubt that the tone and marching orders for Russian intelligence today come from the president's office. Vladimir Putin served in the KGB from 1975 to 1991, earning his stripes primarily in East Germany, where he worked closely with the East German Stasi in joint operations to steal Western technology. Putin speaks fondly of his days in the KGB, and all signs point to his continuing direct involvement in intelligence operations, particularly to repress political opposition and to eliminate perceived enemies of the state.

Putin has a special hatred for the Chechen separatists who defy his authority and carry out deadly terrorist attacks against Russians. A particular thorn in his side was the Chechen writer and political leader Zelimkhan Yandarbiyev. Yandarbiyev joined forces with al-Qaeda to intensify Chechen resistance to Russian rule and helped finance the Moscow theater hostage crisis in October 2002, during which 130 hostages were killed.[7] Putin branded Yandarbiyev a terrorist and made several unsuccessful efforts to have him extradited from Qatar, where he lived, to stand trial in Russia. One can imagine Putin's anger and frustration when his legal initiatives failed. Yandarbiyev was killed in a car bomb attack in Qatar on February 13, 2004. Two Russian GRU officers were convicted of the crime in June 2004 and sentenced to life in prison. Under heavy diplomatic pressure from Moscow, Qatar agreed to extradite the prisoners to Russia to serve out their sentences. The GRU officers were received warmly in Russia and immediately released.

Anna Politkovskaya was a Russian journalist who sharply criticized Putin for his handling of the Second Chechen War. In 2004 she published a scathing indictment of Putin and his autocratic rule in her book *Putin's Russia: Life in a Failing Democracy*. Friends and associates of Politkovskaya warned her that there were threats on her life, but she persisted in her criticisms of Putin. In September 2004, she wrote the following in an article in *The Guardian*: "If you want to go on working as a journalist, it's total servility to Putin. Otherwise, it can be death, the bullet, poison, or trial—whatever our special services, Putin's guard dogs, see fit." On October 7, 2004, Politkovskaya was shot to death in the elevator of her apartment building in Moscow: two shots to the chest, one to the shoulder, and one to the head, professional assassination style. Despite numerous indications of FSB involvement, the legal proceedings that followed failed to identify the person or persons who ordered the killing. Some commentators noted, coincidence or not, that the murder of Politkovskaya took place on Vladimir Putin's birthday.

Alexander Litvinenko was an FSB officer who publicly accused his FSB superiors of plotting the assassination of Boris Berezovsky, a wealthy Russian businessman and political opponent of Vladimir Putin.[8] Litvinenko was arrested on charges of official malfeasance. In 2000 he fled to the United Kingdom to escape the harassment and legal proceedings against him. Working as a journalist in London, he continued his assaults on the FSB and Putin personally, specifically accusing Putin of having ordered the murder of Anna Politkovskaya in 2004. Litvinenko died in London in November 2006, the victim of radioactive polonium 210 poisoning. The circumstances of his murder remain unclear, although the evidence pointed clearly to former KGB officer Andrey Lugovoy, who had met with Litvinenko on the day of his poisoning. The Russians refused a British request to extradite Lugovoy so he could stand trial in the UK. Litvinenko's widow mounted a public relations campaign to seek justice for her deceased husband. An official British inquiry examined all the evidence and determined in January 2016 that the FSB had been responsible for his assassination. An intelligence operation of this kind, involving so many political and legal risks, could not have been carried out without the personal approval of President Putin.

In March 2018 former Russian GRU officer Sergei Skripal and his daughter Yulia were poisoned in Salisbury, United Kingdom. The poison used was Novichok, known to be in Russia's arsenal of chemical weapons. Skripal and his daughter were in comas for weeks but survived. From 1995 to 2004, Skripal worked for British intelligence in Moscow as a penetration of the GRU. He was arrested by the Russians in 2004, convicted of treason, and sentenced to thirteen years in prison. In 2010 he was released as part of a spy exchange and settled in the UK. The British accused Moscow of the crime and expelled several Russian diplomats in London in retaliation.

The Yandarbiyev, Politkovskaya, and Litvinenko killings and the attempt on the Skripals are strong evidence that the intelligence services of post–Cold War Russia remain powerful, dangerous, and ruthless. They also show that it is potentially life-threatening for anyone in Russia to cross Vladimir Putin. The "wet affairs" of the KGB era, including Shadrin and Markov, have not gone away.[9]

Any hopes that we in the CIA had that the end of the Cold War would lead to less nastiness between the KGB and the CIA were quickly dispelled. The initial optimism, however, was real. There was even a belief in some quarters that we could forge a new relationship between the two spy services on the basis of trust and cooperation, particularly in areas of common concern, like counterterrorism, narcotics, and organized crime. Some of the early talks between representatives of the two services were so encouraging that the US side decided it did not want to jeopardize this potential intelligence détente by getting caught in any kind of provocative spying against our new "friends."

This attitude came to a head in 1992, when the CIA rejected the overtures of a former KGB archivist, Vasili Mitrokhin, who wanted to pass to the CIA the voluminous files and notes he had accumulated during his many years of service at the KGB. Could this be a Russian test of the CIA's commitment to a new relationship? Would it torpedo any hope of future cooperation between the CIA and the SVR if the Russians found out that the CIA had provided comfort and support to a hated defector? Was it out-of-date information with little or no current intelligence value? In any event, Mitrokhin was turned away by the CIA and made his way to the British embassy in Riga, where he was received with open arms by MI6. The information Mitrokhin provided was a gold mine of documentary intelligence on Russian espionage operations from the revolution until the mid-1980s. It answered a lot of questions the West had only been able to speculate about previously.[10] As CIA chief of counterintelligence at the time, I had the unenviable task of going to London, with hat in hand, to ask MI6 to let us into an operation that should have been ours in the first place.

And then came the avalanche of bad news to prove once and for all that it was business as usual for the "new" Russian intelligence services. Operations against the United States had never ceased and, in fact, may have intensified. The most devastating counterintelligence loss became known in 1994, when CIA officer Aldrich "Rick" Ames was arrested for spying for the Russians. Ames had volunteered his services to the KGB in 1985 and stayed in place as a penetration of the CIA for the next nine years. He betrayed up to thirty Russians who were working secretly for the CIA. The full extent of his treachery is hard to pinpoint because his access to some of these cases overlapped with the access of other America traitors, most notably Edward Lee Howard.[11] Regardless of how it happened—and Ames clearly bears the bulk of the responsibility—the CIA's human and technical operations in Moscow were virtually wiped out. A key point here is that Ames's spying for the Russians did not miss a beat during the transition from the KGB to the SVR in 1991. It is obvious that despite the feel-good talks between the CIA and the SVR, the Russians never intended to curtail their spying operations against the United States.

I considered Rick Ames a friend and worked directly with him at the CIA on several occasions. I admit that I did not initially see through Rick's duplicity and sociopathic personality. For me, his betrayal was personal. How could someone I knew so well betray me and all his colleagues at the CIA? How could he condemn to execution so many courageous Russian agents who had put their lives in our hands? How could he sell out the country to which he had sworn an oath of allegiance? I am grateful for one thing: Rick Ames was ultimately a stupid spy. His ability to spy against us without being detected for nine years was more a function of weak counterintelligence on our part than brilliance on his. For one thing, his tradecraft was atrocious. No competent spy would throw drafts of operational notes and a printer ribbon in his trash, where an FBI "trash run" could retrieve them. A good spy must also know when to cut and run. As a counterintelligence professional, Rick should have known that it was suicidal for him to continue his spying for the Russians after the breakup of the Soviet Union in 1991. In the turmoil that followed, he should have anticipated that the CIA would be the beneficiary of several recruitments or defectors from the former KGB, any one of whom could reveal his identity. If Rick had taken his money, gone to ground, and destroyed the evidence of his espionage in 1991, as he should have, it is unlikely we would have caught him or been able to prosecute him. He could not quit, though, because the money was too good.[12] In Rick's case, his greed was our friend.

Next came the arrest of CIA officer Harold James Nicholson in November 1996. At the time of his arrest, Nicholson had served in the CIA's Directorate of Operations for sixteen years, performing successfully in a series of overseas assignments. In quick succession he was posted to Manila, Bangkok, and Tokyo. By 1990 he was the CIA chief of station in Bucharest, a plum assignment for a still relatively junior officer. Nicholson was on the fast track, a near lock for a future senior management position in the clandestine service. His personal life, however, was not going nearly as well as his professional life. His wife, Laurie, had not adapted well to the strains of the undercover lifestyle and to a husband consumed by his demanding job. They separated when Nicholson moved to his next assignment as deputy chief of station in Kuala Lumpur in 1992. The three Nicholson children went with their father to Malaysia; Laurie stayed in the States to continue her education. The Nicholsons' divorce became final in 1994.

Sometime toward the end of his assignment in Kuala Lumpur, Nicholson volunteered his services to a senior SVR officer serving in Malaysia. It was a straight cash-for-secrets deal. Nicholson was aware of Ames's arrest in February 1994, of course, and probably reasoned that the SVR would be in the market for a replacement penetration of the CIA.

Nicholson's access was not nearly as good as Ames's had been, but he still had something to sell. His next assignment in 1996 was to be as an instructor at the CIA's training facility in Virginia called the Farm. In that position he would be able to pass to the Russians the identities of all the undercover CIA trainees who passed through the Farm on their way to their first overseas assignments. The SVR leaped at the offer, and Nicholson's lucrative career as a Russian spy took off in earnest. The money Nicholson received from the SVR never reached the levels of Ames's payments, but it did help him deal with the financial burdens of his divorce, his responsibilities as a single father, and the discontinuation of his overseas allowances.[13] His arrest was the result of superior CI work by the CIA and FBI, financial analysis, failed polygraphs, surveillance, and his own suspicious behavior, namely, his transparent efforts to expand his access to Russian-related information that was not required for his job. He was convicted of espionage in June 1997 and sentenced to twenty-three years and seven months in prison. How bad was the damage he did? Hundreds of young CIA case officers had been compromised even before they completed their operational training. The Nicholson case was a coup for the SVR. Just two years after it had lost Aldrich Ames as its best-ever penetration of the CIA, it had another well-placed and even more senior CIA officer on its payroll.[14]

Is the SVR that good, or is it just lucky? My verdict is mixed. In the first place, both Ames and Nicholson were volunteers. They were not chosen because of skillful spotting, assessing, and developing by KGB or SVR case officers. It is not hard to recruit when high-priority targets walk in your door and offer their services. Ames and Nicholson both sold out for money—lots of it—and unfortunately earned the cash with the quality of the information they provided. The skill in these cases came in the form of the professional handling and tradecraft by the KGB and SVR handlers. There, I give them high marks. Ames was in place for nine years and Nicholson for a little over two years. They both could have stayed longer if they had not made their own fatal mistakes.

Earl Edwin Pitts was another member of the Russians' hit parade of key US government penetrations. Pitts, an FBI special agent for thirteen years, was arrested by the bureau in December 1996 on charges of espionage on behalf of Russia. He had volunteered his services to the KGB in New York in 1987 while he was working in the FBI's New York field office as a counterintelligence specialist. Pitts's access to the FBI's programs against the KGB in New York gave the Russians a decisive edge in countering FBI surveillance and other monitoring techniques. Like Ames, Pitts foolhardily continued to work for the Russians after the transition from the KGB to the SVR in 1991. In 1992 Pitts's spying entered a three-year hiatus, not because of well-advised caution on his part but because of a change in his FBI duties that offered him less access to sensitive information. It was too late. A former Russian official who had knowledge of Pitts's initial approach to the KGB began cooperating with the FBI in 1995 and identified Pitts as a spy. The FBI cleverly initiated a "false flag" operation against Pitts, in which an FBI employee posing as a Russian SVR officer "reactivated" Pitts as a source and began passing him money for his resumed espionage.[15] Pitts fell for it completely and incriminated himself repeatedly during the sixteen months of the false flag operation. In 1997 he was sentenced to twenty-seven years in prison.[16]

The US military was also hit by Russian espionage. George Trofimoff was born of Russian parents in Germany in 1927. He fled Nazi Germany in 1944, lived in France, and then immigrated to the United States in 1947. He joined the US Army and was commissioned as an officer in the Army Reserve in 1953. From 1959 to 1994, he worked for US Army intelligence, held a top-secret security clearance, and rose to the rank of colonel. Trofimoff was the chief of the US Army unit at the Joint Interrogation Center in Nuremberg, Germany, from 1969 to 1994. In that position he had access to refugee and defector debriefing reports and to finished intelligence on Russia and Eastern Europe.

Sometime in the early 1970s, Trofimoff was recruited for the KGB by his Russian "foster brother," a close boyhood friend who had become a bishop in the Russian Orthodox Church.[17] The recruitment started slowly, with small "loans" from the friend in return for Trofimoff's willingness to talk about his classified work, but quickly escalated into full-fledged espionage with Trofimoff providing photography of large quantities of secret and top-secret documents. The Russian friend was Trofimoff's primary handler, but testimony at Trofimoff's trial indicated he met once, possibly more often, with staff KGB officers. This was the state of play for the next twenty-five years. The KGB considered Trofimoff a productive and highly valuable agent. He was paid a total of about $250,000.

Everything came crashing down when Vasili Mitrokhin defected to the

British in 1992 and provided documents that pointed to Trofimoff as a longtime Russian spy. The Germans arrested Trofimoff in 1994 but could not make the case against him because of flimsy evidence and the expiration of the German statute of limitations. It was a close call, but Trofimoff thought he had dodged the bullet. He retired from the Army Reserve and moved with his wife to a retirement community in Florida. They had a limited income and quickly ran into financial difficulties that were exacerbated by Trofimoff's reckless spending. The stage was set for the FBI to strike.

The FBI was convinced that Trofimoff had committed espionage against the United States, but it needed more evidence. In the absence of admissions or contemporaneous evidence, espionage is a difficult crime to prove. How about a false flag operation? It had worked against Pitts a few years earlier, and maybe Trofimoff could be lured into incriminating himself in a similar sting. The operation worked like a charm. The FBI impersonator did a brilliant job of breaking down Trofimoff's reticence and convincing him that the SVR was there to help him with his financial problems. After about a year and a half, Trofimoff was so desperate for money that he ignored his reservations and began bragging about all the great things he had done for the KGB. The FBI got it all on tape. Trofimoff was arrested in June 2000, convicted of spying for Russia, and sentenced to life in prison in 2001. He died in prison in September 2014. I give Russian intelligence an A+ for its subtle use of the bishop as Trofimoff's recruiting officer, its patience in drawing him more and more deeply into espionage, and its tradecraft in keeping the operation alive for so many years.

It goes on and on. Another blockbuster occurred in 2001, when FBI special agent Robert Hanssen was arrested on charges of spying for Russia since 1979. How could that be? The CIA was severely criticized for allowing CI officer Aldrich Ames to go undetected for nine years. Hanssen worked for the KGB and later for the SVR at the heart of FBI counterintelligence for twenty-two years. US counterintelligence was asleep at the switch, missed numerous clues, and even wasted four years in a misguided witch hunt against an innocent CIA officer.

Robert Philip Hanssen was born in Chicago in 1944. He was the only child of Howard, a Chicago police officer, and his wife, Vivian. The family was at the lower end of the middle class. With the help of a scholarship and part-time jobs, Hanssen attended Knox College in Galesburg, Illinois, and graduated in 1966 with a degree in chemistry. He did not know exactly what he wanted to do next, but he knew he did not want to get drafted. He decided, more for the deferment than for any real passion, to attend dentistry school at Northwestern University. He stuck it out for three years but finally decided dentistry was not for him. He toyed with going to medical school to become a psychiatrist but quickly abandoned that idea in favor of studying accounting at Northwestern, where he obtained an MBA degree in 1971 and soon thereafter his CPA certification.

While still in dentistry school, Hanssen married Bonnie Wauck, the daughter of a successful psychology professor. Bob and Bonnie came from vastly different backgrounds. Her family was wealthy and upper class, in sharp contrast to Bob's decidedly modest upbringing. Another real difference was that Bonnie was a devout Catholic, whereas Bob was a nominal, nonpracticing Protestant. To please Bonnie, Bob converted to Catholicism and even joined the ultraconservative Catholic organization Opus Dei, in which Bonnie and most of her family members were fervently active. From that point on, Hanssen attempted to insert his newfound religion into every aspect of his life, even proselytizing his friends and future colleagues.

Working in intelligence or law enforcement had long been in the back of Hanssen's mind. He applied to the NSA but, to his extreme disappointment, was turned down. Bob and Bonnie were starting a family (they eventually had six children), and Bob desperately needed a job. He joined the Chicago Police Department, from which his father had recently retired, in 1973. All along, however, Bob viewed his CPA and local law enforcement experience as stepping-stones to something bigger and better. After three years as a Chicago cop, Hanssen joined the FBI in 1976. He had finally achieved his goal.

Hanssen's FBI career did not turn out to be what he had dreamed it would be. Hanssen started in Gary, Indiana, not exactly a glamorous posting for an ambitious young special agent. He wanted more action and welcomed his transfer to New York City in 1978, even though he knew the cost of living there would be a real stretch for his FBI salary. In 1979, under the financial strain of supporting his family and perhaps owing to his disappointment at the slow pace of his FBI advancement, Hanssen sold out to the Soviet GRU. His counterintelligence job in New York gave him excellent access to information on Soviets who had been recruited by the US, technical operations against Soviet facilities and personnel, and surveillance procedures. The GRU paid Hanssen approximately $30,000 for his information. This might have gone on indefinitely, but Bonnie caught Bob in the act of preparing a message for his GRU handler and forced him to confess what he had been doing. She was horrified, and Bob promised that he would stop his spying, confess his sin to an Opus Dei priest, and donate his ill-gotten gains to Mother Teresa. As far as Bonnie knew, that was the end of it.

In 1981 Hanssen was reassigned to FBI headquarters in Washington, DC. His first job was in the budget office, but after two years he moved to a position more to his liking: Soviet analysis. There is no indication that Hanssen was involved in espionage during this period; he had at least temporarily kept his promise to Bonnie. But his status changed when he was transferred back to New York in 1985. The same financial pressures resurfaced in New York, and in October 1985 Hanssen volunteered his services to the KGB in a note to a senior KGB officer. He concealed his identity from the Russians, a ruse he maintained for the remainder of his espionage career. Hanssen began delivering documents to the KGB via dead drops, and he received payments in cash and diamonds in return. The KGB had hit the jackpot; Hanssen revealed the identities of Russians working for US intelligence, the existence of an FBI tunnel under the new Soviet embassy in Washington, and the identities of Americans suspected of being spies for the Russians. Only two years into his second assignment in New York, Hanssen engineered a return to FBI headquarters in Washington, where the mother lode of counterintelligence information was to be found. He singlehandedly decimated FBI counterintelligence. Determining how much he was paid by the KGB is difficult, but the total was clearly over a million dollars.

Where did the money go? Some of it went to remodeling the Hanssen's home in suburban Virginia—and some went to a bizarre relationship Hanssen had with a Washington stripper. Hanssen befriended Priscilla Sue Galey in 1990 and showered her with lavish gifts of jewelry, cash, and a Mercedes. There was apparently no sex in the relationship; Galey said later that Hanssen was just a kind and generous man (no kidding) who wanted to help her change her ways and, hopefully, find religion. Hanssen withdrew his support from Galey after two years, when she left town and returned to a former lover in Columbus, Ohio. The bulk of Hanssen's income from the KGB (and after 1991 the SVR) cannot be traced. It did not go to Bonnie, who was unaware of her husband's extracurricular activities and extra income.

Bonnie was a victim, not only of Hanssen's treason and infidelity but also of his abuse. Hanssen pressured Bonnie to pose for nude photos, which he posted on various blogs. Some of Hanssen's blog activity included sexual fantasies in which he identified Bonnie by her true first name. He also concealed a video camera in their bedroom and videotaped their intimate moments. He later shared the video with his best friend.

The CIA and FBI were aware of a major leak of counterintelligence information to the Russians, but the lead was fragmentary and inconclusive. The FBI, perhaps egged on by Hanssen himself, was convinced that the spy was at the CIA and zeroed in on a good friend of mine, Brian Kelley. Kelley went through hell for over three years as the FBI pressured him to confess and harassed his family and friends. It was not until 2000 that the FBI purchased from a former KGB officer the KGB file on the US mole. The price was $7 million. The file did not include the spy's name but did contain a tape recording of a phone call the spy had made to his KGB contact and fingerprints from a plastic garbage bag he had used to wrap his dead-drop material. Hanssen was arrested by the FBI on February 18, 2001. He pleaded guilty to espionage and was sentenced to life in prison without the possibility of parole. He is serving his time in solitary confinement at the high-security US penitentiary in Florence, Colorado.

Hanssen has defied the best efforts of FBI and CIA psychologists to profile him. He does not seem to fit any of the categories observed in previous traitors. Money was a factor, for sure, but it did not appear to be his primary motivation. Was it revenge, thrill seeking, an insatiable ego, or simply a need to show he was smarter than everyone else? What we do know is that Hanssen was able to separate his life into an amazing number of conflicting compartments: husband, father of six children, senior FBI special agent, devout conservative Catholic, sexual pervert, kinky benefactor of a stripper, and traitor. I hope we never see his like again.[18]

There was a great deal of publicity in March 2009 when US secretary of state Hillary Clinton met with Russian foreign minister Sergey Lavrov in Geneva to discuss ways to improve US-Russian relations. Clinton presented to Lavrov a small box with a button on it to symbolize the "reset" of the relationship that the Obama administration said it desired. Lavrov pushed the button, and everyone had a good laugh. If there was any shred of sincerity on the Russian side about a new relationship, it did not apply to spying against the United States.

On June 27, 2010, the FBI arrested ten Russian illegals—professional intelligence officers living in the US under false identities—in New York, Massachusetts, and Virginia.[19] These Russian spies had been in the US for several years, attending US universities, raising families, and working for US companies. The group consisted of four couples and two singles. Eight of the spies were using false identities, but two were using their true names, which was highly uncharacteristic of Russian illegal operations. The well-trained Russian illegals blended into their environment and made a point of doing nothing to attract attention to themselves. The one exception was Anna Chapman, an attractive divorcée with dual Russian-UK citizenship who was socially active in New York and highly visible on social media.

The FBI acknowledged that it had been working on this counterintelligence operation, which it referred to as "Ghost Stories," for over ten years. It has not been revealed how this investigation began, but the presumption is that the FBI or the CIA had a source inside the SVR. Anna Chapman and others believed they were betrayed by Alexander Poteyev, who was the deputy chief of the American illegals branch at the SVR. Poteyev reportedly began cooperating with US counterintelligence before or during his SVR assignment in New York in the early 1990s. In any event, in May 2011 Poteyev was convicted in absentia by a Russian court of desertion and treason, apparently for his role in the compromise of the ten illegals in the US. He was sentenced to twenty-five years in prison. Let's hope he never does the time and is safe and well somewhere in the US.

For at least a decade, the FBI surveilled the suspected illegals, tapped their phones, and read their emails. The spies were observed making brush passes, servicing dead drops, and carrying out other clandestine acts. There was no doubt that they were engaged in espionage, but for what purpose? That is the big and still unanswered question. The SVR made a tremendous commitment to train, backstop, place, and handle ten illegals in the United States, and its return on investment for this commitment appears to be little to none. The press reported a lot of uninformed speculation that the illegals' mission was to spot, assess, and develop US policymakers for possible recruitment as spies for Russia. The FBI's public statements echoed this objective, but no specifics were provided. Did the illegals ever produce any recruitments of Americans? Were any American officials even under serious development by the spies? There was no credible evidence of any of that. Illegals are often used to handle highly sensitive penetrations of the host country on the theory that they will not have the kind of close counterintelligence scrutiny that diplomatically covered spies receive. If that were the case, how is it possible that the FBI's surveillance of the ten illegals missed everything? Why were no Americans wrapped up by the FBI after the illegals were arrested? It does not add up.

My personal view is that Putin was so obsessed with America and loved the spy game so much that he simply liked the idea of having illegals planted on US soil. He did not really care that they were doing nothing of real value; he was just satisfied to know that he was beating US counterintelligence and had spies in place for the long haul who might one day do something worthwhile. That kind of thinking defies reasonable intelligence logic. Who would be mindless enough to spend so much time and money, put loyal Russian spies at risk of arrest, and throw away so much top-notch talent for so little apparent gain? I say shame on Putin and the SVR if their only real purpose was to have sleepers in the US who could be activated at some future date for some undetermined mission. From my earliest days at the Farm, I recall the admonishments of our instructors: "Never operate for the sake of operating." That is true. Spying without a legitimate purpose is immoral.

What really infuriated me as a former counterintelligence professional was that we threw away the opportunity to get answers to our questions. We had ten Russian spies in our hands and held all the bargaining chips. Chapman and the others had no diplomatic immunity and were looking at up to twenty-five years in prison. Why didn't we squeeze them? Are you telling me that not one of them would have broken and spilled the whole story in return for a reduced sentence? Here are just a few of the CI questions, among many, that needed answers: What was their mission? How did they communicate with Moscow and their SVR contacts in the US? How were they paid? How and where were they trained? Who else was involved? Did they have any operational successes in the US? Were they handling any actual agents? Did they ever detect or suspect FBI surveillance? What was their planned end game?

In the end the ten Russian illegals remained in US custody for only twelve days. On July 8, 2010, they were released and sent back to Russia on a chartered plane via Vienna, where they were exchanged for four Russians being held in Russian prisons on charges of illegal contacts with the West. Why such a rush? Was the US so intent on pursuing its "reset" policy with Russia that it did not want to rock the boat with an embarrassing spy scandal? Were there sensitive aspects of the FBI's investigation that the US government did not want revealed in open court proceedings? Or finally, were there compelling source protection equities—for example, an exposed SVR source—that dictated discretion and rapid resolution? Whatever the reason for this unsatisfying CI outcome, it is hard to countenance the ten-for-four trade. I fully understand and respect our humanitarian reasons for rescuing these four Russians, but where is the balance in this deal? We gave up ten professional SVR illegals and received nothing comparable in return. What would have been wrong with a straight ten-for-ten swap? Who negotiated this lopsided deal for us? Were we so eager to get the whole incident behind us that we settled for less than we could have gotten? The truth is that we were the aggrieved party here—and I am convinced we could have gotten a lot more than we did.[20]

The Russian intelligence services supplement their human intelligence collection with one of their most time-tested and aggressive skills: information warfare. Cyber spying is widely used by Russia to interfere in the politics of other countries, to manipulate their populations, to spread disinformation, to conduct unconventional warfare, and to collect intelligence. The Russian objective is to harass, to discredit, to disrupt, to deceive, and to spy on rival states. The last ten years have seen not only a dramatic increase in the frequency of Russian cyber activity, but also, alarmingly, a quantum leap in the brazenness, sophistication, and destructiveness of these attacks.

The FSB has taken the lead in launching denial-of-service attacks on foreign governments and sponsoring anonymous "web brigades" that bombard political blogs and other forums with disinformation and pro-Russian propaganda. The GRU's cyber capabilities are primarily directed at supporting military interventions, but the GRU is suspected of also having carried out cyberattacks on nonmilitary objectives, such as the German Bundestag and a French television station. The lines of responsibility between the FSB and the GRU are blurry and overlap, leading to a possible duplication of cyber efforts. The SVR uses cyber operations to support human intelligence operations. Although it is not as directly involved in cyber operations as the FSB and GRU are, it plays a planning role in overall cyber strategy.

Russian cyber spying first surfaced on the world stage in a big way in Estonia in 2007. Owing to a bitter dispute over the relocation of a Russian war memorial, Russian-Estonian relations sank to a new low in acrimony and recrimination. At the height of the controversy, Estonia was hit by a massive denial-of-service attack on government offices, political parties, banks, and media outlets. A twenty-year-old ethnic Russian Estonian was fined for his role in the attacks, but no one believed he acted alone. The Estonian government announced that the operation had originated in Russia but offered no substantive proof. Russia denied any involvement.

The Republic of Georgia was the next victim. In July 2008, one month before the Russian army invaded Georgia, the country was victimized by a well-orchestrated cyberattack. Georgian Internet services were rerouted and blocked, causing major disruptions in business and communications. Several Georgian websites were defaced with pro-Russian propaganda. Georgian news agencies' websites were attacked and, in some cases, brought down. The timing of these assaults was such that most Georgians believed the Russians were attempting to create disarray in the country as a prelude to Russia's military invasion of Georgia in August 2008. This type of information warfare is consistent with Russian military doctrine. There were several indications of GRU involvement, but Russia denied any responsibility.

The Russian annexation of Crimea in 2014 was followed by waves of sophisticated cyberattacks against Ukraine's central government in Kiev. In December 2015, three different energy suppliers in Ukraine were hit by cyberattacks, causing hundreds of thousands of residents of Western Ukraine to lose electricity. There were renewed cyberattacks on the Ukrainian power grid in February 2017, as well as separate attacks on the Ukrainian financial sector and the Ministry of Defense. Ukrainian authorities stated categorically that Russia was behind the attacks.

A tactic used repeatedly and successfully by Russia to evade responsibility for cyberattacks has been to outsource them to private individuals, organized hacking groups, and cyber criminals. The FSB and GRU have been linked to private hacking networks that do their bidding for them with the help of covert tasking, guidance, technical expertise, and funding from the intelligence services. When the attribution trail gets uncomfortably close to the Russian government, a spokesperson for the Kremlin can concede that "private Russian individuals" may have been involved in the attacks, but they had no support or connection of any kind with the Russian government. That defense, as flimsy as it is, is hard to disprove. What we can say with certainty, however, is that secret partnerships with nongovernmental enterprises serve as a force multiplier for Russia and give it enough deniability to conceal its hand.

A good starting point for determining the culpability for cyberattacks is to look at who had the means and the motive to carry them out. In the cases of Estonia, Georgia, and Ukraine, there is only one answer. Only the Russian government could have done so. For the hacking of the 2015 and 2016 DNC emails, the answer is less clear—and the evidence is either lacking or still classified. But the bottom line is that Russia had the means (it was not hard because the email security practices at the DNC were so weak) and, according to the US intelligence community, the motive (to defeat Hillary Clinton). America deserves answers. The appointment of

Robert Mueller as special counsel to investigate the role of Russia in the 2016 presidential election is a hopeful sign that the truth may eventually come out. Vladimir Putin's statement on June 1, 2017, that "private Russian hackers" could have been behind the interference in the US election smacks of the standard obfuscation used by the Russians in the past to deflect suspicion away from government involvement.

In March 2017, the US Justice Department indicted two Russian FSB officers—Dmitry Dokuchaev and Igor Sushchin—for stealing data from 500 million Yahoo accounts in 2014. The primary purpose of the operation was straight espionage, but it is possible that accomplices of the two FSB officers also used access to Yahoo accounts for fraudulent financial activity. Yahoo subscribers who may have had their personal information and email communications compromised by the FSB included politicians, White House staffers, business leaders, bankers, journalists, academics, and law enforcement officials. This is the largest known breach of a US computer system and the first to implicate a Russian intelligence service directly.

The cases I have cited are by no means a comprehensive listing of all the spying Russia has done against us in the last several years. There are many more examples. And it is important to note also, of course, that these are just the cases we know about. How I would like to be a counterintelligence officer again and to have the challenge of ferreting out these still undisclosed traitors in our midst! Chinese spying is egregious and should make all of us mad, but it is based on cold, objective, and somehow impersonal self-interest. It does not seem to have the same kind of animus toward the United States that Russian espionage has. Vladimir Putin does not like us. His grudge is personal, and he has unleashed his very capable intelligence services against us. I am certain he takes great pleasure in showing his disdain for America by sheltering the contemptible US turncoat Edward Snowden.[21] When the US intelligence community is interviewing applicants for employment today, it sometimes refers to the "Big Five" foreign languages that are in highest demand: Chinese, Arabic, Farsi, Korean, and Russian. That is not surprising. The Russian language is still on the list for good reasons, not the least of which is that the SVR and GRU are all over us. Russia will remain a major counterintelligence concern for the United States for the foreseeable future. We would be naive in the extreme to believe that we could ever expect good faith from Vladimir Putin.

THREE
Cuba

> I believe the main reason that Cuban intelligence was so exceptionally successful, for so many years, is because the supreme Cuban spy master was Fidel Castro himself.
>
> —Brian Latell, former CIA officer

The country that I consider the third most dangerous counterintelligence threat to the United States is Cuba. I rank Cuba only number three on the dangerous scale, but I rank it number one on the obnoxious scale. When I was chief of counterintelligence at the CIA, no foreign intelligence service rankled me more than the Cuban DI (Intelligence Directorate; formerly known as the DGI, or General Intelligence Directorate).[1] It was ruthless, it was devious, and worst of all, it was very, very good. Not only that, but the DGI was Fidel Castro's instrument of choice in carrying out his personal vendetta against the CIA and the United States.

Castro's hatred of America was well-founded. There was, of course, the deep ideological chasm between our two countries, manifested on our side by the crippling economic sanctions we imposed on Cuba shortly after Castro took power in 1959. Next was the failed CIA-led effort to overthrow Castro by an amphibious invasion at the Bay of Pigs in 1961. Castro had tangible proof that President John Kennedy and the CIA would go to extreme measures to eliminate him. As a result, he turned increasingly to the Soviet Union for military and economic aid and authorized the Russians to build a huge listening post at Lourdes, Cuba, to eavesdrop on US communications. Castro desperately needed Soviet help to deter what he thought could be future American aggressions against Cuba. Nikita Khrushchev secretly began sending missiles and nuclear warheads to Cuba, which in 1963 precipitated the near-cataclysmic Cuban Missile

Crisis. Relations between Cuba and the United States could hardly have been worse.

The Cuban DGI was established by Castro in 1961 to preserve the Revolution; to collect intelligence on Cuba's enemies, both foreign and domestic; and to carry out covert action operations as he directed. Castro was aware as early as 1961 that President Kennedy and his brother, Robert Kennedy, the US attorney general, were trying to have him assassinated through a variety of CIA plots, mostly half-cocked, that never came anywhere near fruition. The main task of the new DGI was to strike back against the United States.

The DGI was trained by the Soviet KGB, but like Socrates, Plato, and Aristotle, this was a case of the student surpassing the master. The DGI was far better than the KGB in terms of audacity, tradecraft, and discipline. The CIA could penetrate the KGB and sometimes count on it to make tradecraft mistakes. I wish that had been the case with the DGI, but it was not.

My deep-seated distaste for the DGI began personally. One Sunday afternoon in June 1987, when I was in Vienna, I received a call from the Marine guard at the US embassy; he used the agreed on parole to indicate that we had a walk-in at the embassy.[2] Most walk-ins were of no intelligence value, so I had low expectations for this one as I drove to meet him. As I entered the embassy, I noticed a Latino-looking gentleman sitting in the waiting area. He had with him a young girl who I thought was probably his daughter. I went up to the Marine desk and said, "Corporal, what do we have here?" The guard handed me two official Cuban passports. I went down to talk to the gentleman, but it was difficult because I did not speak Spanish at that time and he had no English. Our only language in common was Russian, and his Russian was elementary at best. Finally, in his frustration he motioned for me to come closer, and he began whispering in my ear the names of several CIA officers undercover, all of which I recognized. He had my attention. I called in one of my Spanish-speaking officers. We took the two Cubans to a safehouse and had them out of the country on their way to the United States the next morning.

This was Florentino Aspillaga Lombard, the highest-ranking defector from the DGI we had ever had. He was at the time the head of the DGI office in Prague. The young lady was his teenaged mistress, the daughter of a Cuban official at the embassy, and they were on the run. Aspillaga's wife and children were still back in Prague. Aspillaga and his girlfriend wanted a new life together in the United States, so they drove to Vienna to offer their services to the CIA.

In his CIA debriefings, Aspillaga told us a shocking story. He said that all thirty-eight of the Cubans the CIA thought it had recruited over the previous twenty-six years were doubles, controlled and run against us by the DGI. This was a devastating indictment of CIA counterintelligence, one of the worst and most embarrassing compromises we have ever had. The DGI beat us—and beat us soundly.

The CIA's damage assessment was long and painful. The intelligence the CIA disseminated from these bogus agents had to be recalled since it was all DGI-concocted disinformation. The CIA's tradecraft in handling the controlled agents had been completely exposed to the DGI, which later ridiculed the CIA in a TV special for the agency's alleged amateurishness and sloppiness. The CIA lost all the clandestine equipment it had issued to the Cuban assets, including a then state-of-the-art burst satellite communications system. Finally, I shudder to think how much of the CIA's cash, paid to the Cuban doubles in salaries and bonuses, ended up in the DGI's coffers.

How could this have happened? I think there were multiple factors. First, the CIA was so eager to have sources on island that it looked the other way when none of them produced any real intelligence of value. Many of the doubles reported that they were "on the verge" of meaningful access, but they never quite got there. The CIA settled for chickenfeed. Second, intelligence officers always want their recruitments to turn out well. They do not want to admit that they were duped by a double. In their desire to succeed against the Cuban target, the CIA's handling officers rationalized away the questionable reporting, anomalous behaviors, and ambiguous polygraph results of their agents. Third, the quality of counterintelligence at the CIA during much of this period was undermined by the poor leadership of James Jesus Angleton, whose obsessive focus on the KGB and overall paranoia blinded him to other counterintelligence threats. And fourth, the CIA grossly underestimated the skill and sophistication of the DGI.

In another sensational revelation, Aspillaga told the CIA that former CIA officer Philip Agee had cooperated with the DGI and had been paid close to $1 million. Agee's role as a DGI agent was later confirmed by former KGB officer Oleg Kalugin in his book *Spymaster*. Kalugin said Agee had walked into the KGB in 1973, had been turned away as a suspected provocation, and then had gone to the Cubans. Agee, a graduate of the University of Notre Dame, joined the CIA in 1957. He served in a series of undercover assignments in Latin America in the 1960s, supposedly becoming more and more disillusioned by what he considered CIA support of right-wing dictatorships. While assigned to Mexico City in 1968, Agee resigned from the agency, moved to Europe, and began his new career of revealing and "neutralizing" CIA activities everywhere. In 1975 he published his book *Inside the Company: CIA Diary*, a detailed description of his clandestine career and an exposé of CIA activities in Latin America. Most damaging of all, he included as an annex the names of 250 CIA undercover officers and foreign agents, thereby disrupting the CIA officers' clandestine careers and subjecting them to considerable personal risk. The foreign agents he identified were exposed to the even worse fate of possible imprisonment or execution. The CIA chief of station in Athens, Richard Welch, was murdered on the streets of Athens in December 1975, shortly after he had been outed by Agee. Agee's guilt has never been proved conclusively, but few CIA officers I know believe that the timing of Welch's killing was a coincidence.

Agee's US passport was revoked in 1979, but he still traveled widely, mostly in Europe, for the next several years using passports provided by the leftist governments of Grenada and Nicaragua. In subsequent books and magazine articles, Agee continued his denunciations of the CIA and the US government and disclosed the identities of an additional one thousand CIA officers and agents. It was clear at that point that he was not operating on his own but was getting help from a foreign intelligence service. Unfortunately, under US law at the time, the unauthorized disclosure of the names of undercover US personnel was not a crime, so Agee could not be indicted and extradited to the United States.[3]

That Agee was operating on behalf of the DGI could not be denied after 1989. Moreover, his involvement with the KGB was a near certainty because of the close relationship that existed between the DGI and the KGB. I have no reason to doubt Oleg Kalugin's statement that he read reporting from Agee that the DGI passed to the KGB. It is inconceivable to me that the KGB would let its client service run a source of this magnitude without inserting itself into the operation.

In 1989 Agee played the key role in a DGI operation against the CIA. He posed as a CIA official from the inspector general's office in a fiendishly clever recruitment operation against a young CIA officer stationed in Mexico City. Agee contacted her and said he was conducting a sensitive investigation of alleged wrongdoing by the CIA in Mexico City, possibly involving senior management. He asked for her help in carrying out a discreet investigation that would not alert the targets. Agee ordered her on behalf of the inspector general not to discuss his approach with anyone. He played his role to perfection and elicited from our officer significant information. When I learned about this brazen but partially successful operation, I was furious. But then, after a few minutes, I could not help but shake my head and say to myself, "Damn, that was good!"

And it would never end. In 1998 the FBI broke up a large Cuban espionage operation in South Florida called the Wasp Network (Red Avispa). This network consisted of fourteen or more Cuban spies who had the mission of penetrating anti-Castro organizations in Florida. Evidence against some of the members was too thin for prosecution, but five ringleaders stood trial and were convicted of espionage and other crimes. One of the Cuban-American groups the Wasp Network infiltrated was an organization called Brothers to the Rescue. Brothers to the Rescue flew aircraft in and around Cuban airspace to assist people fleeing in boats and to drop anticommunist propaganda leaflets. The organization was clearly a thorn in Castro's side. A member of the Wasp Network found out the flight plan of a Brothers to the Rescue flight to Cuba in February 1996. Cuban fighter aircraft shot down the plane in international airspace, and all four Cuban Americans on board were killed.

The senior analyst on Cuba for the Defense Intelligence Agency (DIA), a woman named Ana Montes, was arrested in 2001 on charges of committing espionage on behalf of Cuba for at least sixteen years. During that period Montes passed to the DGI everything she could get her hands on related to US counterintelligence efforts against Cuba. It is no wonder that the DGI completely owned us for all those years. The tradecraft the Cubans used in handling Montes was fantastic, a credit to the art of espionage. It was a brilliant operation. Montes was sentenced to twenty-five years in prison. The Montes case merits closer scrutiny and will be the subject of more detailed CI analysis in chapter 8.[4]

There are numerous other examples of Cuban treachery, but I will limit myself to summarizing just one more case already mentioned briefly in a footnote. In June 2009 a retired State Department official and his wife, Kendall and Gwendolyn Myers, were arrested on charges of having been DGI agents for almost thirty years. Myers joined the US Foreign Service with a top-secret clearance in 1977. Later he was given even higher clearances when he was assigned to the highly sensitive Bureau of Intelligence and Research at the State Department. Myers sympathized with the Cuban Revolution and believed that the United States was subjecting the Cuban government and people to unfair treatment. His response, probably beginning in 1979, was to spy for Cuba. With the help of his wife, Gwendolyn, he engaged in a full-fledged espionage relationship with the DGI. Until Myers's retirement in 2007, he passed top-secret documents and other classified material to the DGI in a sophisticated system of dead drops and brush passes. During their trial, it became known that the Myerses had received personal congratulations from Fidel Castro. The damage they did to US national security was incalculable.

Agee, Montes, and the Myerses were all ideologically motivated to support the Cuban cause. Contrast this with the motivation of the Americans who spied for Russia, which was almost exclusively venal. Russian intelligence officers had a heyday in the US in the 1930s, 1940s, and early 1950s, when they could recruit Americans who were members of the US Communist Party or who were secret fellow travelers. By the mid-1950s this ideological ace in the hole was mostly gone; few Americans continued to believe in the failed communist system. From that point on, recruitment deals were almost exclusively cash for secrets. KGB and GRU officers must have looked at America with contempt when they saw how many American capitalists could be bought. The easiest recruitment any intelligence officer of any country will ever make is one that boils down to negotiating the price.

In their recruitment operations against Americans, the Cubans and Chinese often benefited from nonmonetary inducements, ideological in the case of the Cubans and ethnic in the case of the Chinese. These recruitments can be relatively easy also in that many of the Americans who worked for the DGI and the MSS essentially volunteered their services. Agee's motivation was more nuanced. Although he wanted to present himself to the world as an altruist and anti-imperialist—and some of that was undoubtedly true—he corrupted himself early on by taking large sums of money from the Cubans. Most intelligence officers I know feel some measure of grudging respect for spies, even traitors like Montes and Myers, who have betrayed us as a matter of conscience. That limited respect disappears completely when money changes hands. I will never forget a high-ranking Soviet agent I was honored to work with who was so intent on preserving the purity of his ideological motivation that he adamantly refused any kind of compensation. There were many more like him.

Another noteworthy aspect of Cuban intelligence activity in the United States is the quality of the tradecraft. The longevity of an espionage operation is largely a function of how good the tradecraft is, not only the skill of the handling officer but also the techniques and equipment used to run the operation securely. Agee operated under DGI control for all or most of fifteen years. Montes was a prolific producer for the DGI for sixteen years. Kendall Myers was in place for twenty-eight years. We know little about Agee's handling, but Montes and Myers were trained by their case officers to use a deft combination of dead drops, personal meetings, brush passes, and one-way-voice-link radio messages to communicate with the DGI and to pass their secrets.[5] It was no small feat for the Cubans to run these cases as long as they did and in hostile territory under the noses of US security and counterintelligence officials without getting caught. I hate to say it, but I take my hat off to them.

DGI covert action in Latin America and Africa has been far-reaching and nefarious. Fidel Castro promoted revolution around the world and, in effect, allowed the DGI to serve as a surrogate for the Soviet KGB. Beginning in the late 1960s, the DGI stationed a large contingent of intelligence officers in Nicaragua to provide security support for the Sandinistas. Cuba, through the DGI, forged an alliance with Salvador Allende in Chile in an effort to blunt US covert action in the country. The DGI and the Cuban military had a large-scale presence in Angola from 1975 to 1991 to fight alongside the revolutionary People's Movement for the Liberation of Angola (MPLA) against the South African–backed National Union for the Total Independence of Angola (UNITA) and the National Liberation Front of Angola (FNLA). The Marxist leader of Grenada, Maurice Bishop, benefited from covert DGI support before and during his successful coup in 1979 until his overthrow and execution in 1983. Hugo Chávez almost certainly had DGI support in Venezuela during his attempted coup in 1992 and throughout his presidency from 1999 to 2013.[6]

Pound for pound the Cuban DGI may be the most effective intelligence service US counterintelligence faces. It cannot compete with the Chinese or the Russians in terms of overall damage to US national security, but that is primarily a function of its smaller size, narrower objectives, and limited resources. We are lucky that Cuba is as small as it is—because otherwise we would be in big, big trouble.

The radio-wave attacks on US embassy personnel in Havana that began in late 2016 and continued until at least August 2017 may or may not have an intelligence connection. No one seems to know what the attacks are, where they originate, or what their purpose is. What is incontestable is that more than twenty American officials have been targeted in their homes or hotels and have suffered health effects as a result. The most common complaints are hearing loss, headaches, nausea, and memory lapses. The affected individuals have given conflicting reports about what they experienced. Some heard a high-pitched sound, others chirping like a cricket, and others nothing at all, raising the possibility of signals in the inaudible ultrasound spectrum. The FBI, State Department, and US intelligence agencies are investigating.

I wish I knew what was going on in Havana. Why are Americans being singled out as victims? Are the signals designed to mask listening devices? Is there some other technical purpose we have not yet discovered? Is the Cuban government responsible? Are the Cubans receiving technical assistance from the Russians? We may never know the answers to these questions.

There is another possibility. The radio attacks may be intended to do exactly what they are doing—harming Americans. I would not put that level of enmity and viciousness beyond the DGI that I have come to know and despise. The Havana attacks are reminiscent of the 1970s and 1980s microwave radiation attacks on the US embassy in Moscow, which also had harmful health effects on US officials.

I hope I have made my case. I hate Cuban intelligence, but I still respect and fear it for the formidable adversary that it is. When Fidel Castro died, my hope was that we would be flooded with DGI defectors who could tell us exactly what the DGI has been doing to us since 1959. I think we would be stunned to discover that what we thought we knew—as bad as it was—was just the tip of the iceberg. Unfortunately, this intelligence bonanza has not taken place. Post-Castro Cuba has shown no signs of ending its clandestine warfare against the United States. US counterintelligence would be ill-advised to lower its guard against Cuba.

FOUR

The Ten Commandments of Counterintelligence

O that thou hadst hearkened to my commandments! then had thy peace been as a river, and thy righteousness as the waves of the sea.
—Isaiah 48:18

In the preceding chapters, I summarized the nature and magnitude of spying conducted against the United States by our three principal counterintelligence adversaries: China, Russia, and Cuba. I estimate that these three countries are responsible for 90 percent of the espionage and covert action directed against American targets today, but the other 10 percent cannot be ignored either. We underestimate the activities of the Iranian intelligence services against American interests worldwide at our peril.[1] Even our "friends," as we have seen earlier, have occasionally been caught with their hands in our cookie jar. US intelligence has "special relationships" with a handful of its closest allies, whereby we do not spy on them and they do not spy on us. It is no secret that the *most* special of these special relationships is with Great Britain, with whom we have enjoyed magnificent and historic intelligence cooperation since World War II.

Much was made of the Samuel Loring Morison case of 1984, which was the first breach of this sacrosanct US-UK intelligence accord. Morison was a US Navy intelligence analyst who was arrested in October 1984 on charges of passing highly classified satellite imagery and other documents to the British magazine *Jane's Defence Weekly*. Morison had worked part-time for *Jane's* while he was still employed by US Navy intelligence and was apparently hoping to earn full-time employment by ingratiating himself with the British company. He accepted payment from *Jane's* for the documents with the full knowledge that his actions were illegal. He was convicted of espionage and sentenced to two years in prison. It was never established that British intelligence was aware of or participated in Morison's spying, but it had to know that *Jane's* was receiving classified information from an American source. Still, I am prepared to give our British friends the benefit of doubt, and we can safely eliminate them as an espionage threat to the United States. I cannot and will not say the same for many other countries.

Espionage against the United States is pervasive, highly damaging, and getting worse. I wrote "The Ten Commandments of Counterintelligence," which appeared in *Studies in Intelligence* in 2001, to codify some of the lessons I learned during my many years of doing CI for the agency. I stand by the validity of these principles all these years later but believe they would benefit from some amplification based on recent events. Let's get started.

The First Commandment: Be Offensive

> A major theme in all my books is that the CIA is not only the first line of defense but they should also be the first line of offense.
>
> —Vince Flynn

Counterintelligence that is passive and defensive will fail. We cannot hunker down in a defensive mode and wait for things to happen. I believe we are spending far too much money on fences, safes, alarms, and other purely defensive measures to protect our secrets. That is not how we have been hurt in recent years. Spies have hurt us. Our CI mind-set should be relentlessly offensive. We need to go after our CI adversaries. In counterintelligence, just as in football, a good offense is the best defense.

The key prongs of offensive counterintelligence fall into two main categories: penetration and double-agent operations. If we simply took care of our business in these two areas, we could go a long way toward preventing or quickly detecting the kinds of spying and technology theft that are causing our country so much harm.

It is a simple proposition: the best counterintelligence has been and will always be penetration. "Penetrate, penetrate, penetrate" should be the clarion call of every intelligence service. For each American spy who is out there betraying us, there are several members of the opposition service who know who he or she is. Our job is to find and recruit those people. Even the best CI officers should not have to rely exclusively on their own efforts to catch spies. They need help and lots of it from their HUMINT colleagues.[2] There is a big myth that counterintelligence successes are the result of the tireless efforts of CI gumshoes who sneak around watching everyone, pore over stacks of travel and financial records, tap phones (with warrants, of course), and read emails. There is a place for all of that, but more often than not, spies are uncovered by penetrations of the foreign intelligence services involved. By "penetrations" I refer not only to in-place sources who are still working for their service but also to defectors who have abandoned their countries and who are now safely in our hands. No matter what it takes, we must have penetrations.

There is a wide disparity in how the US intelligence community deals with these two different types of penetrations. When the KGB defector Vitaly Yurchenko gave us the identities of the American spies Edward Lee Howard and Ronald Pelton in 1985, the FBI could proceed with its investigations without any real concern for the source's safety.[3] We have seen how Florentino Aspillaga Lombard revealed Philip Agee's relationship with the Cuban DGI. When Quiangsheng Yu, a senior Chinese intelligence officer, defected to the United States in 1985, he helped US counterintelligence identify Larry Wu-Tai Chin, a Chinese American employed by the CIA, as a Chinese spy.[4] Defectors, as a rule, deliver their information without fear of retaliation from the services they betrayed. They are out of harm's reach. The receiving service, capitalizing on its counterintelligence bonanza, can usually act on the intelligence quickly without worrying about source protection issues.

The situation with in-place penetrations is completely different. When the CIA, for example, recruits an active-duty foreign intelligence officer who agrees to stay on the job, there is a professional and moral obligation to do everything possible to protect that source. I recall a case I worked on in which our newly recruited penetration of a major hostile intelligence service identified a high-level spy with extremely damaging access. We would have loved to pounce on that spy immediately, of course, and to put him out of action, but our source was too exposed. Only a small number of people in his service were aware of the identity of this spy, so if we had wrapped up the case precipitously, our source would have come under dangerous scrutiny from his own CI service. We could not expose him to that risk. He had put his life in our hands, and we owed him protection. We had to wait until enough time and distance had passed to provide insulation for our source. Only then could we arrest the spy. It was not operationally feasible to limit his access significantly during this period without alerting him, so we had to sit back and watch him continue his betrayal for several more months. It was hard, but we made the right decision.

I should not have been shocked, but I was, when I saw firsthand that the Russian intelligence services did not have the same scrupulosity about protecting their in-place penetrations. Aldrich Ames, Edward Lee Howard, and Robert Hanssen all revealed to their KGB or SVR handlers the names of Russians who were secretly working for US intelligence. By rights and as a matter of simple humanity, the Russians should have gone slowly to shield their invaluable American agents from suspicion. But no. They swooped in and arrested the named traitors as soon as they found out about them. Source protection be damned. What is really disturbing, of course, is that the Russians got away with it. All three spies survived the onslaught. It was only later and because of other factors that their espionage careers ended. American counterintelligence can and should do better.

Penetrations are so important for counterintelligence success that I would like to see US intelligence be super aggressive—even in-your-face pushy—in going after them. We should advertise to foreign intelligence officers that our doors and wallets are open to any of them who come forward with information that leads to the arrest and conviction of an American spy. When the Berlin Wall came down in 1989, the CIA was Johnny-on-the-spot knocking on doors and spreading the word that former Soviet bloc intelligence officers could ease their retirement worries by making a deal. When the FBI and CIA hit a roadblock in identifying the mole we knew we had at the heart of US counterintelligence, a $7 million payment was enough in 2000 to flush out a former KGB officer who could get his hands on and deliver to us what turned out to be Robert Hanssen's KGB/SVR file. Money well spent. We call this "hanging out the shingle," and I, for one, would like to see a lot more of it.

Aggressive double-agent operations are essential to any CI program, but not the predictable, hackneyed kind we have so often pursued. We need to push our bright and imaginative people to produce clever new scenarios for controlled operations, and we need more of them. The opposition services should constantly be kept off guard so that they never suspect that we have controlled from the beginning the operations they believe they initiated. When the requirements, modus operandi, and other objectives of the DA operation have been achieved, we should in a greater number of cases pitch the opposition case officer. If only one out of ten or twenty of these recruitments takes, it is still worth it.

US counterintelligence should operate aggressively against our nontraditional and our traditional adversaries. How many examples do we need of operations against Americans by so-called friendly countries before we act? If we suspect for whatever reason that the operatives of a friendly foreign intelligence service are operating against us, we should test them. We should dress up an enticing morsel—made to order for that specific target—and float it by them. If they take it, we have discovered that this nontraditional adversary is not as trustworthy as we had thought. Since we are testing a "friend," plausible deniability must be strictly preserved. We do not want a diplomatic incident. But the fact remains that every foreign intelligence service is a potential nontraditional adversary. No service should get a lifetime pass from US offensive CI operations.

Double-agent operations are such an essential and powerful weapon in the hands of US counterintelligence professionals that I will discuss them in greater depth in a subsequent chapter.

The Second Commandment: Honor Your Professionals

> Spy catching does not lead to a seventh-floor office.
>
> —Gardner "Gus" Hathaway, former chief of CIA counterintelligence

It has been true for years—to varying degrees throughout the US intelligence community—that CI professionals have not been favored to the extent they deserved with promotions, assignments, awards, praise, esteem, or other recognition. The truth is that CI officers are not popular. They are not welcome when they walk in. They are the skunk at the garden party. They usually bring bad news. Do operators really want to hear that there may be problems with their cases?

For much of my CIA career, many of our best people avoided becoming CI specialists. CI was not prestigious. It had a bad reputation. It was not fast track. It did not lead to promotions or good assignments. James Jesus Angleton left a distasteful legacy that for years discredited the CI profession. As a result, unfortunately, counterintelligence became the refuge of some underperformers who could not get a job anywhere else and who liked the less competitive environment. Is it a coincidence that flawed and mediocre performers like Aldrich Ames and Robert Hanssen found a niche in counterintelligence? To the extent that CI became a magnet for incompetence, its reputation suffered even more. Let's be honest. CI was just not very good. Is it any wonder that traitors like Ames and Hanssen could do their dirty work at the CIA and FBI for nine and twenty-two years, respectively?

The 1980s, the Decade of the Spy in America, were an overdue wake-up call for US counterintelligence. Spy case after spy case caused Congress and the intelligence community to realize that CI had been deficient and had to be upgraded. The CIA created the Counterintelligence Center. The FBI raised the status of Foreign Counterintelligence (FCI) and gave it new leadership and additional resources. The counterintelligence functions at the Department of State, the Department of Energy, the national laboratories, the National Security Council, and elsewhere were given more clout and more staffing. CI specialists from the FBI and CIA were sent on temporary duty to other government agencies to assist them in improving their counterintelligence programs.

The downward trend appears to have been reversed, and CI has begun to be rehabilitated as a respected professional discipline. Nevertheless, the battle has not been completely won. Counterterrorism, nonproliferation, and rogue nations are grabbing resources and priorities at the expense of counterintelligence. I fear that our country's CI capabilities are being degraded. We must rebuild our counterintelligence cadre, and once we have more CI specialists on board, we need to treat them well. We must do more to get CI people promoted, recognized, and respected so that our best young people will be attracted to follow us into what we know is a noble profession and where the need is so great.

The Third Commandment: Own the Street

> It would be naïve to believe that the need for rigorous counterintelligence and counterespionage ended with the end of the cold war.
>
> —Mark M. Lowenthal, *Intelligence*

Owning the street is fundamental to CI, but it is probably the least followed of the commandments. Any CI program worthy of the name must be able to engage the opposition on the street, the field of play for espionage. And when we do go to the street, we must be the best service there. If we are beaten on the street, it is worse than not having been there at all. For years, we virtually conceded the streets of the world's capitals—including the major espionage centers—to the KGB, the GRU, and the

Eastern European services because we either did not know how to do good surveillance or were not willing to pay the price for a thoroughly professional, full-time, local surveillance capability. Opposition intelligence officers must be watched, known meeting areas must be observed, and when an operation goes down—often on short notice—undetectable surveillance must be there, identify the participants, and obtain evidence.

Surveillance is excruciatingly difficult. I cannot help but chuckle when I see the Hollywood or TV version of surveillance: a car pulling over to the curb a hundred feet back when the subject pulls into a driveway, or two men sitting suspiciously in a car down the street waiting for the subject to come out of a building. That kind of surveillance would be detected in a heartbeat. The consequences of being "made" can be devastating. What if, for example, an in-place penetration of a foreign intelligence service provides information on the time and place of an operational act to be carried out by his service? It would be tempting to conduct surveillance of the operation to identify the individuals involved, but if our team is observed, we put our source at unacceptable risk. The danger is compounded by the fact that the opposition services pick the time and location of the operational acts, thereby giving them a decisive advantage in mounting good countersurveillance in the area. I tell my students in my intelligence classes at the Bush School, "If you pick the site, you own the action." Any good intelligence service will choose locations that are comfortable; that have infrastructure for countersurveillance, such as an observation post; and that have cover for action for the servicing officer and the countersurveillance teams. My dictum when I was on active duty with the CIA was this: When in doubt about your ability to conduct surveillance safely, stay away. The cost of being made is too high.

There are two main variables in making the decision of whether to attempt surveillance. The first is how sophisticated and skilled the target is. If you are surveilling an ordinary citizen who is suspected of espionage, chances are that he or she will be a relative amateur in spotting surveillance. In those cases you can probably use standard surveillance procedures and not get caught. Many years ago I was walking down Forty-Second Street in New York City near the intersection with Fifth Avenue. I was not looking for anything in particular, but I noticed that I was in the middle of a simple ABC surveillance team.[5] I first observed B, who was closest to me and intently looking down the street. Sure enough, A was just as obvious about a half block ahead. I knew where C would be, and it took only a quick glance across Forty-Second Street to make him as well. My first thought was that I hoped they had a dumb "rabbit." If their target was a trained intelligence officer, adept at detecting surveillance, this team of tyros, whoever they were, would be toast. Needless to say, I could not resist hurrying ahead to where I knew the rabbit would be. He was a middle-aged Asian gentleman who seemed blissfully unaware that anything was amiss around him. My guess is that this surveillance team, as basic as it was, accomplished its objective.

The opposite extreme is when you know or suspect that your rabbit is a pro. If that is the case, you must dig deeply into your bag of tricks and deploy the best technique you have. A complicating factor, of course, is how important it is not to be made. SVR officers in New York, for example, know they are subject to routine FBI surveillance, so it is not fatal if a team occasionally makes a mistake and is detected. In other circumstances, though, detection of surveillance could cause the operation to be aborted or, as mentioned earlier, put an in-place penetration at tremendous risk.

I had an operation once that raised serious concerns about what kind of surveillance to put on a target. We had intriguing, but far from conclusive, indications that a local resident using non-Russian identification was, in fact, a KGB illegal. Our job was to investigate and, if possible, to verify his status one way or another. This situation called for surveillance, but there was considerable risk. If, in fact, this so-called businessman was an illegal, he would be well-trained and on constant alert. If he saw our surveillance, he would stop operating, go to ground, and escape back to Russia. We would lose the operation. I did not want another Margarita Tairova or Edward Lee Howard fiasco.[6] The neighborhood where the suspected illegal lived offered little cover for action, which added even more vulnerability to the surveillance operation. Weighing all these factors, we decided that we would not attempt continuous lockstep surveillance but would instead limit ourselves to low-risk, downstream, static, and when possible, leapfrog tactics. It was a slow and frustrating process, but in the end it paid off. The Russian illegal never saw us and eventually led us to a high-level American spy he was handling.

The second variable in making surveillance decisions is how good your team is. The way surveillance used to be done by US counterintelligence is not good enough. Often in the past, someone would walk through the spaces of a CIA station, an FBI field office, a military unit, or a police department and say, "OK, we need a surveillance team. Let's go." It is true that these professionals probably all had rudimentary surveillance training, but they were far from expert. Good surveillance is not a quickly acquired skill. In fact, I usually insisted that my teams have at least a year of on-the-street training and city familiarization before they could operate against intelligence officer targets. I would sometimes run against them myself as their rabbit in training exercises to confirm their readiness. Those were fun days out of the office.

Just how inexpert surveillance can be was brought home to me once when I was under surveillance by a Bulgarian team. I had never before seen such obvious, clumsy, and bumbling surveillance. The team members were always out of sync, stayed on point too long, used jerky hand signals, and chose terrible stakeout locations. Their performance made me angry, not because I was under surveillance but because the Bulgarians had put such an incompetent team on me. I considered it a professional insult.

The FBI takes surveillance very, very seriously. They are the best of the best. The FBI today is under heavy pressure to increase its surveillance of terrorist suspects, not to mention its continuing responsibility to cover criminals and foreign intelligence officers. I do not think the American public has any appreciation of how labor intensive and expensive professional surveillance is. What does it take, for example, to do twenty-four-hour surveillance of just one terrorist suspect or one foreign intelligence officer? I estimate conservatively that it would require up to thirty people divided into three shifts to provide that level of coverage. The need for competent US surveillance is overwhelming—and growing. To me, as a teacher, I see opportunities for my students and other young Americans who are looking for a way to break into a counterintelligence career. Being on a surveillance team is a good way to start. Let me share with you something I pulled from the FBI's website:

FBI Surveillance Specialist Careers

- The Federal Bureau of Investigation uses a host of support personnel to conduct surveillance operations. These Surveillance Specialists are chosen for their ability to blend in with a crowd, follow the commands of the lead Agent, and perform the challenging responsibilities required to monitor potential criminals and terrorists.
- Despite the many resources that the FBI has at its disposal including electronic eavesdropping, GPS tracking, and satellite surveillance, there is often no substitute for a concerted human surveillance operation. In order to monitor all of the activities and interactions a suspected per-

petrator may conduct, a Special Surveillance Group is often assigned to watch them continuously.

- Due to the evolving sophistication of many terrorist and espionage operations, as well as the public's growing awareness of the capabilities of federal authorities, the Surveillance Specialist jobs have become much more challenging. Because the target is likely to be looking for individuals who are exhibiting suspicious or awkward behavior, the Surveillance Specialists use a variety of intricate maneuvers that allow them to maintain a façade of normality while still obtaining detailed intelligence.
- Surveillance Specialist jobs involve using professional and personal skills to tail a suspect and gather as much information as possible. This may require setting up and manning a static post in an adjacent building or it could mean following the target through the streets of New York on a bicycle. The FBI often requires its Surveillance Specialists to travel to locations throughout the country in order to bring their unique skill set to an operation.
- Surveillance jobs with the FBI will involve performing the following duties:
    - Plan, organize and implement a surveillance operation
    - Covertly establish a surveillance post in a mobile vehicle or at a fixed location
    - Monitor communications between targets and other individuals
    - Take photographs, videos, sound recordings and other types of electronic surveillance for analysis and admission into a legal proceeding
    - Analyze intelligence and distribute it to the appropriate FBI personnel
    - Maintain a high level of attentiveness and professional performance during extended surveillance operations

The kind of world-class surveillance capability the US counterintelligence community *must* put in the field demands extensive infrastructure: vehicles, photo gear, video equipment, concealment devices, disguises, radios, safe apartments, safe garages, warming rooms, observation posts, license plates, night-vision goggles, beacons, drones, aircraft, satellites, chemical tagging, and on and on. There is no such thing as surveillance on a shoestring. The teams must also have gender, ethnic, age, and social diversity to blend inconspicuously into their environment. I admire US

Army Foreign Counterintelligence Activity (FCA) personnel greatly and worked with them successfully on several occasions, but for many years FCA surveillance teams were made up almost exclusively of young, white, short-haired males. Come on, Army, you can do better than that—and I'm sure you are now. One of the best surveillants I ever worked with was a frumpy little grandmother who absolutely personified "non-threatening." Nobody ever looked at her twice, so she could get up close and personal to her targets, shooting film like crazy from her high-speed, silent shutter, low-light bra camera. Never for a second did her targets suspect that she was eating their lunch.

It is up to us. We have a choice to make. We can either devote the resources necessary "to own the street," or we can accept being a second-rate counterintelligence power that China, Russia, Cuba, and others can continue to rob blind.

The Fourth Commandment: Know Your History

> After more than a thousand years . . . an enemy finally broke through. Not because of superior firepower. Not because the Manchus were better fighters or strategists. They weren't. The Manchus breached the Great Wall and took Beijing because someone opened a gate . . . as simple as that. A general, a traitor, let them in and an empire fell.
>
> —Louise Penny, *A Great Reckoning*

I am discouraged when I talk to young counterintelligence officers today to discover how little they know about the history of American CI. When the FBI's David Major, one of the country's leading experts on counterintelligence, gave courses on CI at CIA headquarters, I sometimes sat in to see how he taught the subject matter. What I recall most vividly is that at the beginning of each course, David gave a quiz to the students to determine what their starting point was in terms of CI knowledge. It was shocking. The students were CIA officers of varying ages and grades, some of whom were already in CI jobs or were headed that way. If it had been a graded test, virtually everyone would have failed. The students had only the barest superficial knowledge of the key milestones and personalities of US counterintelligence history.

Counterintelligence is a difficult and dangerous discipline. It does not come to us intuitively; it must be learned. Many good, well-meaning CI people have gone wrong and made horrendous mistakes. Their failures in most cases are well documented, but the lessons are lost if our officers do not read the CI literature. By the same token, the world of counterintelligence has been the home of some truly brilliant men and women, from several different countries, who have honored our profession with some amazing CI successes. How can our officers learn from the mistakes and emulate the successes if they do not even know about them?

I find it inconceivable that any CI practitioner today could ply his or her trade without an in-depth knowledge of the Angleton era. Have our officers read Mangold and Martin?[7] Do they know the Loginov case?[8] How about HONETOL, MHCHAOS, Nosenko, Pollard, and Shadrin?[9] Are they familiar with Aspillaga and the Cuban double-agent debacle? Have they examined our mistakes in the Ames, Hanssen, and Howard cases? Are they staying current with recent CI releases like *The Spy's Son* and *The Billion Dollar Spy*?[10] I believe it is an indispensable part of the formation of any American CI officer—and a professional obligation—to know our CI history.

The many CI courses being offered now are a positive step, but there will never be a substitute for a CI professional's *personal* commitment to read the literature—usually on his or her own time at home. To assist in this process, I have compiled a list of twenty-five books on counterintelligence that had a major impact on my professional development as a CI officer and that I believe are valuable, if not essential, reading for anyone aspiring to a career in this field. See the appendix at the back of the book, "The Counterintelligence Officer's Bookshelf."

The Fifth Commandment: Do Not Ignore Analysis

> It is not enough, of course, simply to collect information. Thoughtful analysis is vital to sound decision making.
>
> —Ronald Reagan

Analysis has too often been the stepchild of counterintelligence. In the CI community, we have consistently understaffed analysis. We have either made it up as we have gone along or have tried to do it on the cheap.

Operators make bad analysts. We are different kinds of people. We are actors, doers, movers, and shakers; we are quick, maybe a little impulsive, maybe a little "cowboy." Our best times are away from our desks. We love the street. Analysis is not our thing—and when we have tried to do it, we have not been good at it.

True analysts are different. They love research. They are more cerebral, patient, and sedentary. They do not seem to mind sitting in a cubicle before a computer screen for long hours every day. If they had not become analysts, they would probably have gone into academia; the psychological profiles of analysts and academics are similar. Analysts find things we operators cannot. They are super smart. They write better.

Many CI organizations in the past have tried to make operators double as their own analysts. As a result, CI analysis in the United States has historically been the weakest part of our business. We know now that the clues to Pearl Harbor were in the masses of intercepts and other intelligence collected, but they were not analyzed in time to provide a warning to our forces. Similarly, if the movements and activities of the 9/11 terrorists had been analyzed in time—particularly their flight training in the US—the tragic outcome could conceivably have been different. For years the National Security Agency failed to exploit to its full potential the magnificent electronic intelligence it collected because it lacked the analytical brainpower to make sense of it, to identify what was actionable, and to disseminate it to policymakers quickly. The FBI was also late in recognizing the power of analysis. Only in about the last fifteen years has it upgraded the analytical career path at the FBI and filled its ranks with good, solid analysts.

That reminds me of Murray, one of my former students at the Bush School, whose dream was to become a special agent in the FBI. When he completed our master's program in national security studies, he applied to the FBI but was told he was not eligible for the special agent track because he lacked the necessary work experience. He somewhat reluctantly accepted a position with the FBI as an analyst, with the expectation that after three years he would transfer over to agent training. I talked to Murray about five years later and asked him if he had made the switch. He said, "You know, Mr. Olson, the FBI treated me so well as an analyst and the work there was so important and exciting that I just couldn't leave."

The Drug Enforcement Agency (DEA) is another example. DEA made its reputation as a world-class law enforcement agency with its street work. Intelligence analysis was there, but more as a side show than as an integral part of the mission. That changed. One of my wife's and my good friends at the CIA, an analyst named Judy, decided to accept a job at DEA in its understaffed intelligence section. We told her not to do it. "They're not committed to intelligence analysis," we said. "Those macho street guys will eat you alive." Not so. Judy helped build a top-notch analytical capability at DEA—and retired a few years ago as chief of DEA Intelligence. DEA became a believer in the power of analysis.

I hope the MSS, SVR, GRU, and DGI are not reading this, because they are making the same mistake we did. Whether the CIA or the KGB had the better human intelligence sources during the Cold War was close to a toss-up, but US intelligence did a far better job of *utilizing* the collected intelligence because of its superior analysis. Good intelligence collection is wasted if it is not matched with equally good intelligence analysis.

Things are getting better in the US counterintelligence community, but CI analysts are still undervalued and underappreciated. I remember watching some of my case officers' getting awards for their outstanding work in breaking a big CI case.[11] That was fine, but the operation would never have happened in the first place if it had not been for the analysts back at headquarters who put them on the right track. These analysts, unfortunately, were overlooked in the awards process. Where would we operators be in chasing potential penetrations of foreign intelligence services without the help of targeting analysts who point us in the right direction? Nowhere. But when we score, the analysts rarely get the credit they deserve.

A good CI program will recruit and train analysts in sizable numbers. When William Donovan set up the Office of Strategic Services (OSS) in 1942, his initial staffing plan was approximately 9,000 operators and 2,000 analysts. "Wild Bill" Donovan is one of my heroes, and I am loath to second-guess him, but I believe his ratio was lopsided. In my professional opinion, it would not be excessive as a rule of thumb for a top-notch CI service to be evenly divided between operators and analysts. Few of our US counterintelligence agencies come close to that ratio.

When Ted Price asked me to be his deputy in setting up the new Counterintelligence Center at the CIA in 1989, we knew that the old ways of doing counterintelligence had to be changed. The 1985 disaster was still hanging around our necks like an albatross. Counterintelligence was in shambles. The best people went elsewhere. The idea was to create a "center," that is, to bring together experts from various components and disciplines to work CI issues together. This was groundbreaking and heretical. A lot of naysayers said it could not be done. We were too different; we could not work together. But Ted persisted. We brought in security officers, psychologists, technical specialists, and military officers. We brought in lawyers—maybe we should have rethought that one! Just kidding. But best of all, we brought in analysts.

And where did we go to find them? Not to the Directorate of Operations. Case officers do a lot of things well, but not analysis. The best analysts in the agency were in the Directorate of Intelligence, the home of the eggheads. We set them up in their own unit, the Analysis Group, and turned them loose on counterintelligence analysis. We discovered that professional analysts are not bound by their subject matter. They may have been working on the North Korean navy or the Brazilian economy before they arrived, but counterintelligence for them was just another issue to learn, to dig into, and to analyze. They were terrific. Why had we waited so long to do this?

Wonderful things happen when good analysts in sufficient numbers pore over double-agent reports, presence lists, signals intelligence, audio and teltap transcripts, maps, travel data, and surveillance reports. They find the clues, make the connections, and focus our efforts in the areas that will be most productive.

Many parts of the US counterintelligence community have gotten the message and have incorporated trained analysts into their operations, but others have not. Across the board, we continue to have serious shortfalls in good, solid CI analysis.

The Sixth Commandment: Do Not Be Parochial

> Only one-eighth of an iceberg, they say, appears above the water; the proportion of detected espionage to the whole is probably considerably less.
>
> —Rebecca West, *The New Meaning of Treason*

More harm may have been done to the effectiveness of US counterintelligence over the years by interagency sniping and obstructionism than by our enemies. I remember when the CIA and the FBI did not even talk to each other—and both had disdain for the military intelligence services. It is no wonder that American CI was ineffectual and that some incredibly damaging spies went uncovered for so long.

The thinly veiled animosities and rivalries of the US intelligence community have a long history. The FBI and the US military services did everything they could to talk President Franklin Roosevelt out of establishing a civilian foreign intelligence service, the OSS, in 1942. They clearly did not welcome a new player and potential rival in the spy business. FDR overruled them eventually, but that did not stop them from criticizing and belittling the upstart OSS at every opportunity. Gen. Douglas MacArthur did not allow the OSS to operate in the Pacific theater, because he considered Donovan's spies reckless and unwilling to accept military authority. J. Edgar Hoover at the FBI complained angrily that the OSS was spying inside the United States (true), which he considered his exclusive domain. Donovan did not help matters by refusing to consult or to coordinate with his FBI and military counterparts.

The battle lines hardened as World War II drew to a close in 1945. Donovan lobbied hard for the establishment of a postwar civilian intelligence service on the model of the OSS, but the FBI and the military convinced President Harry Truman that the proposal smacked of an American gestapo. Not only that, they said, but the OSS had been wasteful and ineffective during the war (not true), Donovan was too close to the British (probably true), and the OSS would try to push the US toward war with the Soviet Union (probably not true). In any event the die was cast: Truman disbanded the OSS eleven days after Japan's surrender and rejected Donovan's recommendation for a follow-on civilian intelligence service. It was not until 1947 that Soviet treachery around the world, particularly in Eastern Europe, convinced Truman that the US once again needed an aggressive espionage and covert action capability. Thus, the CIA was born—but the gripes and suspicions of the FBI and the military lived on.

I had no way of knowing it then, but I would early on experience this FBI-CIA estrangement firsthand. Public service had a strong appeal for me. I applied to several US government agencies, including the FBI and the CIA. The processing appeared to be going smoothly with both organizations, and I was excited about the prospect of serving in either one. I was getting nervous, though, because my funds were running out and I needed a paying job as soon as possible.

My FBI application seemed farther along. I had passed the interviews, the physical exam, the background investigation, and J. Edgar Hoover's silly spelling test, which he had decreed for all special agent applicants. I called my FBI contact and explained my situation to him. He was friendly and helpful at first, but then came the whammy: "Jim, everything looks really good, but a problem has come up. We discovered that you also have an application pending with the CIA." I said that was true. "Well," he continued, "we have a policy at the FBI of not completing action on any application for employment if there is a simultaneous application to the CIA." I was stunned. "Here's what you need to do," he said. "You need to send a registered letter to the CIA officially withdrawing your application and then mail a copy to me." "If I do that," I said nervously, "does that mean I'm in?" "No," he answered, "we can't say that, but everything does look really good." I couldn't believe it. Weren't we all working for the same country? I decided to withdraw my FBI application and hope for good news from the CIA. It luckily came through. Otherwise, I would probably be practicing law in Clinton, Iowa, my fallback option.

Even as a fresh recruit at the CIA, I could see the strains in our relationship with the FBI. I was warned that we had to be careful about what we said around the FBI special agent assigned as the sole authorized liaison to the CIA. He was a fine man, but we had no doubt why he was there, namely, to report back on what the CIA was up to and to keep the CIA out of the FBI's business.

A big part of the problem is that the intelligence, law enforcement, and military communities have different missions, authorities, and personalities. Spies want to collect intelligence and protect sources; cops want to collect evidence and make arrests; soldiers want to seek and destroy. There is an inherent incompatibility in these activities, often leading to turf wars and personality conflicts. We do not always trust one another, so it is not surprising that cooperation, communication, and coordination have suffered.

Recriminations have flown left and right that key counterintelligence information has not always been communicated from one agency to another in a timely manner. There are resentments that larger CI organizations sometimes dominate the smaller ones and do not include them as equal partners in joint operations. Military commanders are not always happy with the unilateral activities of CIA paramilitary teams operating in their area of responsibility. I recall vividly how outraged the FBI was when a senior CIA officer in Germany refused to share with the FBI critical counterterrorism information contained in East German Stasi files obtained by the CIA when the Berlin Wall came down in 1989. I recall just as vividly how angry the CIA was when clumsy FBI surveillance allowed the CIA traitor Edward Lee Howard to escape to the USSR.

Occasionally in my career, I encountered instances of sarcasm or outright badmouthing of other US government agencies by my officers. That kind of attitude and cynicism infected our junior officers and got in the way of cooperation. These comments were usually intended to flaunt our supposed "superiority" by demeaning the other organizations' capabilities. It was considered good fun to laugh at their failures and their sloppy tradecraft. I dealt with these situations by telling the officers to knock it off, and I hope CI supervisors around the community are doing the same thing right now.

CI is so difficult, even in the best of circumstances, that the only way to do it properly is to do it together. We should not let our personalities, jealousies, or turf battles get in the way of our common mission. Our colleagues in our sister services are as dedicated, professional, hardworking, and patriotic as we are, and they deserve our respect and cooperation. Shame on us if we arrogantly insist on going it alone. We are not serving the American people to the best of our ability if we are not working together. The best people I have known in my career have been CI people, regardless of their organizational affiliation. So let's be collegial.

The Seventh Commandment: Train Your People

> While much of the daily work of counterintelligence is laborious and humdrum, its complex and subtle operations are very much like a gigantic chess game that uses the whole world for its board.
>
> —Allen Dulles, *The Craft of Intelligence*

Counterintelligence is a distinct discipline and an acquired skill. It is not intuitive. It requires a retraining of the mind to deal with the ambiguities and dead ends of the CI world. Expertise in counterintelligence is not automatically infused in us when we get our wings in intelligence, law enforcement, or the military. Good CI is not just a matter of applying logic and common sense to operations but is instead a highly specialized way of seeing things and analyzing them. Counterintelligence must be learned.

I do not know how many times in my career I have heard, "No, we do not really need a separate CI section. We are all CI officers; we'll do our own CI." That is a recipe for overconfidence and failure. There are no substitutes for professional CI officers, and only extensive, regular, and specialized CI training can produce them. Such training is expensive, so whenever possible we should do it on a community basis to avoid duplication and to oversee quality.

This sounds good, but we have a problem, a significant one. Who is going to teach it? When I look around the US counterintelligence community today, I am struck by how inexperienced it is. The midlevel and senior personnel in the community who had become CI specialists, in too many cases, moved to counterterrorism, nonproliferation, cyber intelligence, financial intelligence, organized crime, rogue nations, or other areas as priorities shifted. The counterintelligence function in many agencies, particularly after 9/11, was either downgraded or repopulated with undertrained junior officers. We are short on experienced senior managers who have enough time and depth in CI to teach it effectively to others. It is a scramble to find enough qualified instructors to teach the number and variety of training courses we need to form a new generation of CI professionals. How many people do we really have in US counterintelligence today who know the ins and outs of the Chinese MSS or the Russian SVR or the Cuban DGI? Who can teach the fine art of counterintelligence analysis? Who knows the real world of surveillance well enough to build teams that can defeat well-trained foreign intelligence officers on the street? The US counterintelligence bench is weak.

CI is a conglomerate of several disciplines and skills. A typical operation, for example, might include analysts, surveillance teams, case officers, technical experts, and double-agent specialists. Each of these areas requires its own specialized training curriculum. We were only partially successful in building a strong training capability in the early years of the Counterintelligence Center at the CIA in 1989 and 1990. We saw the need for a dedicated training staff, but we were still emerging from the Angletonian legacy of failed counterintelligence and found it hard to find open-minded, untainted, and experienced CI officers to design our curriculum and to teach our courses. The distorted Angleton-Golitsyn worldview still held sway among some of the CI veterans looking for jobs, so it took some finesse and diplomacy to divert them away from training.[12] I did not want our junior CI officers infected by the veterans' outlandish conspiracy theories, for example, that the Soviets controlled everything, Yuri Nosenko was a plant, and the Chinese-Soviet split was a communist plot to deceive the West into letting its guard down. All nonsense.

We began modestly with two courses. The first was on the errors of the past, specifically how Angleton had made counterintelligence useless by chasing phantoms and withholding approval for Soviet operations. I privately called this our "ANA" course, meaning "Angleton Never Again." The second course was a case study of an operation I was involved in during my Moscow assignment. This case smelled to high heaven when I arrived in Moscow, and it only got worse later. I joined forces with another case officer in the station to write a detailed CI analysis that ended with this conclusion: "There is no way this case can be good." In our judgment it was prima facie mala fide. There could be no other interpretation. Unfortunately, the obtuse (sorry, but that is how I saw it) chief of station did not want to admit that one of his operations could be bad. He rejected our analysis and continued to run the case. When I returned to headquarters several years later and joined the Counterintelligence Center, I was curious about what had happened to that operation.

I asked a junior CI analyst to dig up the file and do an independent study of it. I did not announce my views in advance. My tasking was somewhat unusual because the young CI analyst I chose was the daughter of one of the "fundamentalists."[13] She impressed me as a bright and highly talented young officer on her way to a promising career in CI analysis. The study was an excellent opportunity for her to showcase her abilities. It was also, I admit, a chance for me to see if she had inherited any fundamentalist tendencies from her father. She completed the task in about two weeks—and I was blown away by the quality of her work. Her analysis was brilliant and totally devoid of any manufactured conspiratorial tinge.

I attribute our counterintelligence failure in this case in large part to poor training. If we had had competent CI analysts who had learned their CI craft in sophisticated training courses, we could have and should have picked up on this dangle—or enticing volunteer put forward by an intelligence service to lure the opposition into recruiting it—much earlier.[14] It would have helped too if our senior officers, like the station chief in Moscow, had learned better CI awareness as part of their training along the way.

We used the Moscow operation as a case study for our second, more extensive Counterintelligence Center course because it was so rich in CI lessons and could help teach our analysts how to spot the often-subtle signs that a case is controlled by the opposition. And who was the perfect person to prepare and to teach that course? The young CI analyst who had done such a fine job on the initial case study—and yes, indeed she did go on to have a brilliantly successful career in counterintelligence analysis.

It takes a long time to develop CI specialists, and this means a sustained investment in CI training. The early efforts of the CIA's Counterintelligence Center were a start, but they covered only one agency and a limited number of disciplines. Much more needed to be done, and the US took a big step forward in January 2001, when President Bill Clinton established the Office of the National Counterintelligence Executive (NCIX) under the director of national intelligence (DNI). The mission of NCIX is to counter foreign intelligence operations against the United States and to keep American policymakers apprised of counterintelligence threats.

Significantly, NCIX realized immediately that it needed to establish community-wide counterintelligence training programs. I remember going to Washington to lecture in one of the first classes sponsored by NCIX. It was an unforgettable feeling to walk into the classroom on the first day and to look out at the students' name cards with their organizational affiliations: CIA, FBI, DIA, NSA, National Reconnaissance Office (NRO), Department of Energy (DOE), US Army, US Navy, US Air Force, US Marine Corps, DEA, and several others. "Finally," I said to myself, "we're getting it!" Here we had two important commandments of counterintelligence rolled into this one NCIX initiative: Don't be parochial and train your people!

I wish I could report that NCIX lived up to the high hopes the counterintelligence community had for it at its inception. It has had good leadership and has done many positive things, but it has suffered from changing national security priorities, cuts in funding, and smaller staffing. Its training agenda is still good but not sufficient for the size of the CI community or the massive assaults we are experiencing from China, Russia, Cuba, and others. There was also concern among many US counterintelligence professionals when in December 2014 DNI James Clapper established the National Counterintelligence and Security Center (NCSC), in effect rolling "security" into what had previously been the exclusive domain of counterintelligence. The new center was placed under the authority of the national counterintelligence executive, which was reassuring, but NCIX did not receive an overall increase in resources.

Michelle Van Cleave, a former national counterintelligence executive—and one of the best in my opinion—expressed her concern: "Combining counterintelligence and security is part of a flawed historical model for the CI enterprise. . . . Security has an unbounded appetite for dollars and attention. It is the here and now versus the longer, strategic needs of CI. And the here and now always gets priority. . . . This is a surefire recipe for CI funding to be redirected to other purposes."

That was what I was afraid of too. If the "security" responsibilities of the NCSC include, for example, protecting US facilities worldwide against terrorist attacks, its budget will be gobbled up and little will be left for counterintelligence. A good yardstick for measuring what the future will be is to watch CI training. If it goes down, we are in trouble. One of the first things to go in a budgetary crunch is training, but cutting counterintelligence training would be shortsighted—and very costly for our national security.

The Eighth Commandment: Do Not Be Shoved Aside

> If you control counterintelligence, you control the service.
>
> —James Angleton

As noted in the Second Commandment, some people in the intelligence business and elsewhere in the US government do not like counterintelligence officers. When we are doing our job properly, as we must, we are inconvenient. It is in our nature and in our mandate to see problems everywhere. Our image, not good to start with, was almost irreparably tarnished by the CI failures and abuses of James Jesus Angleton, J. Edgar Hoover, and their like-minded subordinates. The practice of counterintelligence—whether in intelligence, law enforcement, the military, or corporate security—is highly susceptible to overzealousness. It is sometimes a fine line between a good, aggressive CI investigation and a witch hunt. Senator Joseph McCarthy crossed that line with his vicious and reckless loyalty hearings in the 1950s. Angleton did the same with his frenzied search for a mole inside the CIA in the 1960s. Hoover disgraced himself with his obsessive harassment and investigation of Martin Luther King in the 1950s and 1960s. Counterintelligence officers must be wary of what I call the "righteousness trap," that is, our objectives cannot be so righteous and our motives so pure that we can justify inappropriate and even illegal methods.

Senior officers and decision makers everywhere do not like having someone looking over their shoulder. CI officers can cause headaches. We are the classic "black hatters."[15] Entire operations, programs, and other activities can be delayed or even canceled if the counterintelligence office sees problems and refuses to sign off.

Case officers, special agents, commanders, and other managers have a natural tendency to resist outside CI scrutiny. They believe they are practicing good CI themselves and do not welcome being second-guessed or told how to run their operations by so-called CI specialists who are not directly involved in the operations and not in their chain of command. I have seen more examples of this in my CI career than I care to remember.

By the same token, defense contractors and other civilian bureaucrats running sensitive US government programs have too often minimized CI threats and resisted professional CI intervention. I hope no offense is taken, but in my experience scientists and engineers, including at our national laboratories, tend to regard information sharing as the norm and are often slow to attribute ulterior motives to their foreign interlocutors. CI officers, in their view, stir up problems and overreact to them. CI officers' "successes" in preventing problems are invisible, and their damage assessments after compromises are overblown. Counterintelligence professionals create uncomfortable heat. It is not surprising, therefore, that CI officers are often viewed as a net nuisance.

When necessary a CI service must impose itself on the organizations and groups it is assigned to protect. A CI professional who is locked out or invited in only when it is convenient for the host cannot do his or her job. This is a particularly sticky issue for a CI naysayer who is in the chain of command of the operational decision maker. Counterintelligence, to be effective, must be honest, independent, and steadfast. It must be immune from command or political influence. A counterintelligence officer worthy of the name must be prepared to speak unpopular truth to power, even at the potential cost of poor performance appraisals or missed promotions. It is not an exaggeration to say that a good CI officer must be a nag—and as we all know, imperious managers do not like persistent and vocal dissent. At the end of the day, however, those of us who choose counterintelligence as our calling must live with ourselves, and if we do not call it the way we see it, we betray not only ourselves but also the CI profession.

I faced this problem head-on when we were setting up the Counterintelligence Center at the CIA in the early 1990s. Even after Angleton's stranglehold on counterintelligence had been broken by 1975, the bitter aftertaste of his reign remained in the minds of many operators. The old Counterintelligence Staff continued under new management, but the counterintelligence function at the CIA for the most part devolved to the geographic divisions, which organized or built up their own in-house CI components. Those units were staffed by operations officers who were home-based in that division so that the command pressures and subtle biases discussed previously came into play.[16] In effect, the divisions were policing themselves in terms of CI scrutiny. The inevitable result was poor CI.

Under Ted Price's leadership, the upstart Counterintelligence Center proposed a new model. It would post its own personnel, called "referents," inside the geographic divisions and other components to give them outside, independent counterintelligence support. This meant, of course, that the CI specialists from the center would have to be given unrestricted access to the sensitive cases being run by the area divisions. That was revolutionary, and the area divisions reacted just as expected. There was no way, they said, that they would allow "outsiders" from the CI Center to be read into their compartmented operations. Their reasons were predictable. First, they argued, it was poor security to expand knowledge of these cases beyond a strict need-to-know regime. Second, officers from outside the division would be unable to understand the distinctive culture, history, psychology, and other particularities of their region. Finally, and most vigorously, the divisions asserted that they were doing their own CI, thank you very much, and did not need our help. They threw up roadblock after roadblock.

Our referents began reporting back to me that they were being treated brusquely by their host divisions and were being denied access to the case files. The "barons" who ran some of the frontline area divisions were particularly resistant to opening their doors and operations to CI officers who were not answerable to them. And that was precisely the point, of course. Whether the area divisions accepted it or not, they needed independent, hard-hitting CI analysis by CI experts who did not have a professional stake in the outcome of the review. It took several heart-to-heart talks, diplomacy, reassurances, and yes, trips to the seventh floor (home of the deputy director of operations) to override the area divisions' objections and to get our people in. The upgrade in the objectivity and overall quality of CI analysis quickly became apparent to everyone, and a new healthier mind-set toward CI became the norm. The referent system was expanded beyond the doors of the CIA. The CI Center sent its officers out as referents to the National Security Council, the Department of Energy, the Department of State, the National Reconnaissance Office, the Department of the Treasury, the National Security Agency, and elsewhere. The response from these organizations was overwhelmingly positive; they appreciated our help. I recall several productive and cordial meetings at the Department of Energy, which was totally committed to enhancing its counterintelligence capabilities, both at headquarters and at the national laboratories. I was pleased to see that the FBI was doing something similar, that is, sending its foreign counterintelligence experts to other agencies and government contracting firms to give them closer CI support.

My advice to my CI colleagues has always been this: If you are blocked by some senior, benighted, anti-CI officer, go around or through him or her by going to higher management. And document all instances of denied access, lack of cooperation, or other obstruction in carrying out your CI mission. If you don't, when something goes wrong, as it likely will in that kind of environment, you in CI will take the blame. Do not be shoved aside.

The Ninth Commandment: Do Not Stay Too Long

> The game attracted strange men and slowly twisted them until something snapped.
>
> —David C. Martin, *Wilderness of Mirrors*

Counterintelligence is a hazardous profession. There should be warning signs on the walls of CI offices around the intelligence community: "A steady diet of CI can be dangerous to your health."

When I joined the CIA, one of my first interim assignments was with the old CI Staff. I did not know any better, and I found it fascinating. I was assigned to update a history of the Rote Kapelle, the Soviet espionage network in Nazi-occupied Western Europe during World War II. Thirty years after the war, NSA, with its expanded computer power, was breaking the messages sent between the NKVD (People's Commissariat for Internal Affairs) in Moscow and the clandestine radios of the Rote Kapelle cells in Western Europe.[17] Incredibly, these messages came to me. There I was, a brand-new junior officer who had not even been to the Farm yet, and I was literally the first person in the CIA to see the day-to-day traffic from these life-and-death operations. The fear, heroism, and drama in these messages affected me deeply. Above all I felt privileged to have the opportunity to read them.

Building on the CI Staff's earlier study of the Rote Kapelle, I spent several months working on a draft that incorporated the new material. To my great surprise, this study was well received by my immediate superiors, and I was told that I would be rewarded with a personal interview and congratulations from James Jesus Angleton, the head of the CI Staff. Naturally, I had visions of a commendation, a note in my file, and a terrific start to what I was already seeing as a fairy-tale career.

Angleton's office was on the second floor of the Original Headquarters Building. I arrived at the appointed time and was ushered into an outer office, where Angleton's aides briefed me on how to conduct myself. Then I went alone into the inner sanctum. The room was dark and filled with smoke, the curtains were drawn, and there was just one small lamp on Angleton's desk. I had heard that Angleton had eye trouble and that the light hurt his eyes, but I was convinced the real reason for the semidarkness was to add to his mystique. It worked on me! All I could see through the haze and dim light was a pair of owlish glasses staring at me.

I nervously briefed Angleton on my study, and he listened without interrupting, just nodding from time to time. He had not asked me to sit down, so I was standing at attention in front of his desk. When I finished, he methodically attacked every one of my conclusions. Didn't I know that the Rote Kapelle traffic was a deception? Had it not occurred to me that Leopold Trepper, the leader of the Rote Kapelle, was a German double?[18] I was humiliated. Angleton went on and on, getting further and further out, but relentlessly dismissing the research I had done. Even I, a counterintelligence neophyte, could tell that this great mind, this CI genius, had lost it. I thought he was around the bend. It was one of the most bizarre experiences of my career.

When the meeting was over, I was glad to get out of there. As I was walking down the hall, I was crushed, absolutely convinced that the high hopes I had had for this exciting new career were gone forever. How could anyone survive a lashing like that? I vowed to myself that in the unlikely event my CIA employment somehow survived this excoriation, I would never again go anywhere near CI.

I did not keep that vow. In my overseas assignments with the agency, I found myself drawn toward CI operations. Nothing seemed to quicken my pulse more than good CI. I was delighted when I was called back to headquarters in 1989 to join the new Counterintelligence Center as Ted Price's deputy. When Ted moved upstairs in early 1991 to become the associate deputy director for operations, I was named chief of the center. Today, many years after that first disagreeable encounter with CI, I find it hard to believe that it is my picture on the wall of the CI Center conference room at CIA Headquarters, where the photos of all former CIA counterintelligence chiefs are displayed. There I am, number seven, in a row that begins with James Jesus Angleton.

I do not believe anyone should make an entire, uninterrupted career of CI. All of us who have worked in counterintelligence have seen it: the old CI hand who has gone spooky. It is hard to immerse oneself daily in the arcane and twisted world of CI without falling prey to creeping paranoia, distortion, warping, and overzealousness in one's thinking. It is precisely these traits that led to some of the worst CI disasters in our history. Angleton and his coterie succumbed, with devastating results. Others at the CIA and elsewhere in the CI community have as well. The danger is always there.

Clare Petty is a good case in point. Petty was a career counterintelligence officer and a fine man who had done superb CI analysis for many years. When I was a junior officer, I remember seeing him locking himself into a vault and clanging a big safe-like door behind him every morning. I wondered how he could even breathe in there. I knew Petty was in counterintelligence, but of course, I had no idea what he was doing. Many years later I found out. He had become a victim of his CI craft; he had lost his way. For over two years, he had secretively and obsessively done CI research—totally on his own—to prove that the mole inside the CIA was *Angleton*. Certainly Angleton had many faults, but being a Soviet spy was not one of them. Petty's famous twenty-five-count indictment of Angleton made for interesting reading but did not withstand scrutiny. In retrospect, it is ironic that Angleton could hardly have done more damage to the CIA's operational program against the USSR if he *had* been a Soviet mole. But Petty's painstaking analysis was sadly off base.

One of my first acts as the new chief of the Counterintelligence Center was to drive to Bethesda, Maryland, to have lunch with George Kalaris, who had recently retired from the CIA. Kalaris had replaced Angleton as the CIA counterintelligence chief in 1975, and I was eager to tap into his experiences and to solicit his advice. He was generous in sharing with me his thoughts on what he found after Angleton's departure: safes filled with recruitment proposals, walk-ins, defectors, and technical operations that had been ours for the taking but were turned down by Angleton because he was too smart to fall into the KGB's traps. Kalaris said he was aghast to see this documentary confirmation of how Angleton had literally destroyed the CIA's operations against the Soviet Union for twenty years.

At the end of our lunch, Kalaris said something to me that I have never forgotten. He said, "Jim, after doing CI for just two years I felt the occupational madness closing in on me. I had to move on and do something else before I lost my bearings." Two years may not be the right benchmark for every CI practitioner, but I understood and took to heart George's warning.

My wife, Meredith, who was working at the CIA when I met her, knew all about the reputation of counterintelligence. When I was serving overseas and received a cable from headquarters offering me the position in the Counterintelligence Center, I discussed it with her that evening during a walk around our neighborhood. Her response, I thought, was right on the mark. "Okay," she said, "but don't stay too long."

Sensible and productive CI needs ventilation and fresh thinking. There should be systematic and constant flow through. Non-CI officers should be brought in regularly on rotational tours. Particularly valuable are transfers from other agencies and the military who will inject different approaches and help the receiving agency avoid insular thinking. It is imperative that CI units build in rotational assignments outside CI for their CI professionals. They should leave and spend two or three years with the operators or with the groups they are charged to protect. They will come back refreshed, smarter, and less likely to fall into the nether world of professional CI: the school of doublethink, the us-against-them mind-set, the nothing-is-what-it-seems syndrome, or as Angleton rightly called it, the "wilderness of mirrors."

The Tenth Commandment: Never Give Up

> There is one evil that I dread & that is their Spies. . . . I think it is a matter of some importance to prevent them from obtaining Intelligence of our Situation.
>
> —George Washington

The tenth and last commandment is the most important. Counterintelligence requires tenacity and persistence. It is a slow, plodding process that rarely rewards its practitioners with instant gratification. If you pursue counterintelligence as a career, you should know up front that you are choosing a profession in which you will go for months and even years without perceptible progress or accomplishments. A typical CI investigation starts with a kernel, a fragment, or a hunch that is hard to grab onto but that demands attention. A penetration of a foreign intelligence service tells us that his service is receiving reporting on US nuclear weapons technology, but his direct access is limited and he cannot be more specific. A US State Department team is negotiating a sensitive agreement with the Iranian government and is convinced the Iranians have inside information on US government negotiating positions. That is not much to go on, but a perspicacious CI officer would consider that information may be leaked because the Iranians have a source inside the State Department. A CIA officer is ambushed in Moscow while putting a dead drop down for a valuable agent inside the Russian Foreign Ministry. We are certain that our officer was "black"—free of surveillance—when she was ambushed, so that means the agent had already been arrested and the KGB had his communications plan.[19] The KGB knew in advance when and where the drop was to take place, which allowed the agency to set up a professional ambush. It is possible, of course, that the agent compromised himself with reckless behavior, but a good CI officer will not ignore the possibility that there was betrayal from within. Who in the CIA or elsewhere in the US government was aware of this operation? Is there any reason to suspect any of them of espionage? In each of these situations, the CI investigation begins.

The point is that counterintelligence investigations usually start with little and face an uphill fight. They are excruciatingly difficult. Just when you think you might be making a little bit of headway, you hit another impasse. The temptation to concede defeat and to turn one's attention to something else is great. It is no fun to go into the office every day, to stare at the Gordian knot, and to realize at the end of the day that it remains totally uncut. You cannot help but feel that you have wasted another day. Your frustration is high and your job satisfaction is low.

When the CIA's Soviet operations were wiped out in 1985, a major CI investigation was inevitable, but where to start? The first serious investigation concluded that each of the compromised operations had flaws that could account for the agent's arrest. That verdict seemed implausible and unsatisfactory to me and to many other CI officers; the simple laws of probability argued against the virtually simultaneous disappearance of so many Russian agents. Next, the CIA investigators looked at the possibility of a technical explanation. Could the Russians have penetrated the CIA's encrypted communications systems or implanted a listening device inside the CIA's Moscow Station? The KGB mounted a disinformation operation to steer the CIA in that direction, a transparent effort to have the CIA focus on a technical problem rather than on a mole.[20] In fact, the Russians had been incredibly reckless in wrapping up without delay the Soviet spies identified by the traitors Rick Ames and Robert Hanssen, both of whom were still in place. By doing so they placed their two prize penetrations of US counterintelligence in considerable jeopardy. Sadly, however, Ames and Hanssen survived because of the disarray and ineptitude of US counterintelligence at the time.

To be fair, the task was daunting. At least 200 people had access to information on the missing agents, and investigating these people posed serious problems. The potential suspects inside the CIA and the FBI were intelligence and law enforcement professionals who could be expected to be alert to any indication that they were being investigated. If the guilty party or parties sensed they were under suspicion, they would go to ground and destroy all contemporaneous evidence of their crime, making a successful prosecution difficult, if not impossible. Moreover, US law severely limited intrusive surveillance of the suspects without probable cause, a warrant, and Foreign Intelligence Surveillance Court (FISA Court) approval.[21] The CI investigators, therefore, despite their desire to do so, could not go willy-nilly into the banking, credit card, tax, and travel records of the 200-plus mole candidates. Without more specific probable cause than they had, their hands were tied.[22]

By 1991 the CI investigation into the 1985 losses had gone moribund. But the new CI Center was not ready to give up. It reinvigorated the investigation, strengthened the team, and invited the FBI to join the CIA's mole hunters. To commemorate the occasion, I found a stuffed mole, tied a rope around its neck, hung it from my office ceiling, and added a sign in Russian saying, "*Smert' Krotam*" (Смерть Кротам), which means "Death to Moles." If the traitor in our midst ever had the occasion to visit my office and understood Russian, I wanted him or her to know that our mole hunt was deadly serious.

I often ask myself what would have happened if the Ames investigation had in fact died after six years instead of going on for three more years. It is no exaggeration to say that the first six years accomplished nothing; the investigators went down blind alley after blind alley. We could easily have decided that any further effort to unravel this intractable mystery would be pointless. But we plodded on. After Ames's arrest, US counterintelligence was soundly criticized by Congress and the press for taking nine years to catch him, but I believe this criticism misses the point. The key point for me is that we never gave up. The same can be said about the lengthy search for a mole inside the FBI. The FBI investigation that eventually uncovered Special Agent Robert Hanssen as a Russian spy went on longer than it should have and wasted time chasing an innocent man, but in the end it succeeded. The FBI never gave up.

The FBI is making CI cases against Americans today that involve espionage committed in the 1960s, 1970s, 1980s, and later. The case of Ronald Pelton, the NSA analyst, is a good example of counterintelligence persistence. The FBI had a telephone intercept of an American who contacted the Soviet embassy in Washington, DC, in 1980 to offer his services as a spy. FBI investigators were unable to make a definitive identification from the voice alone, but they kept the investigation alive until they could nail Pelton in 1985 with the help of defector Vitaly Yurchenko and painstaking CI analysis. The army's Foreign Counterintelligence Activity and other military CI units are doing the same. The name of the game in counterintelligence is doggedness. CI officers who are impatient need not apply.

What if, in my own experience, we had discontinued a certain surveillance operation after five months instead of continuing into the sixth? Our surveillance team hated this operation because the target lived in an out-of-the-way part of the city, there was little cover in the area, and nothing was happening. Not only was I getting grumbling from the surveillance team, but headquarters was turning testy about the time and expense of an operation that was going nowhere. We stuck with it, however, and hit the jackpot in month 6 when we identified a senior US government official who was passing secrets to the Russians. CI history is full of such examples.

There is no statute of limitations for espionage, and we should not create one by our own inaction. Traitors should know that they will never be safe and will never have a peaceful night's sleep. It galled me when I was chief of the CI Center to know that the atom spy Theodore Hall, who had betrayed the US at Los Alamos in 1944 and 1945, was living quietly in England and had never paid for his crimes. Hall was interviewed by the FBI in the 1950s but escaped prosecution because the evidence against him was considered insufficient. Only with the release in 1995 of the Venona transcripts, which had been strictly protected until then, did American and British counterintelligence have enough to make their case against him in court.[23] By then, however, the seventy-year-old Hall was suffering from Parkinson's disease and cancer, and Scotland Yard decided not to prosecute him on humanitarian grounds, even though he admitted that he had passed atom secrets to the Russians. It may sound cruel for me to say this, but my repugnance for American traitors is such that I hope Theodore Hall at a minimum lived his life in a state of constant high anxiety, with one ear always cocked, waiting for the proverbial knock on his door. Know this, all of you spies out there: US counterintelligence never gives up.

If we keep a CI investigation alive and stay on it, the next defector, the next penetration, the next tip, the next piece of CI analysis, the next wiretap, the next surveillance report, the next communications intercept, or the next clue will break it for us. If US counterintelligence ever had a mascot, it should be the pit bull.

In Conclusion

These are my Ten Commandments of Counterintelligence. Other CI professionals will have their own priorities and exhortations and will disagree with mine. That is as it should be, because as a country and as a counterintelligence community, we need a vigorous debate on the future direction of US CI. Not everyone will agree with the specifics, or even the priorities. What we should all agree on, however, is that strong CI must be a national priority.

I have chosen the term "commandments" because I believe the basic rules of CI are immutable and should be scrupulously followed. In my view it makes little difference whether the adversary is the Chinese, the Russians, the Cubans, rogue American citizens, or others. It likewise makes little difference whether we are talking about 1980, 1990, 2000, 2010, or 2020. Unfortunately, as I watch CI today, I am deeply concerned that the principles I consider fundamental for effective CI are not being followed as carefully and consistently as they should be.

These commandments were not handed down to me from a mountain, and I make no claim that they are inspired or even definitive. They are simply the culmination—for what they are worth—of my experience in counterintelligence.

FIVE
Workplace Counterintelligence

> A nation can survive its fools, and even the ambitious. But it cannot survive treason from within. An enemy at the gates is less formidable, for he is known and carries his banner openly. But the traitor moves amongst those within the gate freely. . . . For the traitor appears not a traitor; he speaks in accents familiar to his victims, and he wears their face and their arguments. . . . He rots the soul of a nation. He works secretly and unknown in the night to undermine the pillars of the city. . . . A murderer is less to fear. The traitor is the plague.
>
> —Marcus Tullius Cicero

As a former practitioner and now as a professor of intelligence studies at the Bush School, I have been involved in personally or studied indirectly hundreds of espionage cases. Over time I realized that I was seeing some common themes in these cases, specifically three workplace failures that led to serious CI compromises. The preeminent goal of any counterintelligence professional should not be to *catch* spies but to *prevent* spies. Whenever I helped break a CI case in my career, it was bittersweet. First, I felt a rush of jubilation that my CI colleagues and I had done our job well; we had caught a spy. But then, at the same time, I turned somber realizing how much harm this turncoat had done to our country. How could this damage have been prevented or at least limited? Our success in finding the spy was overshadowed by our failure to prevent what had happened. As I pointed out earlier, in counterintelligence work our successes are often our failures.

I remember an unusual case in which we had a penetration of a major foreign intelligence service at a relatively low level. Our source was not a case officer but was instead responsible for carrying out operational support tasks for his service. In this instance he was doing casings and setting up countersurveillance for a meeting his service had with an important agent.[1] He knew the date and time of the meeting and the location of the initial contact, but he did not know the name of the agent or even the agent's nationality. We set up careful surveillance of the meeting site with the primary objective of identifying who the agent was. It was a tense moment when the report came in from the surveillance team. On the one hand, I was hoping the spy was an American because that would be the biggest CI coup possible. On the other hand, I dreaded the idea of another disastrous penetration of our government. I was frankly relieved when the spy turned out to be a senior official from a NATO country—not an American. I would not have welcomed the recriminations that invariably follow the arrest of a major American spy. How could we have let this happen? Our critics are right. If we are as good as we should be, we will stop traitors from spying before they can start. Most CI professionals will say the same. Prevention is the ultimate counterintelligence goal. Stop it before it can hurt you. In counterintelligence as in medicine, Erasmus was right: "Prevention is better than cure."

I tell my students that if the Three Principles of Workplace Counterintelligence are practiced consistently we can prevent many of our counterintelligence losses. The Ten Commandments are the framework; workplace counterintelligence is the practical application.

Every spy is an employee. The venue of his or her spying is the workplace. The scene of the crime is the office. That is where we need to focus our counterintelligence attention. Thus, the Three Principles of Workplace Counterintelligence are (1) select your personnel carefully, (2) supervise them properly, and (3) promote individual responsibility.

Selection of Personnel

> Treachery has existed as long as there's been warfare, and there's always been a few people that you couldn't trust.
>
> —James Mattis

Many Americans who have served in US government or contractor positions with the highest-level security clearances should never have gotten in the door in the first place. Hiring and clearance procedures vary from agency to agency and from company to company, but they have one thing in common: they are inadequate. Far too many people with questionable backgrounds, extensive drug histories, character flaws, and personality disorders are getting hired and cleared. Christopher Boyce was a college dropout and a regular drug user when he was hired by the high technology company TRW and given CIA, Department of Defense (DOD), and NSA clearances. His father, a former FBI special agent, had asked a friend at TRW to give his wayward son a job as a personal favor. Aldrich Ames passed supposedly rigorous psychological screening and was hired by the CIA despite his sociopathic personality. His father, a CIA officer, had pushed for his son's employment. Jonathan Pollard was hired by US Navy intelligence and given a top-secret security clearance despite a failed CIA polygraph, heavy drug use, a falsified academic record, and multiple lies about his own and his father's background.[2] Robert Hanssen was hired by the FBI and given high-level clearances despite his history of quirky behavior, his impersonation of a psychiatrist when he was employed as a hospital orderly, and as later revealed, his split personality. Ana Montes was hired by the Defense Intelligence Agency and put in charge of sensitive Cuban intelligence programs even though she repeatedly expressed anti-American and pro-Castro views while she was a graduate student. Edward Lee Howard was hired by the CIA and selected for an ultrasensitive assignment to Moscow despite an admitted history of drug and alcohol abuse. What were we thinking? Unfortunately, these are not isolated examples. We have had and continue to have too many bad apples in the US government.

Screening applicants for employment in the vast US government and contractor world is a massive and arduous process. Mistakes will inevitably be made, but we can do more to minimize them. For one thing, standards can be tightened. When my wife, Meredith, and I were being screened for hiring by the CIA many years ago, even a single use of a controlled substance was disqualifying. US society has evolved since then, and it would be hard to hire to that standard today, but we are now letting people in whose drug histories raise serious questions about their suitability. I have similar concerns about what I believe is a more permissive attitude toward drinking, cheating, shoplifting, and credit card abuse. We have all done stupid things that we regret and will not do again, but applicants who've exhibited certain behaviors—especially repeated behaviors that indicate a character flaw—should be screened out. In most cases I do not advocate disqualifying candidates for "single stupidities," unless they are serious violations of the law, abusive, or grossly disrespectful of others. But any indication—even a slight indication—that the negative activity in question is part of a pattern should be resolved in favor of the government and against the applicant.

Sexual orientation is in a separate category. Intelligence community veterans of my generation who were required to take full-scope polygraph examinations, as Meredith and I were, will recall the uncomfortably probing questions about our sexual practices. Homosexuality was disqualifying, with no exceptions. For many years the FBI under J. Edgar Hoover disqualified special agent applicants who had engaged in heterosexual cohabitation. It was a different time. It was not until the early 1990s that attitudes began to change at the CIA. CIA director Robert Gates commissioned a CI study of how many American spies had been recruited by opposition services because of their homosexuality. The basis for the CIA's policy of rejecting homosexual applicants had been the assumption that they would be vulnerable to blackmail by foreign intelligence services. Director Gates wanted to see the evidence in support of this assumption. It was not there. We could not find a single instance in which homosexuality had played a role in an American espionage case. The policy was changed.

This next topic is controversial and impossible to quantify, but I fear that affirmative action has in some cases resulted in a lowering of standards. The US government has been so intent on improving diversity—a laudable goal—that some hires, I believe, have been based more on demographics than on objective qualifications. I have heard intelligence community recruiters tell me that on certain recruiting trips, they have been directed to look at women and minority applicants only. Well-qualified white male applicants were not even interviewed on those trips. Government leaders will deny that this hard push for diversity has resulted in any lowering of standards, but it stands to reason that de facto quotas based on race and gender will eliminate from consideration some equally or better qualified applicants who are not in those categories. Demographics can and should be considered for operational requirements, such as language ability and cultural knowledge, but not at the cost of lowered standards. The US intelligence community has a vital mission of national security to perform and needs the best and brightest Americans available, regardless of race, gender, or sexual orientation. Excellence should be the hiring standard, not an imposed preference for certain categories of Americans. And, I am pleased to say, with few exceptions, excellence *has* been the standard.

The CIA's website, for example, correctly zeroes in on the qualifications that produce such a result: integrity, dedication, flexibility, interpersonal and communication skills, adaptability, creativity, and so forth. My wife, Meredith, and I agree that we have never known finer people than the people we served with in the US intelligence community.

There are exceptions, but in general eligibility for a US government security clearance at the confidential or secret level requires the National Agency Check with Law and Credit (NACLC). The applicant submits a detailed residence, education, and employment history, usually for the previous seven years, and the government uses this information to check the applicant against law enforcement and credit databases. Unless the candidate has a criminal record or a bad credit history, the process usually ends with a clearance.

US government clearances at the top-secret and sensitive compartmented information (SCI) level (or at the Q level in the Department of Energy) require a background investigation (BI) and, in certain cases, a polygraph examination. Background investigations are conducted by full-time federal government employees or, more commonly, by contractors. The contractors tend to be former US government employees, often retirees, who are assigned to do the BIs by the sponsoring agency. Other contractors may come from state or local law enforcement backgrounds. The investigators are expected to poke around and to dig up whatever information they can, but in practice they rely heavily on the references provided by the applicant. These self-selected references, not surprisingly, are almost always positive. The employment and education verifications are likewise rarely a problem, unless the applicant has been foolish enough to falsify his or her credentials. In short, US government background investigations are relatively cursory and do not often turn up seriously derogatory information.

The efficacy of the BI process is further eroded by the huge government-wide backlog in issuing security clearances. According to the latest figures I have seen, the number of applicants awaiting final clearance decisions is close to 700,000. Long delays of up to nine months or a year are the norm. The effect of this time lag is twofold. First, government agencies are frustrated by the slowness in bringing urgently needed new personnel on board. Second, the government loses out on some top applicants who cannot wait around for months until their clearances come through. As a result, some agencies have resorted to issuing interim clearances based on partial BIs and other checks, thereby giving access to classified information to individuals who have not been thoroughly vetted. The CI risks are obvious. Interim clearances should be eliminated.

The polygraph is a far more effective counterintelligence tool than the BI. It is the polygraph, not the BI, that results in more disqualifications for employment. The polygraph is by no means infallible, but my many years of experience have made me a strong believer in its efficacy. Thank goodness for the polygraph. It has weeded out countless unsuitable applicants for employment at the CIA, the FBI, the NSA, and elsewhere. Even after hiring, reinvestigation polygraphs of active-duty employees have uncovered espionage and other illegal activities that would have otherwise remained unknown. CIA traitors Sharon Scranage and Harold James Nicholson would have betrayed us much longer if they had not been tripped up on their reinvestigation polygraphs.[3] An additional benefit of the polygraph is deterrence. Would-be spies think twice about taking the plunge into espionage when they know they will be periodically polygraphed. FBI spy Robert Hanssen said after his arrest that he would probably not have dared to do what he did if the FBI had used the polygraph in security reinvestigations. The FBI has now incorporated the polygraph into its applicant processing and security reviews.

US government polygraphs come in two varieties: full-scope (lifestyle) and CI only. The latter, used by several agencies, are quicker and easier. They are designed to ferret out counterintelligence threats, such as unreported foreign associations, ambiguous travel to criteria countries, unexplainable income, or contact with known or suspected foreign intelligence officers. To most applicants and current employees, these issues do not apply, so for these individuals, a CI-only polygraph is smooth sailing.

A full-scope polygraph is a different matter. Most of the frontline intelligence community agencies have always used or have later adopted the full-scope polygraph. For most subjects the polygraph is an extremely unpleasant experience. First, it is meant to be aggressive and intrusive. The examiner will likely probe into every nook and cranny of the subject's past and will press for admissions. The tone can quickly turn confrontational if the examiner believes the subject is withholding information or is being evasive in his or her answers. I know from having taken multiple polygraphs in my career that lying is not an option. The machine will get you. As a counterintelligence officer, I was familiar with all the so-called counterpolygraph techniques, but I could not beat the blasted thing even if I had tried. My advice to anyone headed for a full-scope polygraph examination is to be fully cooperative and forthcoming. Let it all out. The minor peccadilloes we all have might be embarrassing to talk about, but if we try to hide them from the examiner, we will likely blip. Besides, these kinds of embarrassing moments are not usually disqualifying in themselves, unless they are indicative of a serious and ingrained character flaw.

Unfortunately, there are occasional cases of false positives in the polygraph process. Some subjects are so nervous, hyperconscientious, or judgmental about themselves that they overreact to the questions. Simply raising certain issues, such as drugs, alcohol, cheating, and stealing, can cause people in this category to show a physiological response—not because they are guilty but because they exaggerate their experiences or find the subject matter personally offensive. As a result some well-qualified and upstanding individuals are unable to get through the polygraph process with clean charts and are not hired. That is a shame, but an exception. In my experience a reading of "deception indicated" on a polygraph means in the vast majority of cases that deception has taken place. It is counterintelligence folly to ignore a bad polygraph.

Is it possible to beat the polygraph? Yes, of course. Aldrich Ames "passed" a reinvestigation polygraph even though he had been working for the Russian KGB and SVR for several years. The results of his examination were ambiguous but fell short of a deception-indicated call. Larry Wu-Tai Chin likewise passed CIA polygraphs during his thirty-plus-year espionage career on behalf of the Chinese MPS. During his postarrest debriefings, Ames said he had been terrified by one of his CIA polygraph examinations and asked his Russian handler for advice. He was told to get a good night's sleep the night before the exam, to relax, and to lie with confidence. My personal view is that Rick passed the exam not because of any countermeasures he took, but because he is a sociopath. Right and wrong have no real significance to him; he is incapable of feeling guilt for his actions. The same may be true of Chin, but I believe there may also have been a cultural dimension to his successful lying. Some nationalities, we know, are particularly difficult polygraph subjects because of different cultural attitudes toward lying and personal responsibility. People who knew Chin commented on his emotional detachment. He was what we call a "flatliner," as opposed to a "reactor." Reactors make good polygraph subjects, and most Americans are good reactors. They have a sense of right and wrong and cannot lie with equanimity.

I advocate an expanded use of the polygraph in national security agencies, national laboratories, and sensitive government contracting firms. Furthermore, I believe full-scope polygraphs should be the norm throughout the government, both for hiring and for reinvestigations. I realize expanding the use of polygraphs will be expensive and time-consuming, but a more rigorous use of the tests in the government will improve the reliability of our workforce with access to classified information and deter would-be bad actors. Counterintelligence could be improved if the US State Department and other outliers in the US government that choose not to polygraph their applicants and employees would reconsider. I would also like to see White House and congressional staffers subjected to full-scope polygraphs before they are given access to classified information. The polygraph is not perfect, but it works.

Our national secrets are only as safe as the people to whom we entrust them. The first line of defense in protecting our secrets is doing a better job of selecting the government employees who will be given access to classified information. That means maintaining the highest possible standards in hiring, improving pre-employment psychological assessments, strengthening background investigations, and expanding the polygraph.

Access to classified US government information is a privilege, not a right. There are no shortages of qualified and honorable applicants for sensitive positions in intelligence, diplomacy, the military, law enforcement, national laboratories, government contractors, and other organizations. We do not have to settle for flawed applicants to fill our ranks. Why should we grant waivers for equivocal issues of past conduct, character, or personality disorder? I propose that CI officers responsible for screening applicants for security clearances apply what I immodestly call the Olson axiom: "When in doubt, keep 'em out."

Supervision of Personnel

> It's the oldest question of all, George.
> Who can spy on the spies?
>
> —John le Carré, *Tinker, Tailor, Soldier, Spy*

It is not enough to hire the right people. We need to supervise them better once they are on board. Counterintelligence history is replete with examples of subpar employees who received inadequate supervision and who spiraled down into betrayal. An alert supervisor could provide early warning of a potential problem; put the employee on notice that he or she is being watched; document the misconduct or aberrant behavior; refer egregious cases to the appropriate security, medical, or counterintelligence personnel; and terminate or reassign (to less sensitive positions) individuals who raise security or suitability concerns.

There is a natural reluctance on the part of US government and contractor supervisors to meet their responsibilities in this regard and to initiate remedial action. No one likes a snooper. In most arenas employees are entitled to privacy and noninterference in their private lives, but in the field of national security, closer scrutiny is required. The best place to start is the immediate supervisor, who is closest to the employee and in the best position to observe anomalies in work performance, security violations, mood swings, and personal problems. Often, however, especially in smaller work units, the supervisor-employee relationship is familiar to the point that the supervisor is not comfortable calling out a "friend" for questionable behaviors or attitudes. The kind of pointed counseling session that should take place in these situations never happens. Good supervisors, however, will maintain professional separation but still develop the kind of rapport with their subordinates that will support frank expressions of concern for their well-being: "I'm worried about you. I've noticed some problems. Are you okay? Is there anything I can do to help? We need to talk."

The all-too-common practice, unfortunately, is for the supervisor to be aloof and uninformed, to look the other way, to avoid confrontation, and "to pass the trash" on to the next supervisor. Even when the behavioral, financial, or psychological problem is observed by a supervisor, no action is taken. It is just easier to let it slide. In that kind of environment, the problem can fester and escalate to illegal acts, including espionage. If only some CIA supervisor had taken decisive action to recommend termination of the low-performing, drunken, and philandering Aldrich Ames, we might have averted the CI disaster that he turned out to be. FBI supervisors knew that Robert Hanssen had hacked into a superior's computer, grabbed a female subordinate by the hair, and generally displayed bizarre conduct, but he remained in a sensitive CI position at the bureau. Sgt. Clayton Lonetree, while assigned to the US embassy in Moscow as a marine security guard, abused alcohol, read pro-Nazi literature, and had a sexual relationship with a Russian woman, all under the nose of his gunnery sergeant superior.[4] One reason for the lack of meaningful supervision was that the gunnery sergeant and the other Marines in Moscow were also drinking too much and violating strict regulations against fraternizing with Russian women. It is no wonder that Lonetree fell into a KGB honey trap.[5] He not only suffered no consequences for his actions in Moscow but also received a cushy onward assignment to Vienna, where his continuing access to highly classified information undoubtedly made his KGB case officer drool.

It is usually not easy to fire a government employee, whether in intelligence, law enforcement, or the military. Reductions in force occur periodically and are not subject to appeal, but terminations for cause can be tricky. If the employee has committed a crime or a serious violation of regulations, the process is easier. The action in these cases may be in the form of a straightforward administrative action, a court-martial, or a nonjudicial punishment. If the grounds are well documented in performance reports, warnings, and memos, the fired employee has little recourse but to accept the decision. Yet, if the grounds are not well documented and the facts can be disputed, the termination process can involve hearings, lawsuits, and acrimony. A disgruntled employee can fight termination by claiming unfairness, discrimination, or retaliation for whistleblowing and other acts of conscience. Nevertheless, good CI requires a willingness and determination to get rid of the security risks, even if the termination proceeding turns out to be lengthy and messy.

A less drastic remedy in dealing with employees who fit disturbing CI profiles is to reassign them to positions of little or no access to classified information. When the CIA and FBI mole hunters zeroed in on Aldrich Ames as a prime suspect, he was reassigned from the Soviet East European Division, where his access was particularly damaging, to the Counternarcotics Center, where his access was less sensitive. This transfer had to be "sold" to Ames as routine and not an indication he was under suspicion. If he tumbled to the latter, he could destroy his espionage materials and weaken or even eliminate our ability to make a case against him. Ames grumbled and tried to finagle his way back to more marketable (to the SVR) access, but to no avail. All he accomplished, in fact, by resisting his transfer to narcotics operations was to heighten our suspicions of him. The transfer option is a good one in problem cases because it is virtually impossible to turn down and there are no legal remedies. I used to joke to my CI colleagues that every US government agency dealing with highly classified information should have a "turkey farm," that is, a place to park its high-risk employees in jobs with no real access.

I wish we had sent CIA officer Edward Lee Howard to a turkey farm instead of summarily firing him when he bombed his polygraph just before he was to get on a plane for his Moscow assignment. Our abrupt termination of Howard caused him to leave with a seething rage against the agency, which ultimately became an overpowering desire for revenge. We paid the price.[6]

Effective supervision in counterintelligence terms can be unpleasant. An intervention with a subordinate that results in his or her termination, demotion, or reassignment is usually devastating to the person concerned. It is no fun. A good supervisor will drop the hammer as gently as possible and allow the employee to save as much face as possible. The CIA was gratuitously harsh and humiliating in how it dismissed Howard. We in counterintelligence can and should learn from that mistake, but ultimately, the supervisor must act decisively to deal with the problem and to mitigate the risk. "Carrying" a high-risk employee on misplaced compassionate grounds is a recipe for a CI disaster. Aldrich Ames and Robert Hanssen are good cases in point.

Some of my worst memories as a CIA station chief overseas are of disciplining officers who became security risks. One of my section chiefs, for example, developed an alcohol problem that was clearly affecting his job performance and reliability. In a tough session in my office, I told him I was sending him home short of tour so he could get treatment. He broke into tears and pleaded with me to reconsider. He said he would stop drinking. I held my ground. Later the officer's wife asked for a meeting with me so she could make the same case. She said my decision would ruin her husband's career and destroy her family. I felt terrible but did what I thought was necessary for the station's security and my officer's health.

I sent three officers—two men and one woman—home short of tour for not reporting romantic relationships with foreign nationals. It is a strict requirement for CIA officers to report any relationships, romantic or otherwise, with foreign nationals. Not doing so raises a serious counterintelligence concern.[7]

In short, US government supervisors have a critical role to play in protecting our country's secrets. If they do their job properly, we will all be safer.

Individual Responsibility

> I have learned to hate all traitors, and there is no disease that I spit on more than treachery.
>
> —Aeschylus

Every US government employee, civilian or military, has an important counterintelligence responsibility: to keep his or her eyes and ears open and to speak up if something does not look right. The best early warning system we have in counterintelligence is an alert and conscientious colleague working side by side with others in the same workplace. Just think of it. If, for example, we have a government office or military unit with twenty-five people in it, that means that everyone in that workplace is subject to being observed by twenty-four professional colleagues. That is a lot of up-close scrutiny by coworkers who are in the same business and who know what anomalous behavior looks like in that context. In almost every case of espionage by US citizens that I have looked at over the last several years, someone saw something but did not report it. In their postmortems of what went wrong, US counterintelligence officials invariably noted that someone who was aware of the traitor's extra income, unauthorized contacts, heavy drinking or drug use, gambling losses, unreported travel, or suspicious behavior in general had not stepped forward in a timely manner.

It is easy to make this call for individual responsibility, but the problem is that ratting out a friend or colleague is a hard sell. When the conduct in question is ambiguous and not glaringly a security threat, the human tendency of most US government employees is not to make trouble for a coworker. We rationalize away our duty to step forward by telling ourselves that it is not our business, that suspicious behavior may have a benign explanation, that being an informant is against our nature, and that an individual's personal and professional reputation should not be impugned by something that may turn out to be unsubstantial. This understandable reluctance to report on others is unusually strong in close-knit groups that are based on brotherhood and sisterhood, like the US military, the FBI, and the CIA. Speaking up is countercultural in these organizations.

I am as guilty as anyone else. Many years ago I was in New York City and met with Aldrich Ames, who was working there. We occasionally went out for dinner together. Rick had expensive tastes, and his favorite restaurants were Gallaghers Steakhouse on Fifty-Second Street and the Oyster Bar in

Grand Central Station. The food in these places was excellent, but it was clear to me that Rick was more interested in drinking his meals than in eating them. After several such dinners, I knew with certainty that CIA case officer Aldrich Ames had a drinking problem. Why didn't I report my observations to the Office of Security? If I had, maybe Rick's assignment to Mexico City, where he met his future wife and accomplice, Rosario, would never have happened. I failed in my individual responsibility as an employee. It never crossed my mind to violate our unofficial code and to blow the whistle on a colleague. I was derelict in my duty—and I regret it to this day.

It is not 1984, and no one wants a Stasi-style police state where everyone informs on everyone else. But there must be a happy medium. In the world of counterterrorism, the catch phrase "if you see something, say something" seems to be gaining wide acceptance. But even there, we have seen failures of individual responsibility. A neighbor of one of the San Bernardino terrorists saw suspicious activity next door but did not say anything because she did not want to be accused of racial discrimination. In the world of counterintelligence, we must break down the barriers to speaking up. We must establish a responsible system of reporting that ensures fairness and confidentiality. Frivolous and vindictive reports can be quickly discarded with no harm done. Serious reports can be discreetly reviewed and may, in some cases, lead to a CI investigation. Everyone should know how to get the CI-relevant information to the appropriate authorities. I would not be opposed to an anonymous hotline that would allow conscientious employees who prefer not to be involved personally to report their concerns. Tip lines have been helpful in law enforcement and may have a useful role to play in counterintelligence as well.

Let's summarize. Workplace counterintelligence can be dramatically improved—and CI losses reduced—if the US government and sensitive contractor firms do a better job of selecting personnel, supervising them, and encouraging employee reporting of suspicious activity.

SIX
Double-Agent Operations

> It is essential to seek out enemy agents who have come to conduct espionage against you and to bribe them to serve you. Give them instructions and care for them. Thus doubled agents are recruited and used.
>
> —Sun Tzu

I believe the most complex and challenging discipline of intelligence is counterintelligence—and I believe the most complex and challenging subspecialty of counterintelligence is double agentry. In *Fair Play* I wrote that double-agent operations are the caviar of counterintelligence operations because, in my opinion, there is nothing more delectable than a good, juicy double-agent operation. It does not get much better for a counterintelligence professional than to dupe his or her adversary, particularly one that prides itself on being clever and sophisticated, with a controlled case. Double-agent operations are such an important element of offensive counterintelligence that they deserve a chapter to themselves.

The first order of business is to define what a double agent is. The term is often misused by popular writers, journalists, government officials, and the public. How many times have we heard Robert Hanssen referred to in the press and elsewhere as "the notorious FBI double agent"? The same terminology is consistently used to describe Edward Lee Howard, Aldrich Ames, Harold James Nicholson, Edwin Earl Pitts, Jonathan Pollard, and many others. All these uses of the term are incorrect. Here is an example from a weekly news magazine:

> Double Agent. A veteran FBI employee with top-secret security clearance pleaded guilty this week in Manhattan federal court to passing information

> to the Chinese government. Kim Shan Chun, 46, also known as Joey Chun, was born in China but became a naturalized American citizen in 1986. He has been an FBI employee for 19 years working as an electronics technician in the bureau's New York office. . . . He faces up to 10 years in prison.[1]

Chun was not a double agent. Let me take a stab at explaining why and offering a correct definition of "double agent." For starters, no one can be a double agent without being an agent first. You will recall that an official of the FBI, the CIA, or any other government agency is not properly called an "agent" in intelligence terms. CIA operatives are "case officers," and FBI professionals are "special agents." The word "agent" used in the latter context can be confusing, but an agent in CI terms is someone who has been recruited by a foreign intelligence service. Robert Hanssen was a Russian agent. Aldrich Ames was a Russian agent. Jonathan Pollard was an Israeli agent. Joey Chun was a Chinese agent. They were not double agents. They would be double agents only if they had allowed themselves to be recruited by the Russians, Israelis, or Chinese as a ruse but were still loyal and responsive to US intelligence.

Let's put it together: *A double agent is an agent who purportedly works as an agent for one intelligence service but who reports to and is loyal to another intelligence service as its agent.*

Here are some examples:

- The FBI finds, recruits, and trains an American engineer with access to classified technology to serve as a double agent. This engineer is directed to walk into a Russian embassy to volunteer his services as a spy for the Russians. The Russians bite. The engineer begins to pass the Russians controlled classified information (feed material), and the operation is off and running. All the while, the engineer double agent is reporting everything back to the FBI and is under full FBI control.
- US Army counterintelligence officers select, recruit, and train a sergeant with access to classified information to serve as a double agent. They dangle him in a bar outside a base in Germany where they know the Russian SVR does spotting for potential recruits. Under army direction the sergeant feigns getting drunk, talking too much, and complaining about his money problems. He expresses disgruntlement with his job and with US policies. Sure enough, the SVR spotter begins to make overtures to him—and the sergeant

slowly lets it happen. He plays hard to get at first but eventually succumbs to the offer of money in return for feed material. The double-agent operation is underway.

- The CIA, working with the FBI and DOE, identifies, recruits, and trains a Chinese-American scientist employed at a US national laboratory. She has access to sensitive nuclear weapons technology in her job at the laboratory. As part of her duties, she travels occasionally to China for scientific conferences and discussions with Chinese officials. On previous trips she noted that the Chinese were cozying up to her, playing on her ethnic and cultural ties to Mother China, and transparently assessing her for possible recruitment as an intelligence source. Under CIA guidance and control, she begins to respond. Eventually she accepts recruitment. We have another double-agent operation.

What are the objectives of double-agent operations? Why do so many intelligence services use them? Why do I love them so much? The benefits of a good double-agent operation are considerable and fall into ten major categories:

1. Spreading disinformation
2. Determining the other side's modus operandi
3. Identifying hostile intelligence officers
4. Learning the opposition's intelligence collection requirements
5. Acquiring positive intelligence
6. Tying up the opposition's operations
7. Taking the opposition's money
8. Discrediting the opposition
9. Testing other countries
10. Pitching the hostile case officer

Spreading Disinformation

Double agents can be used to provide the opposition service with false or misleading disinformation, but this is a relatively infrequent objective. Deceiving the enemy in this manner requires tremendous planning and subtlety because the enemy is not stupid and often has the means to verify the validity of the double agent's reporting. Moreover, if the double agent reports that some action will take place in the future and it does not, the double agent's credibility is seriously undermined. In most cases disinformation in a double-agent operation makes sense only if the stakes are unusually high or the opposition has limited means of verification.

There are, however, some spectacular examples of successfully passing disinformation in double-agent operations. The one that immediately comes to mind is the classic and fantastically brilliant Double-Cross System of World War II. MI5 apprehended and doubled virtually all the German spies sent to England via parachute, submarine, and refugee channels. Some of the spies turned themselves in when they arrived, and others were arrested thanks to good police work and an alert citizenry. The starting point for anyone wishing to understand the art of double agentry is reading the voluminous literature on the British Double-Cross System. One of my favorites is *Agent Zigzag* by Ben Macintyre.[2]

After 1942 most Abwehr (German military intelligence) and SD (German Security Service) spies were captured because the British had broken the German codes and knew when, where, and how the German spies were to arrive in England.[3] Once captured the German agents either agreed to cooperate as double agents or were imprisoned. Some were executed. In an elaborate process run by the so-called Twenty Committee (for XX), the double agents communicated a carefully blended mix of true and false intelligence to their German spymasters via radio or secret writing. The true intelligence was given up reluctantly but was considered necessary to build credibility. It was as undamaging as possible. The main thrust of the false intelligence was to convince the Germans that the Allied landings in France would be at the Pas de Calais and not in Normandy. Most military historians believe that the disinformation from the Twenty Committee's double agents played a crucial role in keeping the Nazis guessing and in contributing to the success of the D-Day landings in 1944. Another notable disinformation success was the double agents' false reports on where the V-1 rockets were landing, which caused the Germans to believe the rockets were scoring hits when they were really exploding in unpopulated areas.

The US Army's double-agent operation against the Soviets to feed them false information on chemical weapons is another example of disinformation as a primary double-agent objective. I recommend David Wise's excellent book *Cassidy's Run: The Secret Spy War over Nerve Gas* for a full account. There are a handful of other examples of successful double-agent disinformation campaigns. These cases, however, are the exception to the rule. Disinformation is not as common an element in double-agent operations as most outsiders assume. In my experience other advantages to double agentry have turned out to be more valuable.

Determining the Other Side's Modus Operandi

A good double agent is in a perfect position to report back on the opposition's MO. For any counterintelligence officer responsible for monitoring and thwarting a hostile service's operations, it is invaluable to know how that service conducts its business. When I was tasked with developing counterintelligence programs for CIA field stations, the first thing I did was review all the double-agent operations that any US government agency had run in that location. What I wanted to learn was how the target services operated. Did they meet their agents in safe houses, cafés, parks, vehicles, or some other location? What time of day did they prefer for their agent meetings? Were there sections of the city they overused? Did they incorporate initial contact points (ICPs) into their MO, and if so, what kind?[4] What kind of equipment and training did they provide their agents? Did they use electronic communications of any kind? Where were their dead drops, and what did their concealment devices look like? What types of signal sites did they prefer?

It is especially helpful, of course, to have double-agent history in the same city where you are operating, but there is value in reviewing any double-agent operations run by the target service anywhere. The case officers of that service have all had the same training and follow the same operational doctrine. They tend to fall into habits and to reuse techniques that have worked for them elsewhere. The result can be predictability—a major vulnerability in spying that can and should be exploited by the opposition's counterintelligence. Thanks to double-agent reporting, for example, the CIA became aware that a major foreign intelligence adversary was operating in a narrow section of a certain city and was extremely unimaginative in varying its tradecraft. That enabled us to anticipate this service's operational activities and to pre-position our counterintelligence resources in a relatively small number of hotspots. As a result, we nailed them. I doubt that even today this service realizes its laziness and predictability caused so many of its compromised operations.

Let us assume that the FBI has put together a neat little double-agent operation against the Russians in California. The principal is a computer engineer working for a high technology company in Silicon Valley. A

Russian GRU officer operating under cover out of the Russian consulate in San Francisco is handling the case. The meetings between the double agent and his Russian case officer take place in small restaurants and coffeehouses in the southern suburbs of San Francisco. The FBI, of course, knows the identity of the GRU officer and can track his movements to some extent through surveillance and observation posts. Over time it becomes clear that his surveillance detection runs average about two hours in duration. On a day, for instance, when he is meeting his double agent at 3 p.m. at a Starbucks in Palo Alto, he leaves the consulate at about 1 p.m. It is logical to assume that the same pattern is used by this GRU officer in his meetings with his legitimate agents. This knowledge of the GRU officer's MO gives FBI counterintelligence a big head start in compromising his operations and identifying the unknown American agents. The FBI has the chance to observe his daytime departures from the consulate and to let him run free for about two hours. He will believe he is black. If he follows the same pattern as he did in the FBI's double-agent operation, he will park his car and proceed to a nearby café or restaurant meeting. Once the FBI finds his car, it can check out the cafés and restaurants in the area and—bingo—find him in the act of meeting with one of his "real" agents.

I can't emphasize enough how valuable it is for US counterintelligence to know how foreign intelligence services operate in the United States and elsewhere. It is an essential first step in beating them. Defectors and in-place penetrations, if we have them, can be a big help, but there is no better window into what is going on right now, right here, on the ground than a cleverly inserted double agent.

Identifying Hostile Intelligence Officers

Foreign intelligence services take great pains to hide their case officers under a variety of covers. They can pose as diplomats, trade officials, journalists, students, businessmen or women, airline representatives, employees of international organizations, and practically any other profession that gives them an ostensible reason for being in the country. US counterintelligence is tasked with piercing those covers and identifying the spies. One of the best tools available for this task is the double agent.

For starters we know who the handling officer is. In some cases the handling officer is the recruiting officer. If the recruiting officer first met our double-agent dangle when he was prowling the spotting and assessing venues in true name, then the double agent can provide a positive identification from the beginning. As standard practice, however, the case officer will use an alias in meeting with the double agent. The double agent can still provide a detailed description of his or her handler and can often make an identification through a photo spread. Also, since the CI service running the double agent operation knows when and where the case officer will show up, for example, to meet the double agent, to service a dead drop, or to mark a signal, it has surveillance and technical options to assist in identification. The case officer usually comes from a known pool of officials from the local embassy, a consulate, the United Nations, a trade mission, or some other official installation. It rarely takes long "to make" who the handler is.

Double-agent operations that go on for an extended period, as many of them do, will lead to further identifications of hostile intelligence personnel. Case officers rotate regularly to other assignments, and their agents, doubled or otherwise, are turned over to a new case officer for handling. It is always exciting to see who the new handler will be. Other case officers are sometimes introduced into the operation as a backup or as a subject matter expert. The primary case officer manages the day-to-day operational aspects of the operation but may not have the in-depth knowledge required to debrief the double agent effectively on a highly technical subject. It is not uncommon in these cases for intelligence services to insert a more knowledgeable debriefer into the operation from time to time.

Hostile intelligence officers can be identified easily if the double agent is being handled completely or partially with impersonal tradecraft, such as dead drops, caches, and signal sites. These operational sites are usually serviced by personnel from throughout the local residency, not exclusively by the primary case officer in the operation.[5] The primary case officer may not be able to get a surveillance break to pick up a dead drop, for example, or may not have cover to mark or to read a given signal. In that event a colleague from the residency is called on to help out—and can be identified by emplaced cameras or other surveillance techniques nearby. In some long-term double-agent operations, as many as twenty or thirty opposition case officers and support personnel have been exposed in this manner.

Things get dicey when the handling or servicing officer of a double-agent operation is an illegal or a nonofficial cover officer (NOC). Case officers in these categories face arrest and imprisonment if they are caught. For that reason illegals and NOCs are used carefully and as a rule handle or support only cases in which the bona fides of the operation are considered airtight. Luring an illegal or an NOC out to show himself or herself in a double-agent operation is a CI coup. The best example I can think of is the SHOCKER case, in which the GRU so trusted the army/FBI double agent Joe Cassidy that it used three GRU illegals to service him. The FBI identified all three and even got clandestine photography of two illegals servicing a SHOCKER dead drop.[6]

Learning the Opposition's Intelligence Collection Requirements

In the cat-and-mouse game of counterintelligence, even the slightest advantage can be the difference between winning and losing. A good double-agent operation can provide a winning edge by alerting the sponsoring service to the opposition's collection requirements. Knowing what the double agent is being asked to provide the handler is a valuable window into what the opposition's priorities and gaps are. How much pressure is being put on the double agent to collect intelligence in a specific area? The range of tasking is limited, of course, to what the double agent professes his access to be, but a good double agent might hint at the possibility of expanded access to smoke out the opposition's response. For example, a high technology double agent might tell his handler that his future duties might include research on night-vision devices. Does the opposition service respond with alacrity or lassitude? The latter reaction could be an indication that this requirement is already being covered by another agent.

Although Edwin Earl Pitts was not a double agent, tipoffs in his tasking surfaced in his debriefings by the FBI after his arrest for espionage in 1996. Pitts was an FBI special agent who spied for the Russians for seven years. He told the FBI that despite his outstanding CI access at the bureau, his KGB and SVR handlers seemed uninterested in broad stretches of his collection capabilities. Why was that? Because the Russians had an even better penetration of FBI counterintelligence in Robert Hanssen and did not want to put the still-valuable Pitts at unnecessary risk to collect what they already had. If the FBI had taken this CI signal more seriously and intensified its search for a mole inside the FBI, Hanssen might not have been able to get away with his spying for another four or five years.

Another ploy that can be used to learn about the adversary's collection priorities is to have a military double agent, for example, announce to his handler that he is up for reassignment and is about to put in his wish list for a new posting. Where would the service like him to go? Where does the service not want him to go? For what kind of billet should he be applying? How the handler responds can indicate the service's collection priorities and gaps and locations where it thinks it can handle the double agent safely.

The British successfully mined the requirements the Abwehr sent to its controlled agents in the UK during World War II to know which industries, locations, military units, and armament were of most interest to German military intelligence. Sometimes the information from the double agents was used effectively, sometimes not. An unfortunate example is the British double agent Dusko Popov, who was sent by his Abwehr controllers to the United States in August 1941 to set up a spy network. He was armed with a lengthy list of collection requirements, a large portion of which concerned Pearl Harbor and the rest of Hawaii. The British notified the FBI of Popov's trip and even arranged for him to be interviewed personally by J. Edgar Hoover. Hoover, however, dismissed Popov as an untrustworthy and immoral double agent and did not take him seriously. As a matter of fundamental counterintelligence, someone somewhere in the US government should have been smart enough to ask why the Germans seemed so interested in Pearl Harbor. Wasn't it likely that the Germans were servicing a high-priority intelligence collection request from their Japanese allies?

Intelligence services do not task their agents haphazardly. The requirements are generated by a systematic process that includes input from all the interested parties. In the United States, for example, requirements for the intelligence community result from an elaborate consultation and give-and-take managed by the Office of the Director of National Intelligence (ODNI). The process is far from casual. Any intelligence service can learn a lot by analyzing the requirements given to its double agents. There is significant meaning in what the opposition service is asking for and what it is not.

Acquiring Positive Intelligence

Occasionally, a foreign intelligence service so believes in the trustworthiness of a double agent that it shares with that double agent positive intelligence information. The purpose may be to give the double agent background information to assist in his or her collection efforts. Or the case officer-double agent relationship may become so cordial that the case officer assumes the double agent's ironclad loyalty and "talks out of school." Or the case officer may try to enhance his or her standing with the double agent by boasting about past or current accomplishments. A good example of misplaced trust in a double agent is the case of Katrina Leung, a Chinese American who was recruited by the FBI as an access agent to report on the Chinese community in Los Angeles, to wine and dine official Chinese visitors to the United States, and to cultivate official contacts inside China itself.[7] Leung was so trusted by her FBI handlers that they shared with her sensitive CI information, including documents, on Chinese intelligence personnel and activities. In CI terms briefing agents is standard practice and has merit, but sharing sensitive information with an agent is almost always poor practice. The fatal problem here was that Leung was a double agent working on behalf of Chinese intelligence. Well-trained and skilled double agents, like Leung, try to ingratiate themselves with their handlers to create the impression that they are sincere fellow-travelers, that is, happy members of the same team. The hoped-for result is a handler's unguarded disclosure of positive intelligence.

Eric Erickson was a US-born businessman who moved to Sweden, established a successful export company there, and became a Swedish citizen. During the early years of World War II, he made huge profits trading with Nazi Germany, particularly in oil. He was recruited by the OSS in 1942 to infiltrate the German oil industry. The OSS asked him to offer to help the Germans increase synthetic oil production for the Nazi war machine. The Nazis bit, and Erickson became a double agent. He sold himself so completely to the Germans, including to Heinrich Himmler personally, that he was given unrestricted access to Germany's synthetic oil plants. After his multiple wartime visits to Germany, Erickson provided the OSS with the coordinates of the secret plants. It is amazing that no one in German intelligence put two and two together to link Erickson to the American and British bombings of the synthetic oil production locations. Erickson was vilified in Sweden and the United States for being a Nazi collaborator, and it was only after the war that his actual work on behalf of the Allies became known and he received the recognition he deserved.[8]

Another notable double agent who obtained valuable positive intelligence is Morris Childs. Childs was born in Russia but immigrated to the United States as a boy. He was an ardent communist who studied in Moscow, where he attracted the attention of Soviet intelligence and was recruited in 1930 as a courier delivering instructions and money to the Communist Party of the USA. He did an excellent job and eventually gained the full trust of his Soviet masters. On his frequent trips to Moscow, Childs became a sounding board and confidant for the Soviet leadership, including members of the Politburo. He was privy to inside information on the politics, personalities, and intrigues of the Kremlin. Unknown to his communist friends and benefactors, Childs was growing disillusioned with communism. He was recruited by the FBI and served as a double agent—literally the FBI's man in the Kremlin—from 1958 to 1977. It was masterful how Childs insinuated himself into the good graces and confidence of so many top Soviet officials and elicited valuable information from them; during his years of operation, he was the best human source US intelligence had on the inner workings of the Kremlin. Childs was so beloved by both sides of the double-agent operation that he received high-level awards from both. Morris Childs, one of the greatest double agents of all time, is the only person in history who could simultaneously display on his mantel the Soviet Order of the Red Banner and the US Presidential Medal of Freedom. I would have loved to have been a fly on the wall when the Soviet Union's top leaders first learned that they had been had.[9]

Tying Up the Opposition's Operations

Every minute an opposition case officer spends on a double-agent operation is a wasted minute. Think of all the time that Katrina Leung's FBI handlers devoted to handling her in the twenty years she worked for them. Her primary handler, FBI special agent James J. Smith, for example, worked virtually full-time on her case during this period and was lost to the FBI for other duties. Also tied up in the operation for no productive purpose were technical teams, linguists, surveillants, and analysts. Multiply all of this by twenty years and the magnitude of the wasted time, energy, and money—in addition to the lost opportunity costs—becomes sadly clear. The Leung case was the centerpiece of the FBI's counterintelligence program in Los Angeles, and for all those years, it was spinning its wheels. Not only that, but the FBI handlers were so indiscreet in sharing sensitive CI information with Leung, including documents, that she was able to pass on to her true friends in the MSS warnings about what the FBI was doing against them. It was a double whammy by a good double agent.

German intelligence, particularly the Abwehr, had the vital mission during World War II of collecting intelligence on the British. The focus of the Abwehr's human intelligence program was to implant spies and saboteurs on British territory. This was a massive espionage undertaking involving hundreds of German intelligence professionals. It was all for naught. It was a colossal waste. All the spies the Germans dispatched to the UK—perhaps as many as sixty—were either arrested or controlled by the British. The Abwehr was neutralized as an effective intelligence force against its British enemy, all thanks to a double-agent program that still stands today as the best example of how this fine art should be practiced.

Similarly neutralized was the CIA's intelligence collection program against Cuba. The assets the CIA thought it had in Cuba were double agents controlled by the DGI. I cannot get over that one.

It is perhaps a perverse but still undeniable pleasure for a US counterintelligence officer to sit back to survey his or her double-agent operations and to gloat about owning a big chunk of that adversary's time and energy. Every useless thing that a foreign intelligence service does in handling one of our double-agent operations leaves less time for it to hurt us with real operations. In the great game of counterintelligence, these are gratifying victories.

Taking the Opposition's Money

Spying can be a lucrative business. Few of us would ever consider risking our lives and freedom by betraying our country for money, no matter how much, but venality is alive and well in America and should never be underestimated. Aldrich Ames, who was motivated almost exclusively by greed, was paid at least $2.7 million by the Russian KGB and SVR. All this money, however, is not doing Rick much good at his current address: Aldrich Hazen Ames, Prisoner No. 40087-083, Terre Haute Federal Correctional Institution, Terre Haute, IN 47808. Foreign intelligence services vary tremendously in how much they pay their agents, but with the right kind of feed material, a good double agent can command big money. The willingness of an adversary service to pay our double agents large amounts of money is a good indicator of how deeply we have set the hook. Just to set the record straight, American double agents do not keep the money they are paid. I am happy to report that in almost every case, Americans who agree to serve as double agents do so out of patriotism and not for personal gain.

The FBI and US Army double agent Joe Cassidy worked against the Soviet GRU for twenty-one years. From the beginning Cassidy made it clear to his Russian handlers that he was in it for the money and nothing else. Of course, he was not in it for the money at all. In fact, he was not even aware of how much the Russians were paying him; he turned the dead drops he picked up from the GRU, usually disguised as rocks, over to the FBI without opening them. Inside the fake rocks, according to the FBI, were baggies with $10,000 in them, sometimes more. Without knowing the actual amounts involved, Cassidy complained repeatedly to his GRU handlers that he was not being paid enough to justify the risks he was taking. This was in keeping with the role he was playing as a money-grubbing amoral American sellout. In fact, foreign intelligence services tend to think that their best hope of recruiting Americans is to buy them. An American double agent who does not press for more money can appear suspect to them. I like double agents who play hard to get and then, once "recruited," drive a hard compensation bargain. We should squeeze these services for every dollar we can get from them.

Double agents working *against* the United States can hit the jackpot as well. Katrina Leung was paid $1.7 million in salary and expenses by the FBI during her twenty-year run as a double agent. It is unclear if the MSS allowed her to keep the FBI's money, but presumably so, because it became known after Leung's arrest that she had half a million dollars stashed in foreign bank accounts—and the pittance the Chinese paid her would not explain that kind of money.

One of the many good things about double-agent operations is that they tend to finance themselves—with a lot leftover in some cases. I do not even want to think about how much the CIA paid to its bogus agents in the twenty-six years of the Cubans' double-agent spree against us. But I should point out that US coffers from successful double-agent operations are not empty either. We have done well. There are many forms of money, but money bilked from a hostile foreign intelligence service through a nifty double-agent operation may be the sweetest money of all.

Discrediting the Opposition

Intelligence services hate to lose face. They want to project to the world an image of competence, professionalism, toughness, and discipline. Any publicity that highlights their failures can undermine their support from their government and demoralize their troops. Anyone who has served in the CIA or the FBI knows, for example, what it means to be vilified in the press for mistakes and wrongdoing. Closed societies, like the former Soviet Union, East Germany, China, and Cuba, were not as accountable to the press and public as Western democratic societies are, but they still did everything they could to protect their reputations. The same is true today of our major counterintelligence adversaries. They do not want to look like the Keystone Cops. Blowing double-agent operations out of the water after they have run their course is a good way to expose the victimized services to the embarrassment and ridicule they deserve. How could they have been so gullible? How much confidence can anyone have in these bumblers? If I am a prospective agent, do I really want to put my fate in the hands of these incompetents? It is questions like these that we want every potential American traitor to be asking about our principal CI adversaries before he or she takes the plunge into espionage.

When Cuban DGI defector Florentino Aspillaga blew the whistle on the Cuban double-agent program in 1987, Fidel Castro knew he could still get some mileage from it. The result was a Cuban TV exposé, replayed all around the world, of how the clumsy Yankees had fallen for the refulgent machinations of the vastly superior DGI. In fact, the film clips of CIA case officers were selected to make their tradecraft look sloppy and obvious as they read signals and serviced dead drops. Castro achieved his objective. It was a disaster for the United States. The CIA was made to look like a laughingstock, the DGI looked omnipotent, and any Cuban would be a fool to cooperate with those American clowns.

The US is reluctant to publicize expired double-agent operations out of fear of revealing sensitive methodology or subjecting the American principal to notoriety. In selected cases, however, I would like to see US counterintelligence be more proactive in capitalizing on the other side's failures. We can make them gun-shy about engaging in future operations against Americans. We can publicize how they fell into our trap and how much they gave away to us in the process. If we can lure them into operating inside the United States, we can do a splashy expulsion of case officers who have diplomatic immunity and arrest those who do not. The hostile service looks bad for letting itself be duped by our double-agent operation and should pay a price for it. It loses some of its operational staff. Its reputation for professionalism suffers. No mistake by the opposition should go unexploited. When a CIA case officer was caught in the act of spying in Moscow in 2013, the Russian FSB had a field day mocking him for his floppy wigs and sunglasses. The Western press gleefully picked up on the ridicule, calling the misadventure "comic" and "more Austin Powers than James Bond." In the eyes of the world, the CIA did not look like a premier espionage service. We looked more like the gang that couldn't shoot straight.

I believe that discrediting the opposition is an often-untapped benefit of a double-agent operation. At some point the previously listed advantages of a double-agent operation have been maxed out or have simply fallen by the wayside. Then why not blow the case up? Bring in the embarrassment specialists. Publicize the case. "Chinese Spies Are Caught in a Double-Agent Sting." "Russian Spies Fall for One of the Oldest Tricks of the Trade." "Cuban Spy Arrested for Trying to Steal American Secrets." Have some fun with it—and hit them hard, very hard, at the same time.

Testing Other Countries

In my discussion of the First Commandment of Counterintelligence—Be offensive—I emphasized the importance of using double-agent operations to test other countries. US capabilities and intentions are important for the rest of the world to know. We are the superpower. We have a history of intervention in the affairs of other countries. We have technological superiority in many spheres, especially in military technology. What we do in the world matters. Any foreign intelligence service worth its salt must look longingly at the treasure trove of secrets to be found in the United States. Our traditional adversaries have been operating here for years. But what about our nontraditional adversaries? They too have sometimes succumbed to the temptation of spying against us. If they are good—and many of them are—they are hard to catch in the act. Is there some way to flush them out? Yes, indeed. Double-agent operations.

Test them. It could be as simple as having an American official, scientist, engineer, or soldier offer his or her services to a friendly foreign intelligence service in return for money or some other favor. If, to our shock, our friend bites, then we learned something we needed to know—and we have an operation. If, as we expect, the friend rejects the proposal, it passes our test, and our CI confidence in that country is at least temporarily affirmed. A friend who not only rejects the proposal but also reports it to us gets an A+! What do Greece, the Philippines, South Korea, Egypt, Ecuador, Liberia, South Africa, El Salvador, Saudi Arabia, France, and Israel, among many other countries, have in common? They have all been caught spying against the United States. It would be hypocrisy for the United States to express outrage about this, because we spy on our friends too. Edward Snowden made that clear to the whole world. But we would be derelict in our CI responsibilities if we did not at least try to find out who, including our allies, is doing what to us. Let the word go out: Those cunning Americans are testing everyone with double agents. Be wary of recruiting Americans. They could be bad.

Pitching the Hostile Case Officer

We have had a good run and have mined a lot of gold from our double-agent operation, but we are not quite done yet. Rather than just shutting down the case, taking our considerable gains, and quietly going home, we should consider finishing with a bang: pitch the hostile case officer. The odds of success are slight, but the simple act of making the pitch has benefits.

The case officer-agent relationship can have a peculiar intimacy to it. The two are joined together in a high-stress enterprise and profess to share common objectives. They can talk openly to few, if any, other people. The case officer values the agent as an important professional accomplishment, one that can lead to promotion and awards. In human terms also, most good case officers feel a personal moral responsibility for keeping the agent safe. It is not a stretch to say that there can be an element of "caring" in the case officer's attitude toward his or her agent.

On the agent's side, too, there can be a strong sense of attachment toward the case officer. The agent depends on the case officer for protection, guidance, and affirmation. Spying against one's country is a momentous decision for anyone, and even a totally venal agent may sometimes feel shame and guilt. The case officer's job is to assuage those feelings by helping the agent rationalize away any reservations about the betrayal involved. The agent's sense of worth is invested in the clandestine relationship. A kind word, praise, or expressions of appreciation from the case officer can go a long way toward helping the agent feel better about himself or herself. It is not uncommon for the agent to develop emotional and financial dependence on the case officer's approval. It would be an overstatement to call the relationship between the case officer and the agent a symbiosis, but both parties do have needs that create a kind of mutual dependency.

Some of the agents I worked with had few redeeming qualities, but I still treated them with respect and consideration. I hoped and believed that they looked at me in the same way, that is, as someone who had their best interests and well-being at heart. More frequently, however, I felt genuine esteem for my agents. They were serving our cause, for whatever reason, and were risking death or imprisonment by working with me. Many of them identified with American values or wanted to strike back against their own oppressive regimes by helping US intelligence. I considered these agents' motives honorable and their courage commendable. I liked them—and I think most of them had positive feelings toward me as well.

An astute double agent will be constantly reporting back to his or her handler on the personal characteristics and vulnerabilities of the case officer. If the operation has been underway for a while, the two of them may have spent many hours together in safe houses or out-of-the-way cafés. Safe house meetings are particularly good for building rapport since they provide a secure and relaxed setting for the two to drink vodka together, to enjoy snacks, to conduct their clandestine business—and also just to talk. They can let their hair down and get to know each other better, particularly during well-lubricated meetings.

The stage is set for the pitch. If the double agent is sufficiently trained, capable, and willing to do it, the conversation can go something like this: "Gennady, you and I have known each other for a long time. I hope you know how much respect and admiration I have for you. I consider you a friend, and that's why it is so hard for me to do what I must do now. I have been a double from the beginning. All the reporting I have provided is worthless feed material. Everything we have done together has been controlled by the service I work for. I am truly sorry for what this will mean for your career and your reputation, but there is a way out. Work for us. We can compensate you royally. Our relationship here can continue and get even more productive. If you want another American recruitment to enhance your career, we can make that happen for you. We want you on our side. What can we do for you? Money, an American education for your children, health care, resettlement in the US? Just tell me."

Can you imagine what is flashing through Gennady's mind as he hears this? "Oh, no! I'm finished. My big American case, the only one I have ever had, is a sham. I fell for it. I'm disgraced. I'll be sent home. And not only that, they pitched me! How am I going to explain that? The first question my bosses will ask is, Why did the CIA think I was vulnerable? They won't ever trust me again. And I've got to report the pitch, because I'm sure those bastards have it on tape." Gennady has assessed his situation accurately. We have put him in a no-win situation. It is almost (but not completely) certain that he will explode with anger and reject the pitch, but at a minimum we have damaged his career, neutralized him as a future CI threat, and discredited the service he works for. All that is good. It is hardball, I know, but everyone plays the game by the same rules.

If the double agent is not comfortable making the pitch himself or herself, an officer from headquarters or elsewhere can be "parachuted" into the operation to make it instead. If the double agent has concerns about his or her personal safety, the pitch can be reserved for a public setting or a place where protective surveillance is possible. In any event, if the target says no, it is a hit-and-run proposition. The double agent will be quickly removed from harm's way and will never see the case officer again.

SEVEN
Managing Double-Agent Operations

> The only safe rule of conduct would seem to be that we are fully entitled to adopt counterespionage measures against any power which indulges in espionage, whether that power be for the time friend or foe.
>
> —J. C. Masterman, *The Double Cross System*

Next, I would like to offer some general thoughts on how to select double agents, how to begin an operation, how to manage it, and from a defensive CI standpoint, how to spot a double-agent operation being run against us.

First, selection of double agents. Not everyone can do it. It takes a special kind of person to pull it off. A double agent must be a good actor, must be able to think quickly on his or her feet, must handle stress well, must be able to read people well, must be observant, must follow directions, and must be a convincing liar. The process usually begins by defining the target and the objective. The US counterintelligence community gets together periodically to discuss where the greatest needs are, for example, which countries, services, and areas of information or technology would benefit from a double-agent operation. Once needs are decided, a profile of a double agent who would fit the bill is created. The various CI agencies then fan out to try to find an appropriate candidate. The candidate is then approached, either directly or through his or her employer, and asked to volunteer to work as a double agent. Not surprisingly, many candidates refuse. If the candidate agrees, then the sponsoring CI service begins the lengthy process of screening, vetting, and training.

Some individuals present themselves as candidates. They report to their security officers at their place of employment that a foreign contact, either in the US or abroad, has been acting suspiciously, asking too many questions, making inappropriate remarks, requesting improper favors, or getting overly friendly. This can be an opening for the security officers to propose to the employee a meeting with CI experts to assess whether a double-agent operation might be started. Occasionally, an individual comes forward who has already been pitched by a foreign intelligence service. If no bridges have been burned and the individual is agreeable and suitable, a double-agent operation can start in this manner.

There are many ways to start a double-agent operation. The trick is to mimic how authentic espionage operations get underway. The most common and classic method is to have the double agent walk in to a foreign embassy, consulate, or other official installation in the United States or overseas, to ask to speak to a security or intelligence officer, and to volunteer. Many of the most damaging American spies in our history, like John Walker and Christopher Boyce, started their espionage careers as walk-ins.[1] Walker walked in to the Soviet embassy in Washington, DC, and Boyce sent his partner, Daulton Lee, to walk in to the Soviet embassy in Mexico City.

Intelligence services, however, are rightfully suspicious of walk-ins because they are so commonly used by adversaries to smoke out intelligence personnel and, if everything goes well, launch a double-agent operation. Many intelligence services have a designated "throwaway" officer, usually an old-timer whose cover is shredded and no longer in need of protection, to meet with walk-ins. The throwaway officer ensures that nothing of value is given up if the walk-in turns out to be a probe or a double. Variations of the walk-in are the write-in or the call-in. Robert Hanssen was a write-in to a KGB officer in Washington, DC. Ronald Pelton was a call-in to the Soviet embassy in Washington, DC.

Walk-ins, write-ins, and call-ins have a place in any counterintelligence service's double-agent program, but varying how the initial approach is made will help to keep the other side guessing. I was always impressed by how some of our most junior officers in the US CI community came up with imaginative curve balls. How about slipping a note to a crew member on a Russian cruise ship? How about doing a study abroad in China and openly bad-mouthing the US government's policies toward China? How about having a US serviceman serving overseas hang out in a bar with international clientele and feign financial problems and political disgruntlement? The FBI and the US Army brilliantly set the hook for a double-agent operation by dangling army sergeant Joe Cassidy to a GRU officer in Washington, DC. The young GRU officer was blatantly spotting US government recruitment targets at a weekly pickup volleyball game in the local YMCA. Cassidy, at FBI direction, joined the volleyball players, made clear that he was in the army (by showing up in uniform), and let nature take its course. The GRU, I am sure, congratulated itself on having so cleverly initiated the successful recruitment of an American soldier. Foreign intelligence services are, as a rule, more inclined to accept the bona fides of a volunteer if the approach is novel or if the service believes it initiated the contact itself after spotting a seemingly vulnerable target.

I love this one. A CI officer colleague of mine in a military service came up with the idea of using a friend of his, a disabled Vietnam War veteran, as a double agent. This individual was wheelchair-bound and worked as a civilian in a US government agency, where he had access to classified information. The idea was to have him go to a foreign installation to volunteer his services as a spy. His story was that he was incensed that the US had sent him to the unjust Vietnam War in the first place, had bungled his medical care, and had then cheated him out of his full disability benefits afterward. He was to conclude by saying that he was stuck in a low-paying job and wanted revenge. The veteran enthusiastically agreed to participate in the operation, played his double-agent role to a T, and convinced the opposition that he was legitimate. He joked to us that he was probably the first "roll-in" in US counterintelligence history. The operation was a success.

A double-agent operation is only as good as the feed material that supports it. Acquiring high-quality feed material is difficult because US government agencies, military services, high technology companies, and national laboratories are reluctant to give up classified or sensitive proprietary information. Trying to get away with doctored information is tricky and rarely successful. The opposition is too smart for that and, in most cases, will kill the operation if nothing can be verified. The cost of running a good double-agent operation is giving up real intelligence—sometimes reclassified to make it look more valuable, but still real. In World War II, the British sprinkled real intelligence—some of it damaging—in their double-agent reports to sell their deception to the Germans. US feed material is reviewed carefully by its owner and the double-agent team involved to ensure that losing it is an acceptable cost of doing business. In double-agent operations, you must give to get. It is pay to play. One military service that I worked with—which I will not name—was so skittish about giving up real information that it refused to clear even "for official use only" documents for use as feed material. Wonder of wonders, this service had no double-agent program.

An ideal double agent should have good access but not spectacular access. If the double agent claims to have in-depth access in a high-priority area, the adversary service will eagerly jump on board but will then demand production that outstrips our willingness to give it up. It is a fine line. The feed material must correspond to the claimed access of the double agent, be good enough to sustain the operation, but not be unacceptably damaging.

"Futures" are a special category. Some services recruit agents who have little or no current access but who might be directed one day into a government job with access. The Russians and Chinese, among others, have been known to recruit young Americans as futures in the hope that they can eventually be steered into employment with the State Department, the CIA, the FBI, the military, or some other national security organization. Recall from chapter 1 the story of Glenn Duffie Shriver, an American college student studying in China when he was recruited by the MSS. Shriver was recruited as a future, and the Chinese paid him to take the US Foreign Service exam with the understanding that if he got in he would spy for China. Shriver failed the exam twice, so the MSS paid him even more money to apply for the CIA's clandestine service, which he did in 2007. The hope was that the CIA would assign Shriver, with his good Chinese language, to Chinese operations, making him a valuable penetration agent. Shriver failed the CIA polygraph and confessed. He was sentenced to four years in prison.

Glenn Michael Souther was a twenty-three-year-old Navy petty officer with the Sixth Fleet in Italy who walked into the Soviet embassy in Rome and volunteered his services as a spy. Souther was a photographer's mate, which gave him virtually no immediate access, but the KGB recruited him as a future. He was paid by the KGB to leave active duty and to major in Russian at Old Dominion University in Norfolk, Virginia. The Russians reasoned that if Souther acquired good Russian-language skills, he would be an attractive candidate for employment with the FBI or CIA after graduation. The scheme worked for a while but fell apart while Souther was still a student. He fled to the Soviet Union.[2] I like futures as potential double agents because so little has to be given away up front, and it is also instructive from a CI standpoint to see how they are directed, paid, and handled.

Double agents require close monitoring and regular debriefing. Even the best ones cannot be left to their own devices. They must be constantly reminded that they are matching wits with a trained intelligence officer whose job it is to look for indications of outside control. A slight slip in demeanor or performance can doom the operation. It is a mistake to overly script the double agent's behavior during meetings with the opposition case officer because spontaneity comes across as more genuine. Nevertheless, each past meeting must be analyzed closely, and each future meeting must be gamed out to anticipate every possible contingency.

The personal safety of a double agent is of paramount concern. The sponsoring service should be alert to any changes in meeting venues or other circumstances that indicate that the double agent is under suspicion and could face trouble. Foreign intelligence services hate doubles and are not above striking back vindictively if they catch one. Double agents being handled inside the United States enjoy a cushion of safety because it is less likely that the opposition service will try anything forceful on our turf. It is a completely different proposition for American double agents being met outside the country. What if, for example, a double agent we are running against the Chinese in the United States is suddenly told by his or her MSS or PLA handler to arrange a business trip to China for a meeting there? Can we risk it? Are there any signs at all that the Chinese are on to us? We do not want an American citizen arrested in China on charges of espionage and forced to sit in a Chinese prison. But by the same token, if we refuse to allow our double agent to travel to China, the Chinese will be suspicious and could terminate the operation. Working as a double agent is not risk free.

Nikolay Artamonov was an American double agent who met a tragic fate. Artamonov was a Soviet navy officer who defected to the United States via Sweden with his Polish girlfriend in 1959. In the United States, he assumed the name Nicholas Shadrin and became a consultant and analyst on the Soviet navy for the Office of Naval Intelligence and the Defense Intelligence Agency. In 1966 the KGB found him in Washington and pitched him to work as a penetration of US intelligence in return for a full pardon and a package of benefits for his family members still in Russia. Artamonov a.k.a. Shadrin reported the approach to US authorities, who convinced him to accept the pitch and to serve as a US double agent. Under FBI and CIA direction, Artamonov began passing the KGB classified information (mostly low-level feed material) to which he had access in his job. The operation continued for nine years, but the KGB finally concluded that Artamonov was not being fully cooperative and was holding back information of real value. It strongly suspected him of being a double. In December 1975 the KGB instructed Artamonov to take his wife to Austria for a ski vacation, a cover for an important meeting with KGB officers in Vienna. He was told that he would be trained in Vienna on a new agent communications system and would also meet the KGB illegal who would be his future handler in the US.

This was enticing bait. It was also the old dilemma, the bugbear of double-agent operators: Do we let our double agent leave the country or not? Artamonov was willing. The FBI and CIA, after long deliberation, decided to allow him to make the trip—in the company of CIA officers who would presumably provide him with protection. The CIA officers deemed actual physical surveillance around Artamonov too risky, however, because, if the KGB detected the surveillance, it would know with certainty that he was a double. The first two days of Artamonov's meetings with the KGB went well, and everyone breathed a sigh of relief. On the third day, however, when Artamonov was informed that he would meet with the illegal, everything changed. He was told that he would be picked up by his KGB friends that evening in front of the Votivkirche on the Ringstrasse. When the KGB car pulled up, two KGB officers jumped out, wrestled Artamonov into the trunk of the car, covered his face with a chloroform-drenched cloth, and injected him with a heavy dose of a sedative. The plan was to drive him across the Austrian border to friendly Czechoslovakia and then to send him to Moscow for KGB interrogation. Everything was going according to plan, except that the sedative was apparently an overdose. When the KGB car crossed into Czechoslovakia, Artamonov was unconscious, and he died a short time later.[3]

Double-agent operations, even the most skilled ones, have flags that should be noticed by a competent counterintelligence service. The CIA has been victimized by several clever—and frankly not so clever—double-agent operations, most notably by the Cubans but also by the East Germans, Russians, and others. That should not happen. No service is ever going to bat 1.000 in ferreting out double agents, but there is no excuse for overlooking or minimizing the telltale signs that an operation is controlled.

Production

The best indicator that an agent is bona fide is without any doubt production. If the agent is consistently producing valuable and verifiable intelligence that is damaging to his or her country's or group's interests, there is a strong presumption that the agent is genuine. Foreign intelligence services do their best to avoid self-inflicted harm by passing high-quality information. In fact, low-level production is a common denominator in most double-agent operations. Double agents do their best to explain away why their production is not better: the good stuff is locked up or out of reach, it would be too risky to go for it, or my duties do not give me access to that kind of information. Production is so important in smoking out double agents that a case officer should not be bashful in demanding from every new or prospective agent up front proof of bona fides in the form of a significant piece of intelligence.

Promises

A double agent who is underproducing frequently promises better production in the future to keep the case officer on the hook. CI officers should be alert to statements from an agent along the lines of "I'm expecting a transfer to a job with better access"; "my best friend works for the Ministry of Defense"; "my office is in the running for a major new project"; or "I think I can get my colleague in another office to talk more openly with me about her classified work." Promises are a dilatory tactic used by weak producers.

Excuses

A double agent can be ingenious in coming up with excuses for why he or she is unable to complete an assigned task: "I'm sorry, my parents stopped by and I couldn't get away"; "I was sick all last week"; "they started exit searches at the ministry"; "I think I'm under suspicion and will have to lie low for a while"; or "the copier is strictly controlled, and I don't have enough privacy to use a camera." Recurring excuses are a big red flag.

Tests

A good case officer will find subtle ways to test his or her agent. One avenue to consider is to task the agent with delivering something that any employee at his or her agency would have: "bring me a copy of your agency's phone book"; "bring me the passwords to your office computer accounts"; or "bring me your organizational chart." If the agent is a double, these are things that the controlling service might not want to give up. An agent who fails simple tests should be considered suspect.

Traps

Another way to test an agent's validity is to rig a trap. Give the agent a package to deliver to a controlled address. Rig the package so it will detect opening or x-raying. If the agent is a double, his or her controlling service will be sorely tempted to know what is inside. A variation of this ploy is to direct the agent to pick up a similarly rigged dead drop. Again, curiosity could cause the controlling service to show its hand by tampering with the package.

Fearlessness

Most bona fide agents show concern for their own safety. This may manifest itself in nervousness or avoidance of risks. Apprehensive agents will most likely bring up these concerns with the case officer, who can then read the tone and body language of the discussion to assess authenticity. Fear is hard to fake. An agent who shows no fear and appears oblivious to risk is either stupidly intrepid or possibly a double. Doubles, of course, face no risk of imprisonment or death. Their indifference to danger may be discernible. The case officer's job is to differentiate between honest fear and feigned fear.

Pushiness

An intelligence service that is running a double agent can be greedy about maximizing the gain from its operation. It therefore tends to task the double agent with obtaining as much information, training, and equipment as possible from his or her case officer. As a result, the double agent may be pushy about expanding the operation's parameters. Here are some examples that could be CI flags: "I'd really like to have some way of communicating with you electronically"; "I'm attending a training session next month on cyber security; can you give me some requirements?"; "Is there some place safer to meet than in cafés?"; or "I might be able to get a bug into my supervisor's office; are you interested?"

Polygraphs

Double agents dread the polygraph. No amount of training in countermeasures by the controlling service can eliminate the risk of failing. A bona fide agent will be uncomfortable with the procedure and may even be hurt by the request but will usually comply. A double agent, on the other hand, will resist: "I don't believe in those things. Everyone knows they're unreliable. Don't you trust me? I really resent your springing this on me now. I'm not sure I even want to continue working for an organization that treats people this way." If the double agent nevertheless submits to the polygraph and the results are inconclusive or deception is indicated, the double agent will ascribe the outcome to nervousness or simply insist that the machine was wrong. The machine is usually not wrong. I am a strong advocate of polygraphing every agent, if possible, especially those with low-level production or other indicators of control. As a rule of thumb, the earlier a polygraph can be administered to an agent the better.

Genesis

How an operation starts is a relevant factor in CI analysis. Counterintelligence officers should be especially wary of walk-ins, write-ins, and call-ins. They are the quick and easy avenues for any intelligence service to get a double-agent operation started. It takes more time and energy to engineer a chance encounter or to patiently dangle the bait in the hope that the target service will spot it and react. The fact that many legitimate operations begin as walk-ins, write-ins, and call-ins will deter the receiving service from rejecting this kind of approach out of hand. Still, several CI questions should be asked: Did the walk-in show up during busy working hours or wait for a quieter time? Did the walk-in express any concern about being spotted by guards or other locals? Did the walk-in ask to leave by a back door or to make his or her departure less visible in some other way? Did the walk-in specifically ask to meet with an intelligence officer?

Did the walk-in have a prepared cover story for why he or she was making the visit? Did the call-in know or suspect that the call could be monitored by local authorities? An authentic volunteer will usually feel and display anxiety about making the initial contact; a double agent might not. Also dangerous are situations in which a person is pitched, seems hesitant and noncommittal about accepting, but then comes back later to accept. The obvious risk is that the person reported the pitch to his or her local authorities and was recruited to move forward as a double agent. If the pitch is too easy or the subject is too compliant, be wary.

Demeanor

The fail-safe in detecting whether an operation is good or not is the case officer's reading of the agent's demeanor. A case officer is trained to notice any anomalies in an agent's voice, eyes, expression, affect, body language, or general behavior. Truthful people react to stimuli in a certain way; liars are different. A liar may get away with it for a while but will eventually slip up. Individuals selected to be double-agent candidates tend to be trustworthy and reliable. The sponsoring intelligence service is looking for candidates who can be counted on to follow directions precisely and to report accurately. Why would you entrust a tricky double-agent role to someone you cannot trust yourself? In other words, the services are usually looking for people who have lived their lives honestly and responsibly. Lying may not come easily to them. Training can help overcome this obstacle to an extent, but many double agents are sent into the fray with only rudimentary lying skills. The case officer's job is to pick up on these poor liars. Most experienced case officers will tell you that, although they cannot explain why, some agents just do not look, sound, or smell right. US counterintelligence should trust those instincts and dig more deeply whenever a case officer reports that something about an operation feels funny.

EIGHT

Counterintelligence Case Studies

Counterintelligence is not an abstract or philosophical exercise. It's a hard-nosed, hard-fought, and high-stakes street fight between two competing intelligence services. Each side studies its successes and failures and adapts its methodology accordingly. We must do this better than our adversaries do it. US counterintelligence professionals will benefit greatly from analyzing the cases. I have chosen the following twelve case studies because I believe they illustrate succinctly some of the most important dos and don'ts of good CI.

Clayton Lonetree

> More men are guilty of treason through weakness than any studied design to betray.
>
> —François de La Rochefoucauld

It was December 14, 1986. I was in Vienna attending the embassy Christmas party with my wife, Meredith. The host was the US ambassador to Vienna, Ronald Lauder, the son of the cosmetics magnate Estée Lauder. The Lauders entertained lavishly and had outdone themselves on this occasion with beautiful decorations, great food, and plenty of holiday cheer.

Toward the end of the evening, I was standing in a small conversation group. I noticed a young man standing off by himself a short distance away, watching me. He was in civilian clothing. I did not know his name, but I recognized him as a Marine security guard. As our group broke up and I moved away, the young Marine moved over to intercept me. He was visibly shaking and agitated. I thought he was having an episode.

With some difficulty he said to me, "I know who you are because they told me who you are." He introduced himself as Sgt. Clayton Lonetree. I ushered him around a corner into a small corridor so we would be out of sight of the other guests. Lonetree told me that he had previously served at the US embassy in Moscow and had gotten himself into trouble. He said he had been in contact there with a KGB officer who had followed him to Vienna and was now pressuring him for more cooperation. Lonetree said he did not know what to do and needed help.

This was a shocking revelation. Marine security guards have virtually unlimited access to embassy offices and activities, including the communications centers, the phone system, the ambassador's office, and the classified burn bags. A US Marine security guard who goes bad is a counterintelligence nightmare. Lonetree was not admitting to much yet, but it was essential to get to the bottom of his story right away.

Clayton Lonetree is a Native American who was abandoned by his mother, spent several years in an orphanage in New Mexico, and then lived with his alcoholic father in Minnesota during his high school years. The Marine Corps was Lonetree's way to break out of a bad environment and to make something of himself. We cannot fault him for wanting to make the most of it. He was given the opportunity but fell into a honey trap in Moscow and betrayed our country.

Lonetree was convicted of espionage in 1987 at a Marine Corps court-martial in Quantico, Virginia, and was sentenced to thirty years in prison. His sentence was reduced to twenty-five years in return for his full cooperation in the damage assessment. He was a model prisoner. Upon petition of the commandant of the Marine Corps, Lonetree was released from prison in 1996, after he had served nine years, because he had shown genuine contrition, had not done significant damage to US national security, and had been put into a situation by the Marine Corps that he was too young and naive to deal with.

I supported Lonetree's release. Yes, he committed espionage and besmirched the reputation of the US Marine Corps—inexcusable acts—but in some ways he was a victim. He should never have been in Moscow. His motivation was love, not greed or some other form of depravity. The damage he did was minimal. Lonetree was not an evil person in the mold of Aldrich Ames or Robert Hanssen. No one died because of what he did. Nine years was enough. I do not know where Clayton Lonetree is now or what he is doing, but I wish him well.[1]

LESSONS LEARNED

- The Clayton Lonetree case showcased failed workplace counterintelligence. For starters Lonetree should never have been selected for the Marine Security Guard (MSG) program. He failed the test to get into the MSG the first time around and was admitted to the program only after Senator Rudy Boschwitz of Minnesota complained, on behalf of Lonetree's tribe, that the test was culturally biased against Native Americans. The Marine Corps had other grounds for rejecting Lonetree in addition to the failed test. He had a reputation for being a loner who was fascinated by Nazi Germany. He was drinking too much. There were serious questions about Lonetree's suitability for the MSG program in general, let alone for the most sensitive post of all, in Moscow. Outside political pressures should never be allowed to interfere in the selection of personnel for national security positions. Our country would have been far better served if the Marine Corps had stood its ground.
- Proper supervision, the second principle of workplace counterintelligence, was an utter failure also. The marines at the embassy in Moscow may have performed their guard duties well, but when they were off duty, all hell broke loose. They drank far too much at the Marine House bar and essentially ignored the policy of nonfraternization with local women. Even the post's gunnery sergeant, who should have been enforcing the rules, was in flagrant violation. The marines, moreover, were always supposed to go out on the town in groups of two or more. Lonetree routinely roamed the city on his own.
- Next, there was a breakdown in individual responsibility. No one stepped forward to report Lonetree's questionable behavior. The other Marines knew that he was seeing a Russian woman, was going out alone, had pro-Soviet posters and books in his room, was drinking too much, and sometimes voiced anti-American views. In theory they could have expressed their concerns to the gunnery sergeant, the regional security officer, the Marine Corps inspection teams, or someone else in authority, but they did not. A marine did not inform on another marine; this would have been unthinkable. The procedures and culture to support whistleblowers were not in

place. Strike three. All three components of workplace counterintelligence (selection, supervision, and individual responsibility) were whiffs.

- The State Department's policy of employing foreign service nationals—that is, locals—in high-threat posts like Moscow, Beijing, and Havana should be reexamined. It makes no counterintelligence sense whatsoever to invite the opposition into your midst. The State Department's rationale is that these local employees will have no access to classified information or spaces inside the embassy. Furthermore, the argument goes, employing locals in these clerical and menial positions, rather than bringing in higher-paid Americans who require housing, education, and other support, for both themselves and their families, is significantly less costly. If this is such a smart policy, why do our adversaries not follow suit? Why are there no Americans employed at the Russian, Chinese, or Cuban embassies in Washington, DC? I am certain the FBI would be delighted to see American citizens working inside these embassies as secretaries, clerks, maids, electricians, plumbers, janitors, mechanics, or chauffeurs.[2]
- Also significant in the Lonetree case was the Sixth Commandment of Counterintelligence: Do not be parochial. From the beginning of the investigation, the CIA had superb support from Ambassador Henry Grunwald, the State Department's regional security officer, the Naval Investigative Service (NIS), and the US Marine Corps. Our organizations' objectives were different, but we all worked together beautifully and stayed in sync. The CIA was responsible for the counterintelligence issues; the State Department was concerned about the physical security of its embassies in Moscow and Vienna; NIS focused on the criminal investigation; and the Marine Corps wanted a hanging. Our differing priorities could easily have led to turf wars and personality conflicts, but that never happened. Do not be parochial.

Sharon Scranage

> It's a little difficult to know when to trust your people and when not.
>
> —John le Carré

Nothing in Sharon Scranage's background suggested that she would be a security risk. She grew up in a solid middle-class African American family in King George, Virginia, where she was active in her church, sang in the choir, did cheerleading in high school, and was an honor student. She obtained an associate's degree from a business school in Roanoke and was hired by the CIA as a secretary in 1976. Scranage started with the Office of Imagery Analysis but moved in 1982 to the Africa Division of the Directorate of Operations. In 1978 she married a security guard, but she was divorced from him two years later. In May 1983 Scranage, then age twenty-seven, accepted an assignment to Accra, Ghana, as an operations support assistant. She said later that she was apprehensive about the move but thought it would be good for her career.

Scranage was not a case officer, but like everyone else in the CIA station in Accra, she had a top-secret security clearance. The station was small and cramped, so there was no real compartmentation. Operations were discussed openly inside the station, and the files were accessible to everyone.

Soon after Scranage arrived in Accra, she met a dapper thirty-seven-year-old Ghanaian "businessman" named Michael Soussoudis. Soussoudis had lived for many years in New York, where he married an American woman, with whom he had a daughter. This marriage ended in divorce, and Soussoudis returned to Ghana. Soussoudis was a Ghanaian intelligence officer; his alleged business dealings were simply a cover. He was smooth, good looking, and sophisticated. He frequented the best restaurants and nightclubs. The quiet, lonely, and sheltered Scranage was flattered by his attention and was soon swept off her feet.

Whether Soussoudis specifically targeted Scranage for recruitment or met her by chance is not relevant, because he quickly realized that she was a great target and was susceptible to his advances. She was an intelligence officer's dream. Scranage and Soussoudis likely were lovers by December 1983, and she probably began passing classified information to him at that time. She revealed to him the identities of CIA personnel in the station and, even worse, the identities of the Ghanaian agents being run by the station. In a clear case of emotional blackmail, Soussoudis told Scranage that he would break off the relationship if she stopped cooperating. She was such putty in his hands, in fact, that he even arranged for her to be debriefed by other Ghanaian intelligence officers. Scranage said later that Soussoudis controlled her with threats of violence, but this accusation was never proved. The truth is that Scranage was totally mesmerized by Soussoudis and did whatever he asked her to do. She was never paid.

One of the most frustrating aspects of this case is that it could have been nipped in the bud before any significant damage was done. All CIA employees are aware of the regulation that requires them to submit a written report to their management and security of any contact with a foreign national. Unfortunately, this requirement is sometimes ignored by employees and management alike. Employees resent the intrusion into their personal lives, and managers are uncomfortable probing into these kinds of matters.

The US government sends thousands of individuals overseas every year to work in the State Department, the CIA, the military, and other organizations. Many of them are single and are placed in locations where social opportunities with Americans are limited. Scranage is a good example. The US embassy staff and the local American community in Accra did not provide much of a dating pool, so inevitably some government employees sought companionship with locals or other non-Americans. Did the US government really expect them to be celibate for the duration of their tour? Government agencies can easily manage the counterintelligence pitfalls of staff contacts with foreign nationals if the employees take seriously their obligation to report these contacts promptly and accurately. Supervisors are to blame too because some of them know what is going on but look the other way. Another shortcoming in this system is that employees sometimes cover themselves with an initial report of what they describe as a casual encounter with a foreign national, but they do not update their report when the nature or intensity of the relationship changes. The result is sloppy counterintelligence. In my view any US government agency involved in classified work, at home or abroad, should strongly emphasize its foreign national reporting requirement, ensure that it is understood by all employees, and impose real consequences for noncompliance. We will have more Lonetrees and Scranages if we do not do this.

In November 1983, when the Scranage-Soussoudis relationship was still in its early stages, a senior Ghanaian government official told the US ambassador that a black female was meeting inappropriately with a Ghanaian citizen and that it should stop. The ambassador passed on this information to the CIA chief of station, who called Scranage in and instructed her to break off the relationship with Soussoudis, which she promised to do. She did not. I fault the chief of station for not making this warning a matter of official record and for not following up with better monitoring of Scranage's activities.

It took an outside intervention for the illicit affair and the espionage to begin to unravel. In mid-1984 a security officer from headquarters was conducting a routine inspection of the Accra station. As was customary the station personnel wanted to show the visitor some local hospitality, which, in this case, included an invitation to visit Scranage's apartment. When the security officer visited the bathroom, he noticed a photo of an unknown male sitting in Scranage's bed with his naked chest exposed above the covers. On the assumption that this individual was a foreign national, he reported the incident to the Office of Security when he returned to headquarters. The security officers discussed recalling Scranage to headquarters for a special issue polygraph exam, but in the end no action was taken. After all, such liaisons were not uncommon. Instead, Scranage was not polygraphed until she completed her tour and returned to Washington in May 1985. She was due for a routine reinvestigation polygraph before she left for her next overseas assignment. In a lengthy series of polygraph sessions, the examiner elicited from Scranage the details of her relationship with Soussoudis and a full admission of her espionage activity in Accra. Not only that, but Scranage disclosed that she was still in touch with her lover and had promised to continue giving him classified information.

At FBI direction Scranage lured Soussoudis to the United States in July 1985 for a tryst at a motel in Virginia, where he was arrested. Scranage and Soussoudis were indicted on several counts of espionage. In a plea deal, Scranage pleaded guilty to reduced counts of revealing classified information and identifying undercover intelligence personnel to an unauthorized person. She was sentenced to five years in prison, a sentence later reduced to two years, and served eighteen months. Soussoudis was convicted of espionage and sentenced to twenty years in prison. He did not serve his term, however, because he was swapped for eight Ghanaian spies who had been identified by Scranage and who were imprisoned in Ghana. I have seen published reports that resettling these eight Ghanaians and their families in the United States cost the US government up to $13 million.

LESSONS LEARNED

- This is a sad case because it was preventable. If Scranage had been supervised more closely, she could have been stopped earlier. Her colleagues in the station were derelict in not reporting her local boyfriend, who had to have been known to at least some of them. The chief of station ran a lax operation. The Office of Security was wrong not to bring Scranage back for a special issue polygraph, potentially uncovering the espionage a year earlier. The entire organization was at fault for not enforcing the foreign nationals reporting requirement more diligently.

- Sharon Scranage is a good reminder to CI professionals that the most damaging spies are not always the highest ranking. A general is great, but a corporal working in communications could be just as valuable in terms of access, maybe more. Scranage was the most junior employee in Accra station, but she had access to everything. Foreign intelligence services are aware that in the US government, access does not always correspond to rank. In fact, a secretary, a clerk, a communicator, or an IT technician can be a gold mine of intelligence. Moreover, they are especially attractive recruitment targets for opposition services because they are lower paid, possibly more prone to financial difficulties, less educated, perhaps less sophisticated, and often underappreciated. Supervisors and CI specialists should keep in mind that their subprofessional and paraprofessional employees are being aggressively targeted.
- Not to be ignored either are employees who do not have direct access to classified information in their jobs but who have physical access to the premises, for example, maids, janitors, electricians, painters, and plumbers. What I would have given in my career to recruit an agent in one of those categories who worked inside a foreign embassy or ministry. Even a menial employee can report on the staff, the layout of the building, alarms, cameras, and concealment possibilities for a technical operation. In many cases these employees can be used to implant listening devices themselves. Individuals like that can be valuable assets to our adversaries and should not be overlooked in CI reviews.
- The polygraph saved the day. Even though the polygraph exam was administered later than it should have been, it uncovered Scranage's espionage. At the time Scranage was still loyal to Soussoudis and subject to being reactivated as an agent of Ghanaian intelligence. Her polygraph-induced confession and subsequent arrest averted what could have been an even worse CI disaster. When an employee's conduct raises CI concerns, we should not be reluctant to conduct a special issue polygraph exam.

- Even small third world countries like Ghana are counterintelligence threats. They will grab low-hanging fruit if a US government employee shows himself or herself to be an easy mark. We know from experience also that some third world intelligence services have close working relationships with larger and more sophisticated services, including traditional adversaries like Russia and Cuba.
- In applying the workplace counterintelligence test to the Scranage case, I have no problem with the first principle, that is, how she was selected. By all indications she was a well-qualified and properly screened recruit. There were, however, total breakdowns in how she was supervised and how her station colleagues failed to report her inappropriate behavior.

Clyde Lee Conrad

> Most of the FBI successes against the Soviets came from the defection of persons who had been involved in Russian intelligence operations.
>
> —Robert Lamphere, *The FBI-KGB War*

Clyde Lee Conrad's name is not well-known to the American public, but it should be. He controlled one of the largest spy rings in the history of US counterintelligence and was responsible for the loss of thousands of top-secret NATO and US Army defense documents. Conrad spent almost fourteen years spying for the People's Republic of Hungary. His story serves as a cautionary tale about the dangers of overlooking or underestimating a "lesser" nation's spying prowess.

Conrad was born in Ohio in 1948. He joined the US Army right out of high school. After a tour in Vietnam, he was assigned to West Germany, where he spent most of the remainder of his career, primarily with the Eighth Infantry Division. In 1969 Conrad married a German woman with two children; he and his wife had a child of their own a few years later. Conrad's salary as an enlisted man (he eventually reached the rank of first sergeant) made it difficult for him to support his family; his wife worked as a cleaning woman to help make ends meet.

By all accounts Conrad was a good soldier. He received superior performance reports and was viewed by everyone who worked with him as conscientious and reliable. He was assigned to his division's War Plans Section, where he and others were responsible for securely storing NATO and army war plans as well as other highly sensitive documents. Another of his duties was to control and keep records of any reproduction of those documents. In time Conrad became the noncommissioned officer in charge of this unit. He was so good at his job that he was somehow able to wrangle staying there, despite the army's usual practice of rotating its personnel to new jobs every three years or so.

The ingredients for big-time espionage were in place: a soldier with a top-secret clearance, access at an amazingly high level, weak workplace counterintelligence, and serious money problems. All that was needed was a spark to set off this volatile mixture. The spark was Zoltan Szabo. Zoltan Szabo immigrated to the United States with his parents from his native Hungary in 1957. He joined the US Army in 1959 and was assigned to Germany, where he spent most of his twenty-year military career. His most significant assignment in Germany was in the War Plans Section of the Eighth Infantry Division, the same unit in which Conrad worked. Szabo had been recruited by Hungarian military intelligence in 1971 and since then had been passing the Hungarians large quantities of top-secret documents. He was not content to limit his spy production to what he could personally get his hands on, so he began recruiting subsources to extend his spy ring's access and to increase production. Szabo was getting very, very rich in the process.

In 1975 Szabo landed his best-placed and most productive recruit: 1st Sgt. Clyde Lee Conrad. Conrad jumped on board enthusiastically, stole thousands of war-planning documents for the Hungarians, and was soon cashing in. He and his wife abruptly and visibly changed their lifestyle: a new home, new cars, porcelain, art, gold coins, jewelry, and so forth. Someone must have noticed the sudden affluence, but no one spoke up. Conrad was so good as a spy that when Szabo lost his access and retired from the Army in 1979, Conrad took over management of the ring and even expanded it with new recruits.

It was shockingly easy. Conrad was an expert at sizing up and recruiting other soldiers with the lure of big money, but some of his pitches did not take. Still, no one turned him in—another total collapse of workplace counterintelligence. Nor was there a problem in getting the documents out. Conrad and his accomplices removed them from the vaults by the stack, even suitcase loads. There was no security, no supervision, no control. Two Hungarian-born brothers living in Sweden, one of whom had worked with Szabo earlier, served as couriers for Conrad, delivering his documents to Hungarian intelligence officers in Budapest. Later, Conrad delivered some of the loads himself, typically in Austria. Meanwhile, the money kept rolling in. The best estimate is that Conrad was paid over a million dollars for his work.

The Hungarian intelligence services, like all the Warsaw Pact intelligence services during the Cold War, were totally subservient to the Soviet KGB. Everything the Hungarians received from their intelligence bonanza in Germany was being passed immediately to the Russians. The stark result was that the Russians had chapter and verse on exactly how NATO forces and the US Army would respond in the event of war. It is horrifying to imagine how cataclysmic the outcome would have been if war had broken out during those years.

US counterintelligence was blissfully unaware that anything was seriously wrong. The devastating espionage losses from Szabo, Conrad, and their accomplices continued unabated. Finally, in 1978 the CIA received a startling report from one of its well-placed sources behind the iron curtain: a Soviet GRU colonel working with Hungarian military intelligence in Budapest. According to this source, the Hungarians were receiving huge quantities of classified documents from the US Army in Germany, including top-secret war plans. The documents, he added, were being immediately shipped to Moscow. One document alone was considered so valuable that the unknown agent was paid $50,000 for it in 1978. The CIA's source, unfortunately, was unable to provide any additional significant information.

This is vintage counterintelligence. A nugget comes in, often not a whole lot to go on, and an arduous CI investigation begins. Where to start? The known facts could apply to thousands of US Army enlisted and officer personnel in Germany. How long had the spying been going on? Was it one person or a network? Why were the Hungarians running the operation and not the Russians? Was the $50,000 windfall something that might be observable?

Army counterintelligence did its best, but it was understaffed and made little headway. By the early 1980s, the investigation was dead in the water. For all intents and purposes, it looked as if the spy or spies in Germany, whoever they were, were going to get away with it. This is the worst frustration of being a counterintelligence officer, that is, to know that there is a despicable traitor out there somewhere and not to be able to get him or her.

This is how matters stood until 1985. By then the hemorrhaging of our vital military secrets had been going on for fourteen years. Our security situation in Europe was even worse than we could ever have imagined. Finally—belatedly in my opinion—the army decided to resurrect the investigation in early 1985 and to assign responsibility for it to the FCA at Fort Meade, Maryland. Some new leads enabled CI analysts to put together a profile of the culprit or culprits: He was likely a senior noncommissioned officer, perhaps an ethnic Hungarian, with a top-secret clearance who had been allowed to homestead in a document controls billet (officers change jobs more frequently). He was probably assigned to the G-3 (Operations and Plans) Staff, responsible for generating and storing war plans, and showed signs of unexplainable income. Furthermore, the documents seemed to point to one of two army divisions in V Corps—one of which was the Eighth Infantry Division. The investigators were getting warmer, but they still had a long way to go. Hundreds of army personnel fit all or some of these criteria. It was not going to be easy.

Every counterintelligence professional will tell you that he or she will never forget what I call the Eureka moment of a CI career. This moment comes after months or even years of painstaking, mind-numbing, seemingly endless analysis and legwork, when you suddenly break through and get the hit. You find exactly what you were looking for: you identify the spy. In early 1986 an FCA agent in Germany had his Eureka moment. In culling through piles of army personnel records, he found a strikingly close fit: Clyde Lee Conrad. Conrad had recently retired from the army but was still living in Germany. The investigators knew that the espionage was still going on, but they thought it possible that Conrad had recruited others to carry on in his place. By rank, time in Germany, clearances, and access to war plans and other specifically identified documents, Conrad fit the bill perfectly. There was even a Hungarian connection in his file; one of his earlier supervisors had been a Hungarian-born first sergeant named Zoltan Szabo. Further research by the FCA team revealed that Conrad had changed his lifestyle dramatically in about 1975, going from heavy debt to lavish spending. FCA was certain that it had its man, but it faced serious legal issues. Conrad lived in Germany and was no longer part of the US military. Unless he could be lured to the United States, he would have to be arrested and prosecuted by German authorities. Not only that, but espionage is an extremely difficult crime to prove, and much of the evidence against Conrad was circumstantial.

FCA started working to make the case. It was a formidable challenge to zero in on Conrad without tipping him off that he was under investigation. Physical surveillance was an integral part of FCA's effort to collect evidence against Conrad that would hold up in court. This type of surveillance was an especially high risk because, if Conrad spotted it at any point, he could flee to the safety of Hungary. A single misstep by a surveillant could ruin everything: no prosecution, no justice, and several years of wasted CI work. What FCA needed above all was proof—probably photographic—that Conrad was in touch with a Hungarian intelligence officer. Contact with a foreign officer was an essential element of the crime of espionage. As a wary longtime criminal, Conrad would likely be alert to his surroundings and looking for surveillance. Moreover, he lived in a quiet residential neighborhood and drove at excessive speeds, so watching his home discreetly and staying with him when he was on the road would be difficult.

While working on surveillance, FCA also began contacting army personnel who had known Conrad in Germany during his many years there, particularly his coworkers at the Eighth Infantry Division. This was a worldwide task because many of them had been reassigned or had left active duty. Also, if one of the people FCA contacted blew the whistle and notified Conrad, perhaps an old buddy, of the approach by army investigators, Conrad could possibly go to ground. The risk was deemed worthwhile, however, because of the need to learn as much as possible about Conrad's activities and attitudes.

One of the people interviewed by FCA was Danny Wilson, an army master sergeant who had worked with Conrad in Germany ten years earlier. Conrad had soft-pitched Wilson about joining him in an undefined but clearly shady "business enterprise" to make a lot of money together. Wilson said he was not interested. FCA saw an opportunity here. Could Wilson, who was stationed in the United States, be sent to Germany on temporary duty, renew his contact with Conrad, elicit information on his activities, and subtly dangle himself as a potential recruit in the hope that Conrad was still in the espionage business? The plan was masterful. Wilson, under close FCA guidance, gained Conrad's friendship and trust to the point that Conrad pitched him on behalf of Hungarian military intelligence. Mission accomplished. FCA had a double agent in place. Wilson gave Conrad actual secret documents, cleared by FCA, to establish his bona fides with the Hungarians. Soon, Conrad was sharing with his new accomplice information about his past activities, communications, and Swiss bank accounts. He also introduced Wilson to his Hungarian-Swedish couriers. FCA surveillance observed and photographed these meetings, and Wilson wore a wire, so the evidence against Conrad was accumulating rapidly. The still missing piece, however, was proof of a direct link between Conrad and his Hungarian case officer. Finally, thanks to a tip-off from Wilson, an FCA surveillance team got the photo it needed of Conrad in a restaurant meeting with a known Hungarian intelligence officer. The case was complete.

On August 23, 1988, Conrad was arrested by German authorities. He was convicted of espionage and treason in a German court in 1990 and sentenced to life in prison. He died in prison of a heart attack in 1998 at age fifty. Several of Conrad's accomplices were rounded up and sentenced to prison terms also. One of the most damaging espionage cases in US history was finally over.

LESSONS LEARNED

- Penetrations are the best counterintelligence. Without the recruited CIA source, there would have been no Conrad operation. There should be special awards for CIA case officers, military intelligence officers, or FBI special agents who recruit opposition intelligence officers. Be offensive (the First Commandment).
- Double-agent operations are a powerful CI tool—and are fun to run. Danny Wilson is a perfect example of a brilliantly conceived and skillfully run double-agent operation. His ability to insinuate himself into Conrad's trust and to elicit from him key operational data led to the evidence that made prosecution possible.
- Own the street (the Third Commandment of Counterintelligence). Despite the many risks and difficulties, the FCA surveillance team was successful in monitoring Conrad's movements and obtaining clandestine photography. Most nonprofessionals fail to appreciate how excruciatingly difficult physical surveillance is, especially vehicular surveillance. Beacons (when possible) and aerial surveillance can be helpful in following vehicles discreetly, but the task remains formidable.
- Do not be parochial (the Sixth Commandment). The Conrad case was a showcase of cooperation and coordination by FCA, the CIA, the FBI, the Department of Justice, and German authorities.
- Never give up (the Tenth Commandment). It was ten years from the CIA's first report in 1978 to the arrest of Conrad in 1988. Once

the army resurrected the investigation in 1985, it stayed with it to the end.

- Poor workplace counterintelligence is a recipe for disaster. Security in Conrad's unit was shockingly bad. He was essentially unsupervised by the officers of his unit. Not a single soldier he pitched or probed with illicit propositions came forward. Conrad's flashy lifestyle also went unreported.
- Do not ignore analysis (the Fifth Commandment). I am in awe of the work of the FCA analysts who compiled the CI search criteria and sifted through the mountains of army personnel files looking for, and eventually finding, a fit. Analysts are our unsung heroes. To all my counterintelligence colleagues and friends at FCA, past, present, and future: Bravo Zulu.[3]

Earl Edwin Pitts

> Assignments to counterintelligence functions were not considered career enhancing, and most good officers avoided them. Thus the ranks of counterintelligence . . . were filled to an unacceptable degree with mediocre case officers and those lacking interpersonal skills.
>
> —Duane R. Clarridge, *A Spy for All Seasons*

Life was hard for FBI employees in New York because of their relatively low government salaries and the high cost of living. Earl Edwin Pitts did not feel that he was being adequately compensated for his long hours, difficult working conditions, and increased expenses. He felt underpaid and underappreciated. Much to his humiliation, he was forced to ask his truck-driver father for monetary assistance to support his wife and himself. Pitts said later that his grievances against the FBI were the motivating factor for his betrayal of the bureau, his colleagues, and his country. In July 1987 he crossed the line from being a disgruntled federal employee to a spy for the KGB.

It was a classic write-in approach. Pitts knew that the FBI did not have a mail cover on Russians at the United Nations, so he felt safe writing a letter to a Russian diplomat assigned to the Soviet delegation there. In the letter Pitts provided some FBI surveillance information as bona fides and asked the Russian (a legitimate diplomat) to put him in touch with the KGB. The diplomat helped set up a meeting between Pitts and KGB officer Aleksandr Karpov at the New York Public Library. The KGB liked what it saw, and the operation was soon underway. For the next two years, Pitts provided the Russians with good, solid inside counterintelligence information on what the FBI knew about Soviet intelligence operations and personnel in New York and elsewhere, FBI surveillance methods, double agents, and assessment data on other FBI employees who might be susceptible to KGB recruitment. Pitts's production in New York was excellent as far as the KGB was concerned, but it began to dry up after Pitts was transferred in August 1989 to a low-access job at FBI headquarters in Washington. Karpov continued to run him as an agent, however, until 1992, when the operation went dormant because Pitts was not producing enough and the SVR had a deeper penetration of the FBI in the person of Robert Hanssen.

Pitts was paid $224,000 by the KGB/SVR during his five years of activity. He stashed much of the money in a private bank account and did not change his lifestyle conspicuously. His wife, Mary, a clerk at the FBI, was not aware that her husband was a Russian spy and had an outside source of income.

Pitts must have felt good about himself. He had gotten away with it. As he later told a CIA psychiatrist, "I was shoved by the bureaucracy, and I shoved back." This was satisfying for him. He had gotten his revenge on his FBI tormentors, and not only that, he had a tidy sum waiting for him in his bank account. If Pitts had been smarter, he would have known that his smugness was premature and his victory would be short-lived. Traitors, even inactive ones, should know that the knock on the door that every spy dreads can come at any time. The standard operating procedure for US counterintelligence is to never sleep and never give up. If you choose to spy against the United States, you are playing Russian roulette. You are vulnerable to the next recruitment US intelligence makes inside the service that is handling you, the next defector that comes our way from that same service, and any mistakes you yourself make in the course of your spying. Spying against the US is a losing gamble, and those who do it tend to think that they are smarter than everyone around them, including US spy catchers, and can succeed where many others before them have failed. They are dumb enough to accept their case officer's assurances that only a few people in the foreign intelligence service know who they are. That's nonsense. Having an American spy is a big deal for any foreign intelligence service, and news of that success invariably seeps out to other case officers, support personnel, communicators, technical staff, and intelligence consumers. My warning to future spies: Do not count on compartmentation to keep you safe; lots of people know who you are, and if only one of them begins to cooperate with us, you're done.

That is exactly what happened to Pitts. In late 1994 or early 1995, the Russian diplomat he had written in July 1987 to volunteer his services to the KGB began to cooperate with the FBI. This diplomat had excellent recall of the offer's circumstances, the write-in's identity, and the subsequent turnover to KGB officer Karpov. The FBI examined Pitts's bank accounts and other records and discovered approximately $120,000 in suspicious deposits from 1987 to 1992. The FBI investigators had little doubt about Pitts's guilt, but the evidence against him was thin and would not support a prosecution for espionage.

It is easy to imagine how much the FBI wanted to get Pitts. The only FBI special agent ever to have been convicted of espionage was Richard Miller in 1990 (the Miller case is discussed later in this chapter). The discovery of yet another traitor inside the FBI must have been infuriating. The FBI, of course, was not yet aware that the worst traitor in its history, Robert Hanssen, was active right under its nose at the heart of FBI counterintelligence.

Pitts was assigned to the Behavioral Science Unit at the FBI Academy in Quantico, Virginia, in 1995. His access there was not especially damaging, but like any FBI special agent, he had secondary and peripheral access to information that might be of interest to the SVR. The FBI put Pitts under surveillance, tapped his office and home phones, installed a camera in the ceiling of his office, and monitored his computer activity. The problem was that Pitts was inactive, so nothing incriminating was coming up. Pitts's wife, Mary, was also being watched on the theory that she might be a spy working with her husband, but her surveillance too came up blank. When the FBI put everything together—no further suspicious deposits to Pitts's bank accounts, his reduced access in recent years, and no evidence of current espionage activity by Pitts or his wife—it concluded that Pitts, for whatever reason, was on ice. Without some form of contemporaneous evidence, it would be virtually impossible for the FBI to charge Pitts with espionage. The prosecution was in jeopardy.

The FBI decided to break the logjam with a false flag operation. This approach suggested itself because the Russian diplomat who had been at the front end of the Pitts case was still cooperating with the FBI and was willing to help. In August 1995 the diplomat knocked at the door of Pitts's home. Pitts answered. It is unclear if he recognized the Russian from their brief interaction in 1987, but in any event the Russian quickly established his bona fides by identifying himself and referring to what had happened in New York eight years earlier. The diplomat said he had a "visitor" who wanted to speak with Pitts. A meeting was set up for a short time later the same day.

The visitor, complete with Slavic features and a thick Russian accent, was one of the FBI's best false flag specialists. He told Pitts that the SVR desperately needed help from inside the FBI and was hoping he would agree to be reactivated. Pitts bit like a hungry carp. He talked about what he had done for the KGB and SVR previously and exaggerated his current access in the hope that the Russians would again pay him top dollar. The agreement was quickly struck. The Russian gave Pitts an envelope with $15,000 in it, and Pitts agreed to do whatever he could to help. From the FBI's point of view, the meeting could not have gone any better.

There was a complication, however. Pitts's wife had witnessed the strange encounter at the door and was perplexed by her husband's nervous state and hasty, unexplained departure. While he was gone, she searched his desk and found compromising material. She confronted him when he returned and was not satisfied with his vague explanation that he was doing undercover work. On its tap of the residence phone, the FBI picked up Mary's distressed calls to her family and friends about what to do. Her dilemma was excruciating: protect her marriage and husband by saying nothing or turn him in as a suspected spy. As the press later described her decision, she chose her country over her husband. The next day she informed her FBI supervisor about what had happened and gave him the compromising material she had found.

Mary's courageous and patriotic decision obviously imperiled the false flag operation. The FBI had no choice but to play the incident out. Pitts was interviewed and allowed to get away with a makeshift explanation that the visitor was a drunken low-level contact from New York who was seeking help for a legal problem. Pitts said he got rid of him as soon as he could. The FBI breathed a sigh of relief. The false flag operation had survived.

Over the next sixteen months, Pitts participated in twenty-two dead drops, nine phone calls, and two clandestine meetings with his fake SVR case officer. He provided the "Russians" with whatever he could get his hands on, including information on colleagues with problems, rosters of employees, classified documents, casing information on the FBI facility at Quantico (badge, door codes, alarms, etc.), and a handset for the US government's top-secret phone system. The FBI had what it needed as evidence, and when Pitts began talking about escaping to Russia, it was clearly time to wrap up the case. Pitts was arrested on December 18, 1996. In April 1997, he pleaded guilty to espionage and was sentenced to twenty-seven years in prison. Mary divorced him shortly thereafter.

LESSONS LEARNED

- Could the Pitts betrayal have been prevented? Probably not. It would have taken an unusually perceptive supervisor in Virginia, New York, or Washington to have picked up on Pitts's frustrations, intervened to assist him with his problems, and addressed his grievances. Likewise, observant coworkers could have identified the warning signs and alerted the appropriate authorities of the potential threat, but they did not. For supervisors and colleagues alike, it is easier simply to look the other way. Insider threats like Pitts have always been bad, but they will be much worse in the future as more and more employees at all levels have access to classified computerized databases.
- Once again a source inside the opposition was the critical element in catching a spy. The FBI's ability to obtain the cooperation of the Russian diplomat was decisive in the Pitts operation. I do not wish to minimize the outstanding surveillance, investigative, and analytical efforts of my CI colleagues, but the fact is that the overwhelming majority of counterintelligence successes come from penetrations, not from grinding inside CI work.
- It is not unusual for CI professionals to learn of spying against the United States that took place in the past but is no longer active. Even Pitts, who was not a particularly smart spy, made it difficult for the FBI to confirm his past spying. He stupidly kept the proceeds from his spying in a bank account under his own name and left incriminating material in his desk, but he refrained from any direct communication with the SVR or overt spying of any kind. The FBI was basically left with two options: a confrontation or a false flag.
- False flag operations that appeal to a spy's greed are often successful. Since most Americans who have betrayed our country since the 1950s have done so for money, the opportunity for them to

cash in again can be irresistible. When Pitts saw the envelope with the $15,000 in it, he fell hard.

- The FBI failed to pick up on what should have been a clear counterintelligence signal. In its debriefings of Pitts, the FBI learned that the SVR seem uninterested in exploiting Pitts's access to the fullest. Granted, his access to classified information had declined, but he was still an FBI special agent. It was counterintuitive that the SVR would underutilize and eventually deactivate any FBI penetration—unless it had something better. The FBI should have reinvigorated its in-house CI investigation.

Chi Mak

> I forgive those who murder and steal because they did it out of necessity, but a traitor never.
>
> —Emiliano Zapata

Chinese intelligence operations against the United States are effective, but they are sometimes prone to one of the cardinal sins of espionage: predictability. Every US counterintelligence specialist should study the Chi Mak case because it provides a template of how the Chinese intelligence services like to operate against the US high technology target. Their chosen method works, so they do the same thing repeatedly: they dispatch Chinese scientists, engineers, and students to the US in the hope that they can eventually acquire US citizenship, gain employment in the government or high technology sector, obtain a security clearance, and then, when all goes well, get access to classified or proprietary information of value to China. Knowing how the Chinese are stealing our technology is one thing; stopping it is another. The onslaught of Chinese spying is so massive that it overwhelms US counterintelligence capabilities and resources. We should never underestimate what is going on. We pat ourselves on the back when we catch a Chi Mak, but the crucial question remains unanswered: How many other Chinese spies like Chi Mak are out there right now operating against us with impunity? My guess is dozens, if not hundreds.

Chi Mak was born in China in 1940 and moved to Hong Kong in the 1960s. There is speculation, but no proof, that he was already working for Chinese intelligence before he moved to Hong Kong. After establishing himself in Hong Kong, Chi immigrated to the United States in the late 1970s. Was this part of a master plan? Did Chinese intelligence believe that Chi could more easily immigrate to the US from a British colony than from Communist China? The FBI later determined that Chi had lied on his immigration application forms. What was he hiding? At his trial Chi admitted that he had been dispatched to the US with the mission of "burrowing in" to US high technology.

After five years of residence in the US, Chi became a naturalized American citizen in 1985. In 1988 he began working as an electrical engineer for the defense contractor firm Power Paragon of Anaheim, California. Power Paragon is a company that focuses on the research and development of advanced propulsion systems and other sensitive technologies for US Navy submarines and surface ships. Chi quickly gained the reputation of being a quiet, hardworking, unassuming, and brilliant engineer. It is puzzling from a CI standpoint that a recently naturalized Chinese American was working for a company like Power Paragon, but Chi was presumably not involved in the most sensitive projects there because his secret US government security clearance did not come through until 1996. If Chi's path to access was orchestrated by Chinese intelligence as far back as the late 1970s, as I believe it was, his handling by his case officer was brilliant and remarkably patient. Chi Mak had successfully maneuvered himself into a fantastic position to serve his Chinese masters.

When I was chief of counterintelligence at the CIA in the early 1990s, I sometimes briefed CIA and defense contractor firms on counterintelligence threats. I recall going to one company in California where I met with the director of security, a friend and former CI colleague. I asked him a question that I knew was politically incorrect but that made sense for a counterintelligence officer: "How many of your engineers with access to our sensitive programs are naturalized US citizens born in China?" I was shocked by his answer of hundreds. He saw my reaction and said, "Jim, I know what you're thinking. It is terrible CI. But what would you have us do? We need engineers, and when we go to the best engineering schools to recruit them, what do we find? Chinese."

Power Paragon was a damaging place for a Chinese spy to be. Delivering sensitive US Navy technologies to the Chinese could change the strategic balance in East Asia. With Chi Mak's help, the Chinese navy could accelerate its modernization program and present a more menacing challenge to US Navy forces in the region. Chi was collecting and delivering huge quantities of sensitive US Navy technical data to China. There were no security procedures in place at Power Paragon to prevent him from doing that.

Something happened in 2003. From an unknown source or sources, the FBI became aware that sensitive US Navy technology was being leaked from Power Paragon to the Chinese. The FBI and the Naval Criminal Investigative Service (NCIS) opened a counterintelligence investigation and soon zeroed in on Chi Mak as the prime suspect.[4] They threw tremendous resources into the investigation. After obtaining the proper warrants, they conducted physical and photographic surveillance of Chi, tapped his home and office phones, examined his financial and travel records, and went through his trash. The trash cover was a long and filthy job, but it finally paid off when the NCIS investigators retrieved a torn-up requirements list from Chi's Chinese intelligence handler. Another torn-up piece of paper contained instructions on how Chi should attend scientific conferences, elicit information from attendees, and scoop up any available documents. There was no doubt that both notes were intelligence related. This was potent evidence, but clearly not enough. How to get more was the problem.

The surveillance coverage of Chi and his wife, Rebecca Liu, revealed that they lived frugally in a small home and rarely went out, other than to visit Chi's younger brother, Tai Mak, and his wife, Fuk Li. Rebecca had assimilated little into American life and spoke minimal English. Chi and Rebecca took their cheapness to ridiculous extremes; they ate their meals on newspapers, used gas station squeegees to wash their car, and went regularly to a lumber yard to drink the free coffee. According to all appearances, they were leading a sad and lonely life devoid of any excitement. There were no signs of gambling, drinking, carousing, or any form of lavish spending.

The FBI and NCIS desperately wanted to get a look inside Chi and Rebecca's home, but Rebecca rarely left the house. The big break came in September 2004, when the Maks took a trip to Alaska. Could this possibly be an operational trip? It apparently was not because the surveillance team that went with them noticed nothing unusual. The Alaska trip provided the long-awaited opportunity for the investigative team to do a surreptitious entry of the Maks' home.[5] The investigators pulled if off beautifully; they got in and out without being detected by nosy neighbors, joggers, or dogs. What they found was shocking: piles and piles of technical documents from Power Paragon, stacked in every corner. Chi was a pack rat. He was storing some 40,000 pages of work-related documents in his home. The documents were not highly classified, but many were export controlled and for official use only. Chi was in flagrant violation of company rules that forbid taking documents of this kind out of the office. The entry team noted that the Maks were poor housekeepers; there was dust everywhere in the house, and moving and photographing everything without leaving marks in the dust was difficult.

The FBI and NCIS knew they were on the right track. Something illegal was definitely going on inside that house. They obtained a warrant for a second surreptitious entry, this time to install concealed cameras and listening devices. The payoff came quickly. Chi and Rebecca were observed working at their kitchen table transferring paper documents onto a CD. Separately, the phone tap on the house picked up conversations between Chi and his brother, Tai, about a trip the latter was planning to take to China with his wife. The tap on Tai's phone added the information that Tai promised to deliver something important to Pei-liang Pu, presumably an intelligence officer, when Tai arrived in China.

It was easy to put this all together. Chi had acquired something important to pass to the Chinese, and Tai was his courier. The investigators could not know for sure what was on the CD but feared that it might involve highly sensitive technology to mask the acoustic signature of US nuclear submarines, something Chi had been working on at Power Paragon. The imperative of preventing what would be a devastating loss to US Navy security forced the team to act. Tai Mak and his wife, Fuk Li, were arrested on October 28, 2005, at Los Angeles International Airport as they were about to board a flight to China. Chi Mak and his wife, Rebecca Liu, were arrested at their home the same day. Under interrogation Chi confessed to having committed espionage.

The prosecution was not a slam dunk. The defense argued that the documents were not highly classified and some were even available to the public. It contended that Chi's prosecution was based on racism and xenophobia and that he had been singled out as a scapegoat for the government's failure to win convictions in other Chinese cases. Chi's confession to NCIS interrogators was damning, but it was essentially useless in court because the NCIS agents had failed to record it, an unimaginable lapse on their part.

Power Paragon itself seemed to line up on the side of the defense. An internal compliance officer for the company testified that no sensitive information had been compromised. A Power Paragon engineer stated that the materials Chi Mak passed did not contain "anything that couldn't be found in graduate-level textbooks." The prosecutors countered that this testimony was intended to protect the company's reputation and interests. If, they said, it became known that Power Paragon practiced weak internal security and handled sensitive information in a careless manner, it could lose the military contracts on which its business depended.

On May 10, 2007, Chi Mak was convicted of conspiring to violate export control laws, acting as an unregistered foreign agent, and making false statements to the FBI. He was sentenced to twenty-four and a half years in prison and a $50,000 fine. The judge said that he meant the sentence to be a warning to China to stop sending agents to the United States to steal our military technology. The following month Tai and Rebecca pleaded guilty to conspiracy and failure to register as foreign agents. Tai Mak was sentenced to ten years in prison and Rebecca to three years. The members of the ring were informed that they would be deported to China after they served their time.

LESSONS LEARNED

- The Chi Mak case highlights the importance of applying good workplace counterintelligence to defense contractors as well as to government employees. Security in US high technology contractor companies has been notoriously bad. The FBI, DOD, and CIA have programs dedicated to educating company employees and enforcing proper security procedures, but they cannot control what happens once they leave. It is probably an overgeneralization, but one I stand by, that scientists are often oblivious to security. They live in a world where other scientists in their field, regardless of nationality, are assumed to be friendly. Sharing research data is what good scientists do. Counterintelligence officers should never assume that scientists or, by extension, engineers have even a basic understanding of how espionage targeting works.
- The efforts of the Chinese intelligence services to send Chinese emigrants or recruit immigrants for espionage are pervasive. Their number one target without question is US military-related high technology. It would be ignoring the obvious and, in my opinion, a dereliction of duty for a counterintelligence professional to treat all national security employees the same. Chinese Americans who work in national security, particularly those born on the mainland,

require additional CI scrutiny given how China's intelligence services operate.

- I liked how the FBI and NCIS worked together on the Chi Mak case. They were the furthest thing from parochial. Their cooperation, sharing of information, and mutual respect were exemplary.
- Go for a surreptitious entry as early in a CI investigation as possible. Once the evidence is sufficient to obtain FISA approval, consider going in. Do not give the suspect the chance to determine that he or she is under surveillance or being investigated and then to destroy the evidence. Get what you can as soon as you can. There is more than likely a smoking gun in there somewhere.
- I hate to say it, but NCIS bungled the initial interrogation of Chi Mak. The first confrontational meeting with any suspect in a CI case, before or after arrest, must be meticulously planned. Investigators, prosecutors, and even psychologists should participate in the planning. Under no circumstances should an interview take place without videotaping and recording. Every CI team has a member who is particularly adept at conducting interviews of this kind—and that person should be given the lead. CI interrogations are filled with evidentiary and legal pitfalls and should be handled by experienced personnel only.

Ana Montes

> My firm belief is that hardly anyone becomes a traitor for money alone.
>
> —Markus Wolf, *Memoirs of a Spymaster*

I am of a mixed mind on ideological conviction. On the one hand, I admire people who are steadfast in their beliefs and are willing to sacrifice everything—perhaps even their lives or their liberty—to further their cause. In my classes at the Bush School, I tell my students that I cannot help but respect Julius and Ethel Rosenberg for their fervent commitment to communism and their readiness to accept death in the electric chair rather than to abjure their beliefs. I do not agree with their cause, of course, but I can still recognize and honor the depth of their conviction.

On the other hand, as a counterintelligence professional, I hate ideological conviction because it makes spies so much harder to catch. Spies of conviction, often referred to as ideological spies, tend to fly under the radar and to cover their tracks better than venal or amoral spies. It is less likely that ideological spies will attract attention to themselves by profligate spending and other forms of reckless behavior. These spies of conviction must conceal their true beliefs from everyone around them, and they become skilled at doing just that. They are chameleons. They blend in as model employees and solid citizens who are totally loyal to their country. No one would ever suspect that they are secretly seething with anger, disillusionment, and susceptibility to treason.

Ana Montes was the classic spy of conviction, or as she was called by Scott Carmichael, the Defense Intelligence Agency spy catcher who led the way in nabbing her, a "true believer."[6] Montes worked for Cuban intelligence for sixteen years. I am not sure she would ever have been caught if she had kept her mouth shut. She stupidly attracted attention to herself by spouting off to coworkers, friends, and family about how strongly she was opposed to US policies toward Cuba. It was foolhardy in the extreme for her to reveal her pro-Cuba sentiments. Moreover, Montes was so eager to please her Cuban handlers that she gradually inserted herself as an agent of influence in the US intelligence community to try to shape US government attitudes toward Cuba. If she had kept her feelings to herself and had only provided positive intelligence to the Cubans instead of engaging in subtle activism, she might have avoided the spotlight and survived the subsequent investigation.

Ana Montes was the oldest of four children born to a US Army psychiatrist and his wife, both of Puerto Rican ancestry. Ana was born in Germany in 1957 but moved with her parents to the United States as a child and was raised primarily in an upper middle-class home in Towson, Maryland. Her father had a private psychiatric practice. Montes alleged later that her father was authoritarian and abusive, which may or may not have been true. Montes's sister countered that their father was in fact stern but also loving and supportive. The parents divorced when Montes was fifteen, and she lived with her mother until she left for college.

In 1979 Montes graduated from the University of Virginia with a degree in foreign affairs. At the University of Virginia, during a study abroad in Spain, she reportedly began to harden her radical political views. She became convinced that the United States supported dictatorships around the world, especially in Latin America, and imposed its will on weaker nations. Her family and friends noted that she became decidedly leftist in her worldview. After graduation Montes worked for a short time as a legal assistant in Puerto Rico, and then in 1980 she accepted a job as a clerk at the US Department of Justice, where she was granted a top-secret security clearance. Her family and friends were surprised that she agreed to work for a government she appeared to despise. There is no indication that Montes was thinking of espionage at this point; the mostly likely explanation is that she just needed a job. How she could obtain a top-secret clearance with her anti-American views is still a mystery, but I suspect that the background investigation was deficient.

While working at the Department of Justice, Montes started taking night classes at the Johns Hopkins School of Advanced International Affairs (SAIS) with the goal of eventually obtaining a master's degree. She was smart and ambitious. She made no secret of her leftist views and was outspoken in her criticism of President Ronald Reagan and his support for the Contras. It was obvious to all of Montes's classmates that she aligned herself politically with the Sandinistas in Nicaragua and Fidel Castro in Cuba.

Now it starts. Someone at SAIS was apparently a spotter for Cuban intelligence and saw in Montes a prime candidate for recruitment. This unknown intermediary arranged for her to meet with a Cuban intelligence officer in New York, probably in December 1984. The Cuban, like any good case officer, originally intended to move slowly toward a recruitment pitch, so as not to scare Montes off, but it was soon obvious to him that she was ripe. He pitched her, and she accepted.

I am sure Cuban intelligence was delighted at how eager Montes was to become an agent and how valuable she would be as a cleared US government employee. Her access, however, at the Department of Justice left a lot to be desired. Not only that, but Montes was raw as an agent and needed specialized training in clandestinity. The brazen solution was to have Montes travel secretly to Cuba for further indoctrination, motivation, and training, which she did in March 1985. The Cubans urged her upon her return to apply for a job with better access to sensitive information concerning Cuba.

True to her word, Montes applied to several national security agencies and hit pay dirt with an offer to work as an intelligence analyst for the Defense Intelligence Agency. She began her job at DIA in September 1985, initially working on El Salvador and Nicaragua. Once again US workplace counterintelligence failed. DIA did not polygraph Montes (its practice at the time was not to polygraph new employees), did not uncover her misrepresentation about her academic credentials, was duped by her lies concerning foreign travel, and ignored—if it even knew about them—her anti-American politics. Montes was viewed as an excellent employee and rose quickly in the ranks. In 1992 she became the senior DIA intelligence analyst on Cuba.

In the meantime Montes was spying away. She was careful about not getting caught, so she did not photograph any documents at the office or take them home with her. Instead, she memorized the contents of the important classified documents she saw, typed summaries on her laptop at home, encrypted the text onto diskettes, and then (she thought) erased all the incriminating material from her computer. She received instructions from Havana via encrypted shortwave radio broadcasts, which she deciphered on her laptop using a special program provided by Cuban intelligence. She was also able to send messages to her handler by calling him from a public phone booth and leaving a brief coded message on his pager. The biggest risk Montes took was having dinner once or twice a month with her Cuban case officer in a restaurant in the Washington, DC, area to hand over the diskettes and to bask in the praise and affirmation that Cuban intelligence was lavishing on her. As a purely ideological spy, Montes was never paid for her services.

In 1996 an alert DIA employee, practicing good workplace counterintelligence, reported his concerns about Montes to CI officer Scott Carmichael. The employee noted that Montes appeared sympathetic to the Cuban cause and was inappropriately aggressive in seeking expanded access to sensitive intelligence on Cuba. Carmichael interviewed Montes, who openly admitted her disagreement with US policy toward Cuba but insisted she had done nothing wrong. Since Carmichael could find nothing about Montes's statements or behavior that would justify further action, he let the matter drop—but his CI sixth sense was aroused, and he filed away his suspicions of her for future action.

In 2000 Carmichael became aware that the FBI was looking for a Cuban mole inside the US intelligence community. Little was known about the identity of the spy, except that he or she was using a Toshiba laptop computer to communicate with Cuban intelligence. Carmichael immediately thought of Montes, but he had so little evidence to support his suspicions against her that he had great difficulty in convincing the FBI to open an investigation. The FBI was aware of Montes's secret visit to a US Army Special Forces camp in El Salvador and of a Cuban-supported guerrilla attack against that same camp a few weeks later. A US Special Forces soldier was killed in the attack. Equally suspicious was Montes's strange behavior related to the Cuban shootdown of two Brothers to the Rescue aircraft in 1996, in which three US citizens and a permanent resident alien were killed. Rather than condemning the Cuban government for the murders, Montes seemed to be pushing the line that Brothers to the Rescue, a U.S.-based anti-Castro group, was to blame for ignoring Cuba's warnings. In 1998 Montes edited a major intelligence assessment to downplay the severity of the threat Cuba posed to the United States. Her input and tone impressed some of the other participants as an apologia for Cuba.

Carmichael was admirably persistent in pushing the FBI to open an investigation (never give up), and his efforts finally succeeded. In May 2001, the bureau threw a full court press at Montes, starting with extensive physical surveillance. It did not take long for the FBI to conclude that she was involved in illegal activity. First, she was obvious and amateurish in her surveillance detection routes, often entering a store by one door and quickly leaving by another. Second, she made a succession of one-minute phone calls from public phone booths, even though she owned and carried with her a cell phone. Montes's behavior was suspicious enough for the FBI to obtain approval for a surreptitious entry of her apartment on May 25, 2001. She was away on a weekend trip with her boyfriend. The FBI knew that this entry would be particularly dicey; if Montes was in fact a Cuban-trained spy, she could have trapped her apartment to detect an intrusion. There was, however, no evidence of trapping, and the entry was successful. The FBI team found a shortwave radio of the type used by spies to listen to encrypted broadcasts and also the telltale Toshiba laptop. On the hard drive, which the FBI drained, were multiple messages from the Cubans to Montes commenting on her intelligence reporting, giving her additional tasking requirements, and coaching her on her tradecraft. I am sure the FBI computer experts chuckled when they read the instructions from the Cubans to Montes on how to erase everything incriminating from her hard drive. She either did not follow the instructions or they did not work because the FBI recovered a treasure trove of espionage traffic. One message thanked Montes for identifying an undercover US intelligence officer who was being assigned to Cuba. It was later determined that she gave the Cubans the names of other US intelligence personnel in Cuba. She blew their cover and sabotaged their mission.

The FBI continued its surveillance of Montes for another four months in the hope of identifying her Cuban handler or handlers. That effort was not successful, but the FBI was able to search her purse when she was out of her DIA office to attend a meeting. Inside her purse the FBI found more incriminating material, including the pager phone number she used to send short coded messages to the Cubans. Obviously, all these investigative techniques, especially the physical surveillance, had to be flawless. If Montes detected surveillance, she could flee. In fact, it was later revealed that the Cubans had given her an escape plan to use if she felt threatened.

Under normal circumstances the investigation might have gone on longer to collect more evidence, but when Montes was on the verge of gaining access to US war planning for Afghanistan in the aftermath of 9/11, the FBI and DIA decided they could wait no longer. Montes was arrested at DIA headquarters on September 21, 2001. She pleaded guilty to espionage and was sentenced on October 16, 2002, to twenty-five years in prison. Montes was defiant and unrepentant to the end. In her statement to the court, she said US policy to Cuba was "cruel and unfair." She concluded, "I obeyed my conscience rather than the law."

There was an unconfirmed report in March 2016 that the US moves to normalize relations with Cuba might include a prisoner exchange. The Cubans reportedly had Montes on their list. She has several years left on her sentence, and I personally hope she serves every day of it.

LESSONS LEARNED

- Montes should never have received a top-secret clearance from the Department of Justice and the Defense Intelligence Agency. The background investigation should have picked up on her anti-American views. We cannot be the thought police, but Montes's well-known extremism should have been disqualifying. Many US government applicants and employees are privately opposed to the policies of the political party in power, and that is fine. But when dissent reaches the point of being a significant risk of disloyalty, leaking, or worse, clearance should be denied.
- DIA was wrong not to require polygraphs of its new employees. (This deficiency has since been corrected.)
- It should be sobering to all of us in counterintelligence that a polygraph of Montes when she entered on duty at DIA in 1985 might not have uncovered her duplicity. We know that Montes was trained in counterpolygraph measures by her Cuban handlers, and she passed a DIA reinvestigation polygraph in 1994. She told her interrogators that the technique she used involved tensing her sphincter muscles. We should ask ourselves how the Cuban double agents who were run against us successfully for over twenty years

were also able to beat the polygraph. The Cubans are doing something against us that we need to understand better and then defeat.

- Bravo to DIA for having a policy in place that encouraged employees to come forward with any workplace counterintelligence concerns they had. The report of Montes's suspicious behavior in 1996 turned out to be inconclusive but still served the purpose of putting her on Carmichael's CI radar.
- Cuban intelligence is very, very good. I am tremendously impressed by the quality of the tradecraft used in the Montes operation. The computer program to decipher the radio messages eliminated the need for one-time pads, which, if found, are incontrovertible evidence of espionage. The paging system, when used properly, was a good and safe alternative to signal sites. The encrypted diskettes were an extra level of security. The personal meetings in Washington and Montes's secret travel to Cuba were risks, but well-managed ones.
- The Cuban case officers recruited and handled Montes brilliantly. They recognized and exploited her sympathy for the underdog, her sense of justice, and her need for acceptance and recognition. The Cubans were her family. She became emotionally attached to her case officers and craved their approval. There was no one else she could talk to.
- Scott Carmichael, his team at DIA, and the FBI special agents involved epitomized the best of the counterintelligence art from beginning to end. Hats off.
- Penetration is the best counterintelligence. Without the FBI source to raise the alarm and to put Carmichael back on the scent, Montes might still be in place. She would be approaching retirement age by now—and would probably be in line to receive the Career Intelligence Medal. That is enough to make any CI officer cringe.

Richard Miller

> Miller was a marginal agent at best and had been shunted around from position to position, never doing anything well. How and why he was put on a counterintelligence squad is still murky in the annals of the Bureau.
>
> —Oliver "Buck" Revell, *A G-Man's Journal*

FBI special agent Richard Miller was the laughingstock of his office. His FBI colleagues scratched their heads in disbelief that he had been hired in the first place. In the buttoned-down world of the FBI, he was totally out of place. He was poorly dressed and noticeably careless with his grooming. His weight and physical fitness did not meet the FBI's rigorous standards. At 5'9" tall and weighing as much as 250 pounds, he never came close to matching the stereotypical profile of the trim and athletic FBI agent. Richard Miller was an overweight misfit.

To make matters worse, Miller was hopelessly incompetent. He begged his FBI colleagues to give him assets because he was incapable of developing any of his own. At various times he lost his FBI credentials, gun, and office keys. His performance reviews were consistently bad, but somehow his career chugged on. Miller was part of an FBI culture that did not turn on its own, even at the cost of carrying deadweight. In that regard he was similar to the CIA's underperforming Aldrich Ames, who should have been fired for unsuitability long before he committed treason. In both cases Miller's and Ames's supervisors were aware of their employees' deficiencies but failed to take decisive remedial action.

Richard Miller was born in Los Angeles in 1936. He graduated from Brigham Young University, where he majored in English and minored in Spanish. His Spanish language ability was presumably a factor in his being hired by the FBI in 1964. In quick succession he served at FBI field offices in San Antonio, New York, Puerto Rico, and Tampa, finally landing in Los Angeles in 1969. He started off doing criminal work in Los Angeles but was so unsuccessful that he was transferred to Foreign Counterintelligence, where it was thought he would receive closer supervision and mentorship from the FCI chief, who was a fellow Mormon. Unfortunately, in those years counterintelligence was often seen as a dumping ground for underperforming employees. CI was not highly regarded, and the best people stayed away, leaving noncompetitive vacancies for the likes of Ames at the CIA and Miller at the FBI.

Miller was married and the father of eight children. He was going nowhere in his FBI career, and his prospects for promotion were nil. Money in the Miller family was tight. Miller was on the lookout for ways to increase his income, and as a result he began to cut ethical corners. He stole money from his uncle in a far-fetched invention scam. He pocketed money from the FBI that should have gone in authorized salary to an elderly woman asset, thereby cheating her out of money to which she was entitled. He illegally used bureau resources to run license plates and other checks for a private investigator who slipped him up to $500 for each inquiry. He sold Amway products out of the trunk of his official FBI vehicle to colleagues and friends. How pathetic is that? Finally, in what he thought was going to be the answer to his financial problems, he pulled together enough money to purchase an avocado farm outside Los Angeles. He spent his free time trying to make it profitable; he failed.

After he was transferred to FCI, Miller's job was to monitor the large Russian émigré community in Los Angeles. To do that he was expected to mingle with the Russians and to develop sources inside that community who could keep him informed of any indications of Russian espionage. It is not hard to imagine how this big, sloppy, and bumbling FBI agent was perceived by the Russians with whom he came into contact. There is no indication that Miller ever did anything of significance during this period. In fact his career and his personal life were spiraling downward. As he would later tell investigators, he sometimes took three-hour lunches at a 7-Eleven store, reading comic books and eating shoplifted candy bars. His behavior was becoming increasingly erratic. The FBI knew that it had a grossly substandard employee on its hands and did what it considered appropriate to try to help him. Miller received counseling from his sympathetic FBI supervisor and was referred to a psychiatrist in 1982 for a mental health assessment. The psychiatrist diagnosed Miller as emotionally unstable, prone to irrational acts, and unreliable. He recommended that Miller be placed in a "harmless post" and watched closely until his retirement. No action was taken. Miller stayed in the same job.

In January 1984 Miller was excommunicated from the Church of Latter-Day Saints for adultery. His wife, Paula, a schoolteacher and the mother of their eight children, did not immediately leave him but eventually filed for divorce in 1988. Everything was coming to a head for Miller in 1984. He was a train wreck waiting to happen. In April 1984 he was suspended for two weeks for failure to meet FBI standards of weight and performance. His goal was simply to hang on until he became eligible to retire in two years at the age of fifty. Out of compassion and professional courtesy, the FBI was willing to let him do that, that is, finish his time and then fade away. But Miller would not go quietly.

In May 1984 Miller received a phone call from a woman with a thick Russian accent named Svetlana Ogorodnikov. Miller likely knew who she was because Svetlana and her husband, Nikolai, had been fixtures in the Los Angeles Russian émigré community since their immigration to the United States from the Soviet Union in 1973. Svetlana had been a low-level source for the FBI a few years earlier but had been dropped for lack of production. She asked for a private meeting with Miller.

Svetlana is a mysterious figure. The evidence strongly suggests that she was dispatched by the KGB in 1973 to infiltrate the Russian community in Los Angeles and, if the occasion presented itself, to spot, assess, and develop Americans for potential recruitment. Svetlana's husband, who was seventeen years her senior, worked as a meatpacker in the United States and played only a minor role in their espionage activity. Svetlana was the mover and shaker. She made occasional visits to the Russian consulate in San Francisco, presumably to check in with her KGB contact. Among the other Russian émigrés in Los Angeles, Svetlana and Nikolai were known as being outspokenly pro-communist.

When Svetlana met Miller at a restaurant in Marina del Rey in May 1984, she was in her midthirties and attractive. What exactly transpired at the meeting is unclear. Miller later claimed that he was in effect dangling himself to Svetlana in the hope that the KGB would recruit him through her and he could work as a double agent on behalf of the FBI. That cockamamie idea made no counterintelligence sense whatsoever. First, an FBI special agent knows far too much to be dangled to the Russians. Second, a sensitive operation of this magnitude would never be freelanced by a single agent without the full knowledge and approval of his superiors. Miller's explanation of what happened clearly smacks of an after-the-fact effort to attribute some exculpatory operational motive to his actions.

Far more likely is that Svetlana was the predator from the beginning. She may have known from her contacts in the émigré community that Miller was a sad sack whose life and FBI career were reeling out of control. The timing of her call indicates that she probably had some knowledge that he was in trouble and possibly vulnerable. My hunch is that the KGB had good assessment data on Miller and tasked Svetlana to call him. The seduction part did not take long. Miller was an easy mark. Sex between the two began almost immediately and was frequent. Svetlana was in control and on the verge of landing a major recruit for the KGB. She must have been excited.

Instead of reporting her progress to the KGB via the San Francisco consulate, Svetlana chose to go to Moscow in June for consultations. She met with Miller again in Los Angeles in August, and their conversation turned irrevocably to cash for secrets. Miller gave her a secret FBI document to prove his bona fides. He was hooked; there was no going back. Svetlana arranged for Miller to meet with a KGB officer on August 15 to negotiate the terms of the deal. It was a gutsy call by the KGB to agree to a meeting in the US at such an early stage of an operation. The KGB fears provocation by the FBI and does not like to expose an officer unless the bona fides of a case are ironclad. In this case the KGB's reasoning must have been that the FBI would not dangle a special agent and would not allow a controlled operation to go sexual. Also, of course, Miller was "big game" for the KGB and justified some risk. Miller agreed to provide classified FBI documents to the KGB in return for $50,000 in gold and $15,000 in cash.

For some reason the KGB was not yet fully satisfied with Miller's sincerity. It wanted more proof that he was who he said he was. The solution was for Miller and Svetlana to travel together to San Francisco. Miller gave Svetlana his FBI credentials so that she could show them to her KGB contact inside the Russian consulate, which she did. Miller himself did not go into the Russian consulate, but his ill-advised trip with Svetlana to San Francisco was the beginning of the end for him.

Miller and Svetlana were planning a trip to Vienna, probably in October, to meet with a senior KGB officer. The KGB's purpose in setting up the trip was to solidify Miller's recruitment, debrief him on FCI, and train him in tradecraft. The trip never happened, however, because the FBI was rapidly building its case against Miller and would soon be ready to pounce. Something had happened in San Francisco; I cannot be more specific than that. The result was that the FBI became aware that Miller had an unauthorized and unreported relationship with Svetlana. It obtained approvals for wiretaps, a bug in his car, and physical surveillance. The Ogorodnikovs received similar coverage.

The case broke wide open on September 27. Miller panicked. He either realized he was in way over his head as the Vienna trip approached—or else he picked up on the FBI's surveillance of him. In either event he knew he had to find a way out. What he came up with was typically lamebrained. He went to his FBI supervisor, gave him a bowdlerized account of his contacts with Svetlana, and requested approval to continue the operation as a way to penetrate the KGB. The FBI saw through the subterfuge, of course, and gave Miller a polygraph exam, which led to several admissions, including the admission that he had given Svetlana a secret document. A search of Miller's home revealed a stash of classified FBI material that he had taken from the office and apparently intended to parcel out to the KGB once the operation was underway.

The FBI arrested Miller and the Ogorodnikovs on October 3, 1984. Svetlana and Nikolai pleaded guilty of conspiracy to commit espionage in

1985 and were sentenced to eighteen and ten years in prison, respectively. Svetlana was released in 1995 and Nikolai in 1990. Miller's prosecution and conviction took considerably longer. The result of his first trial in November 1985 was a hung jury. At the second trial in June 1986, Svetlana testified on Miller's behalf and categorically denied that any espionage had taken place. The jury did not buy her story. Nor did it buy Miller's contention that he was trying to resurrect his flagging FBI career by using Svetlana in a bold effort to penetrate the KGB. Miller was convicted of espionage in June 1986 and sentenced to two life terms plus fifty years. His conviction was overturned, however, in 1989 on the grounds that the trial judge had improperly allowed polygraph results to be admitted into evidence. Miller, who had been in prison for five years by that time, probably had the vain hope that the government would give up and set him free, but that was not the case. He was again convicted of espionage in October 1990 and sentenced to twenty years in prison. His sentence was later reduced to thirteen years, and he was released in May 1994. Miller has reportedly remarried and is living in Utah to be close to his children.

LESSONS LEARNED

- The Miller case is another glaring example of failed workplace counterintelligence. Common denominators in case after case of espionage against the United States are poor hiring and poor supervision. Regarding the former, Oliver "Buck" Revell, the former associate deputy director of the FBI, wrote in his book that one of the first things he did when he assumed his position in 1985 was to order an internal investigation into how someone like Miller could ever have been hired by the FBI.[7] He wanted to know why the FBI's preemployment screening had been so bad that an applicant as intellectually, physically, and ethically flawed as Miller could get through the process. There was no good answer.
- No one believed that Miller was smooth enough or smart enough to conceal his shortcomings when he was being interviewed by FBI recruiters. Did no one during his background investigation comment that he was not very smart and more than a little goofy? Was there a subtle preference given to Mormon applicants, as some have suggested?[8] Was Miller sheltered from the kind of on-the-job scrutiny he should have received because of an overly

protective Mormon supervisor? J. Edgar Hoover's FBI had the reputation of selecting only the best and brightest to become special agents. Something went terribly wrong in the hiring of Miller.

- It is even harder to understand or to excuse how FBI supervisors let Miller stay on duty after his multiple personal and professional failures became known to everyone. I cannot fault Miller's office mates for failing to report his aberrant behavior, because it was so obvious. They saw no reason to report something that was common knowledge in the office. The fault lies with Miller's managers, who knew how bad he was but still did nothing. A problem employee like Miller, who is allowed to fester in place in a sensitive position, is an unacceptable counterintelligence risk. It is misplaced kindness to keep grossly subpar employees on the job indefinitely and not to intervene. At a minimum, they should be moved to jobs with less damaging access.
- The Second Commandment of Counterintelligence—Honor your professionals—comes into play here. If counterintelligence as a discipline had not fallen into such disfavor because of the excesses of J. Edgar Hoover and James Jesus Angleton, it would not have become the refuge of incompetents like Miller and Ames. The word was out at the FBI, at the CIA, and in the military that if you wanted good promotion prospects, stay away from CI. I saw a rehabilitation of CI in the aftermath of the "Decade of the Spies" in the late 1980s and early 1990s, but I am not sure how long it has lasted. Resources have been shifted throughout the intelligence community to counterterrorism and nonproliferation, sometimes, unfortunately, at the expense of CI. The CI professionals I talk to today tell me that counterintelligence is severely understaffed in relation to the enormity of the threat.

Harold James Nicholson

> Son: Was my father a traitor, Mother?
> Lady Macduff: Ay, that he was.
> Son: What is a traitor?
> Lady Macduff: Why, one that swears and lies.
> Son: And be all traitors that do so?

> Lady Macduff: Every one that does so is a traitor and must be hanged.
>
> —William Shakespeare, *Macbeth*

I would have expected CIA officer Harold James "Jim" Nicholson to use better tradecraft in his spying against the United States. After all, he was a fourteen-year veteran of the CIA's clandestine service and was teaching tradecraft to CIA trainees at the Farm. The FBI would probably have caught Nicholson anyway, but his sloppy tradecraft contributed to his downfall. Nicholson reminds me a lot of the other CIA traitor, Aldrich Ames, who made some of the same fundamental operational mistakes that doomed Nicholson. I would like to thank Jim and Rick for making the job of US counterintelligence easier by their often sloppy tradecraft.

Nicholson would take great offense at my characterization of him as stupid. He was the ultimate fast-tracker, the golden boy, the gung ho army ranger, and the superspy. He had a high opinion of his intellectual acuity; a clear case of hubris led him to take unnecessary risks and to underestimate the ability of US counterintelligence to catch him. In the beginning Nicholson showed great promise, and the real tragedy of his case is that he succumbed to personal financial pressures to throw everything away.

Jim Nicholson was born in Oregon in 1950. His stepfather was an airman in the US Air Force, and Nicholson grew up on a succession of air force bases. He attended Oregon State University on a Reserve Officers' Training Corps (ROTC) scholarship and was commissioned as an army officer upon graduation in 1973. While in college Nicholson met Laura Cooper, and they were married on June 10, 1973. Their life together began with airborne training for Nicholson, followed by cryptography school in Massachusetts and an assignment with the Army Security Agency in Okinawa. By all accounts Laura, or Laurie as she was called, was a dutiful army wife and moved from base to base without complaining. A son, Jeremiah, was born in 1978.

For years Nicholson's dream had been to serve in the CIA. Even as a boy, he had shown a fascination with spying. Nicholson maneuvered the latter part of his army service toward intelligence in the hope that he could ultimately make himself more attractive to the CIA. He left the army in August 1979 and submitted his application to the agency. The process was slow, however, and Nicholson, with a wife and child to support, needed income. He accepted a job with Hallmark and moved his family to Kansas City. At about this time, Nicholson, who had been raised a Presbyterian, converted to the Church of Latter-Day Saints. Finally, the long hoped-for offer from the CIA came through, and he entered on duty with the agency in October 1980. The Nicholsons' daughter, Star, was born in 1981.

After operational training at the Farm and language training in Washington, DC, Nicholson was assigned to Manila in 1982. He did well, and his career in the clandestine service seemed to be off to a good start. A third child, Nathan, was born in 1984. On the personal front, however, all was not well. The Nicholsons' marriage was increasingly troubled.

The CIA moved Nicholson quickly from assignment to assignment to broaden his experience base and to expand his area knowledge. He served in Bangkok from 1985 to 1987 and in Tokyo from 1987 to 1989. In Bangkok Nicholson was so aggressive in his nighttime derring-do that his CIA colleagues gave him the nickname "Batman," a sobriquet he seemed to wear with pride. He was receiving glowing performance appraisal reports, and it was clear to everyone that he had a bright future.

Nicholson was thirty-nine years old and just ten years into his CIA career when his first real professional breakthrough occurred; he was named chief of station in Bucharest, Romania, in 1990, a plum assignment for any upwardly mobile CIA case officer. Bucharest was an important posting because Romania was on the verge of transitioning from communist to democratic rule—and the CIA station there would be responsible for monitoring events closely. Nicholson threw himself into his operational and managerial duties to the extent that he was often out at night and on weekends, neglecting his family in the process. The Nicholsons' marriage, strained for several years, was now falling apart.

In July 1992 Laurie filed divorce papers. She felt neglected, betrayed, and stifled in her marriage with Jim and wanted a new life of independence and self-fulfillment. Her college education had been interrupted at the time of their marriage, and she now wanted to go back to school. Nicholson was awarded custody of their three children since he was the wage earner and she was unemployed. He was ordered to pay for Laurie's college education and an additional $700 a month for her living expenses.

Meanwhile, that same summer, Nicholson was preparing to move with his three children to Kuala Lumpur for his next assignment as deputy chief of station. His reassignment from a chief of station position in Bucharest to a deputy chief of station position in Kuala Lumpur might seem to have been a demotion, but the station in Kuala Lumpur was larger and the move was probably no worse than career neutral. Nicholson continued to perform well on the job and seemed to relish his new role as a single father. He eased back on his obsessively long hours and became more of an engaged presence in the lives of his children than he had been before.

In Kuala Lumpur Nicholson was once again the handsome and vain pretty boy and ladies' man he had been in his previous assignments. He wore expensive tailored suits from Hong Kong, visited tanning salons, wore a Rolex watch, and took pride in his perfectly groomed beard and impeccable hair. His divorce from Laurie was not yet final, but he nevertheless began a romantic relationship with a Chinese-Malayan woman named Lily who worked in the US embassy. He announced to his children his intention to marry Lily, but he backed down when the two older children strenuously objected.

The pressures were mounting on Nicholson. He knew that his relationship with Lily was doomed. He also knew that his divorce settlement with Laurie, which was about to be finalized, was going to be messy and costly. There were acrimonious battles over alimony, child support, custody, visitation travel, and distribution of property. Nicholson was ordered to pay airfare for the children's twice-yearly visits to their mother in Oregon and to continue paying for Laurie's college expenses. The financial settlement was ruinous for Nicholson. His big hope was that he would be approved for a third year in Kuala Lumpur, but his request was denied.

In the spring of 1994, Nicholson received headquarters approval to meet with the SVR *rezident* in Kuala Lumpur.[9] Meeting with the *rezident* is something an aggressive CIA case officer like Nicholson would be encouraged to do; the agency would want to size up the opposition and to collect assessment data on him. The assumption was that a CIA officer could never be subverted but that a Russian might somehow be enticed into making a deal. In Nicholson's case, this assumption was horribly wrong. The timing strongly suggests to me that Nicholson went into the meetings with the *rezident* with the intent to negotiate a sellout. He had four authorized meetings with the SVR officer, and after each meeting he submitted anodyne reports back to headquarters on what had happened. What he did not tell headquarters was that at the first meeting on June 17, 1994, he told his Russian interlocutor that he would work for the SVR in return for $25,000 in cash up front. The *rezident* must have been beside himself; this was too good to be true. Over the next three meetings, the SVR confirmed that the offer was real, paid Nicholson the requested amount, and set up a meeting with him in New Delhi in December 1994. After Nicholson's fourth meeting with the Russian on June 29, 1994, he wired $12,000 to his credit union in Oregon.

The charade of meeting with the senior SVR officer to assess him gave Nicholson the perfect cover to offer his services in a safe setting. Not only did he pull it off, but he got his relationship with the SVR formalized before he left Kuala Lumpur for reassignment to the United States on July 5, 1994. He was well on the way to solving his financial problems. It was brilliant. Batman must have been very proud of himself.

Nicholson's next assignment was to the Farm, where he was to be a tradecraft instructor for future case officers. When Nicholson went to the Farm in 1994, there was no stigma. He was not being demoted.[10] Moreover, he convinced himself that the Farm's bucolic, calm setting would be better for his children than suburban Washington, DC. I am mildly surprised that Nicholson persuaded the SVR that a training assignment would give him enough access to classified information to justify big payments. He must have been convincing, however, because the Russians eagerly moved forward and paid him well. Perhaps they were anticipating bigger and better assignments for Nicholson in the future. As it turned out, his access at the Farm eventually proved to be a gold mine.

When Nicholson began his treason in June 1994, he knew all about the Aldrich Ames case. Ames had been arrested on February 21, 1994, and had pleaded guilty to espionage on April 28, 1994. Nicholson later told his FBI interrogators that he was "inspired" by the Ames case. It is not hard to imagine how Nicholson's avarice kicked in when he heard how much Ames had been paid by the Russians and how confident Nicholson would have been that he, the superspy, could duplicate what Ames had done—but do it better and without getting caught.[11] Nicholson may even have reasoned that his timing was perfect because the SVR would be in the market for a replacement for Ames and would likely pay top dollar.

Nicholson settled into his training duties at the Farm, moved into comfortable housing, and enrolled his children in school. Everything looked good, but how could he keep the SVR's money coming in? He was no longer on the front lines of clandestine operations, so his access was limited. As an instructor at the Farm, he saw some current intelligence reporting, but nothing of the juicy kind that the SVR would most covet. His concern about how he could keep the Russians interested in him was soon allayed when he realized that he could pass to them the names and biographical profiles of the trainees at the Farm, all of whom were destined for operational assignments. He knew that the SVR would be keenly interested in knowing who the CIA spies were even before they arrived at their first overseas postings. It was shockingly callous and selfish of Nicholson to betray these young officers at the outset of their careers.

Nicholson put in for personal leave to travel to London, New Delhi, Bangkok, and Kuala Lumpur in December 1994. He returned to Bangkok and Kuala Lumpur to visit old haunts and friends, including a girlfriend from his time in Bangkok. The New Delhi stop, of course, was to meet with his new SVR case officer. Nicholson's plan was to travel to Asia twice a year to meet with the SVR; he apparently had dismissed any concern that this travel pattern could look suspicious to US counterintelligence.

Unknown to Nicholson, events in 1994 were quietly working against him. Spy catchers at the CIA and FBI joined forces to improve US counterintelligence in the aftermath of the Ames case. It was an unprecedented level of cooperation. The new head of the counterespionage branch at the CIA was an experienced FBI special agent. There was some predictable grumbling inside the CIA about this FBI "takeover" of CIA counterintelligence, but the new formula worked—and worked well. The quality of counterintelligence took a quantum leap forward. The CI team began compiling a list of CIA officers who fit the sketchy profile provided by a penetration. Nicholson, among many others, was on the list.

Nicholson's trip to New Delhi was a big success. Upon his return to the US, he made deposits or payments to his various accounts and credit cards in the amount of $28,000. Like clockwork, he then traveled to Singapore, Kuala Lumpur, and Jakarta in June and July 1995, to Bangkok and Phuket in December 1995, and to Singapore in June 1996. After each of these trips, he disbursed unaccountable income in roughly $25,000 increments. As Nicholson transited Zurich in December 1995, he stayed long enough to open a numbered Swiss bank account with a deposit of $61,000 in cash. It is still fuzzy how much Nicholson received from the SVR in all, but it was probably close to $300,000 for his two and a half years of espionage.

On October 16, 1995, Nicholson was given what was billed as a routine reinvestigation polygraph.[12] Although he reportedly received counter-polygraph training from the SVR in New Delhi, he showed "deception indicated" on the subject of concealing contacts with a foreign intelligence service. A second polygraph on October 20 had the same result. At a third polygraph on December 4, Nicholson tried using irregular breathing techniques to foil the machine—and was told to stop it. The CI investigators, who were watching all of this closely, decided to call a break and to mislead Nicholson into thinking he had passed the test. This artifice must have worked because Nicholson was off to Zurich and Bangkok just two weeks later. He was so smug and arrogant that he apparently believed he had outsmarted the polygraph examiners, just as he was sure he was outsmarting everyone else.

Not so fast. The FBI-CIA team was zeroing in on Nicholson. It received FISA approval to conduct physical and electronic surveillance against him and to access his financial records. The team quickly matched Nicholson's foreign travels in 1994 and 1995 with his unexplained deposits to his accounts. A curious turn of events tightened the noose even more. In March 1996 an SVR officer in Washington made an official request to the FBI for any information it had on Chechen rebels, a subject of keen interest to the SVR. The following month Nicholson drove to headquarters from the Farm and made the rounds of his buddies working on Russia to request information on Chechnya, ostensibly for an exercise he planned to run for his trainees at the Farm. The request was bogus and transparent. Nicholson was clearly servicing an urgent request from his SVR masters.

The CI investigative team wanted Nicholson closer for better observation, so it engineered a transfer from the Farm to a branch chief job in the Counterterrorism Center (CTC) to begin in July 1996. Nicholson was promoted to GS-15 to make it look as if his career were still on solid ground. His deputy in the center was recruited to report on his every move. Nicholson requested personal leave in June and July 1996, before he assumed his CTC duties, to visit Singapore and Bangkok. The case against Nicholson was firming up, but the mole hunters needed one last piece to ensure a conviction: a direct link between Nicholson and a Russian intelligence officer.

Singapore provided that opportunity, but the risks were enormous. Catching Nicholson in the act of meeting his SVR handler in Singapore required physical surveillance of a trained intelligence officer in an unfamiliar foreign city. Any surveillance of Nicholson had to be done by a visiting FBI/CIA team or by Singaporeans. If Nicholson made the surveillance team—and he was trained to do exactly that—he would cease all espionage activity, destroy any contemporaneous evidence, and perhaps even flee to safety in Russia, as Howard had done. In other words, Nicholson could wipe out the entire case before it came to investigative fruition. The details of what happened in Singapore are sensitive, but suffice it to say that Nicholson was in fact observed meeting with a Russian intelligence officer.

Back on the job at CTC, Nicholson obliged the CI team by giving them even more evidence. He did computer searches on Russian topics that had nothing to do with his CTC duties. He mailed two alias letters to an

SVR accommodation address to report his status and to set up a future meeting—all while he was under FBI surveillance.[13] He stored classified documents on his personal computer. He requisitioned a special camera for document photography from the CIA's Office of Technical Services—and then used it in his office to photograph secret documents. The pinhole camera the FBI installed in the ceiling of his office picked up everything.

In Nicholson's second letter to the SVR, he requested a meeting in Zurich in November 1996. His trip to Zurich was declared as personal leave at the end of an official CIA trip to Africa and Europe. The FBI arrested Nicholson at Dulles Airport outside Washington, DC, as he was about to board a plane for Europe. He had with him film, diskettes, and a money belt to be filled in Zurich. In his wallet he had the business card of his Swiss banker, on the back of which he had conveniently written his secret account number. Nicholson was convicted of espionage on June 5, 1997, and sentenced to twenty-three years and four months in prison.[14]

LESSONS LEARNED

- Do not be parochial (the Sixth Commandment of Counterintelligence). The close cooperation between the CIA and the FBI in carrying out the Nicholson investigation was exemplary. These two organizations, known to have been insular in the past, did not let turf battles, personalities, or mission conflict get in the way of working together. The Nicholson case should be the blueprint for future interagency CI cooperation.
- Own the street (the Third Commandment of Counterintelligence). Surveillance is extremely difficult, but the FBI team beat Nicholson on the street. I am not privy to how they did it, but my hat is off to them. I would love to know more about how many people they used, how many vehicles they had, what technical aids they had, and what their techniques were.
- Hooray for the polygraph. It is not infallible, but in more cases than not, it works. Nicholson's stumbles on the polygraph paved the way for more intensive investigation.
- Find the money. Most Americans who have spied against the United States since the 1960s have done it for money. (Ana Montes was an exception.) Nicholson and Ames were both reckless in how they spent their ill-gotten lucre. CI investigators should do everything they can to access a suspect's financial records as

early as possible. The US Patriot Act of 2001 has been a big help in this regard.[15] Not only is it possible to get access to an individual's financial records with a lesser showing of probable cause, but the banks, credit unions, credit card companies, brokerage firms, and other institutions are forbidden by law to reveal to anyone that the information was requested and provided.

Glenn Michael Souther

Though those that are betrayed
Do feel the treason sharply, yet the traitor
Stands in worse case of woe.

—William Shakespeare, *Cymbeline*

The case of Glenn Michael Souther is one of the strangest I encountered in my counterintelligence career. I am still puzzled by many aspects of Souther's betrayal. Specifically, how did this once conservative and religious young man from the Midwest become so disenchanted with the United States that at age twenty-three he sought Russian citizenship? How could he turn his back on what appeared to be a successful start to his career as a US Navy enlisted man? Finally, how could he get away with his espionage on behalf of the KGB for as long as he did—six years?[16]

Souther was born into a middle-class family in Indiana on January 30, 1957. His parents divorced when he was six, and Souther eventually moved to Maine to live with his father. He graduated from high school in Maine in 1975. He was not keen about going to college, but his father pressured him to enroll at Purdue University Calumet in Hammond, Indiana. Souther lasted a semester before he defied his father by joining the US Navy in January 1976. After boot camp at Great Lakes, Illinois, Souther was assigned to photography school in Pensacola, Florida, to pursue the specialty he had declared as his primary interest when he enlisted. After completing his schooling in June 1976, the nineteen-year-old Souther reported for duty aboard the aircraft carrier USS *Nimitz*, which at that time was deployed to the US Sixth Fleet in the Mediterranean.

While in port at Naples, Souther met a young Italian woman named Patrizia Di Palma, and the two were married in April 1978. Neither was ready for marriage, and their relationship was strained from the beginning. Souther was an indifferent husband, began to drink heavily, and developed an avid interest in communism. He filled the bookshelves of their apartment with communist literature and told Patrizia that he admired the Soviet Union and its communal way of life. Souther frequently voiced his resentment of his Navy superiors and his disagreement with US government policies. The apolitical Patrizia did not fully understand what he was saying and paid little heed to his rants. Despite their unhappy marriage, Patrizia gave birth to a son in September 1981.

What Patrizia did not know was that sometime in 1980 Souther had walked into the Soviet embassy in Rome and had requested Russian citizenship because he felt alienated from America and admired the USSR. He was received by the same KGB officer, Boris Solomatin, who had recruited and handled John Walker, the US Navy warrant officer who worked for the KGB from 1967 to 1985. Solomatin did not perceive much intelligence access of value in the twenty-three-year-old Navy photographer's mate, but as was standard KGB practice, he recruited Souther as a future who could possibly be steered into a position of intelligence access. It is not clear if Souther was requesting immediate defection and a new life in Soviet Russia, but it would have been child's play for an experienced case officer like Solomatin to persuade the American to stay in place. In any event, the deal was made. Souther was welcomed with open arms by his new comrades, promised citizenship, trained in clandestine tradecraft, and directed to return to the United States in pursuit of a US government position of greater intelligence value. In the meantime, Souther began reporting to the KGB whatever he could pick up in his low-access job as a photographer's mate.

Souther's access was apparently good enough for the KGB to issue him a clandestine communications plan. Patrizia observed her husband receiving one-way-voice-link messages from the KGB, and in the fall of 1981, he admitted to her that he was working for the Russians. Souther also showed Patrizia a pen concealment device that contained his rolled up onetime pads.[17] The KGB obviously had high hopes for Souther and wanted to train him in clandestine tradecraft before he returned to the United States. Souther was promoted to photographer's mate first class in February 1982, a rapid ascent through the ranks. His performance evaluations were consistently excellent.

In April 1982 Souther was transferred to the Naval Air Station in Patuxent River, Maryland. He originally told Patrizia that their marriage was over and she should remain in Italy with their son, but he relented and they accompanied him to the United States. It was not to be for long, however, because Souther was an unfaithful and abusive husband. In May 1982 Patrizia and the eight-month-old baby returned to Italy, where she was stranded without any significant support or communication from Souther. Abandoned and bitter, Patrizia had too much to drink at a New Year's Eve party on December 31, 1982, and told her brother-in-law, US Navy lieutenant Jeffrey Smallwood (married to Patrizia's sister), that Souther was a Russian spy. Smallwood passed the information to a Naval Investigative Service officer in Naples, but NIS dismissed the report as the drunken ramblings of a vengeful spouse. No action was taken. In fact, there was no reporting whatsoever of the incident in NIS files.

Souther was discharged from active duty by the navy at the end of 1982 and entered Old Dominion University in Norfolk, Virginia, in the spring of 1983. He transferred to the Navy Reserve and began drilling one weekend a month at a nearby naval air station. Although Souther's divorce from Patrizia did not become final until October 1983, he had a series of affairs with co-eds at Old Dominion. He was indiscreet in telling some of his girlfriends that he was involved in some form of spying, but he did not admit, at least initially, that he was working for the Russians. One girlfriend recalls that he complained in this period about not being able to find a dead drop in the Washington, DC, area. Souther's hints about leading a double life were not simply bravado to impress women; he was actively spying. Perhaps the best evidence of this is that he was living far beyond his visible means. On the surface Souther's only sources of income were the GI bill and his small salary from the Navy Reserve, not nearly enough to account for his tuition, rent, heavy drinking, and habit of picking up the drinking and dining tabs for his friends.

The KGB got a good deal in Souther; he was living up to his end of the bargain to do everything he could to enhance his access. The information he was providing from his billet at the naval air station could not have been exciting to the KGB, but better days were ahead. Souther was majoring in Russian at Old Dominion and was an active participant in the university's Russian Club. With a college degree and Russian language on his résumé, his prospects for a sensitive job in US national security were good. In May 1983, when classes were over for the summer, Souther and his girlfriend traveled to Italy. He made no effort to see his wife or son. The purpose of this trip was to report to the KGB on his progress and to get his marching orders for future steps. To impress his girlfriend, Souther could not resist flashing to her the $10,000 in cash he received from the KGB. The KGB was making a serious investment in its "future" recruit.

Upon his return to Norfolk, Souther dug into his Russian studies, applied for an upgraded security clearance at the top-secret-SCI level, and began the application process for Navy Officer Candidate School. His access to highly classified information would be far greater as an officer than as an enlisted man. Souther's Russian was getting markedly better; he could converse comfortably in the language and write papers in Russian for his literature courses. He could not wait to return to Italy with his girlfriend in January 1984 to let the KGB know that everything was proceeding according to plan. On this trip his girlfriend saw him mark a signal on a wall and carry out outlandish measures to detect surveillance. (There was none.) She was also aware that Souther received another large infusion of cash from his "friends." Was it the Mafia, drug dealers, undercover work for the US government, or foreign espionage? She did not know but eventually strongly suspected espionage.

In April 1984 Souther was inexplicably involved in a bizarre incident on campus. Without provocation of any kind, he attacked a female student, pinned her to the ground, and bit her neck. There were witnesses. Souther was arrested and charged with assault. The charge against him was eventually reduced on appeal to disorderly conduct, and he got off lightly with a six-month suspended sentence and a small fine. On the recommendation of the Student Conduct Committee at Old Dominion, he was suspended from school for a semester.

None of this slowed Souther down. He spent the summer of 1984 at the Russian immersion program at Norwich University in Northfield, Vermont. At the end of the summer, his TS-SCI clearance was approved. How in the world did the background investigation by the Defense Investigative Service (DIS) not turn up Souther's criminal conduct, his unexplained income, his sleazy abandonment of his wife and son, his drinking, and his often-professed anti-American views?[18] The reason, I submit, is that DIS was overwhelmed by a huge backlog and insufficient staffing, which unfortunately led to perfunctory background investigations. I am not sure the situation is much better under OPM today.

Souther should never have been cleared at the TS-SCI level, but the damage was done, and with his high-level clearance, Souther was eligible to transfer to the Fleet Intelligence Center, Europe and Atlantic (FICEURLANT), in Norfolk to do his weekend Navy Reserve duty. FICEURLANT processed the most sensitive satellite imagery for the United States Navy. Souther could not have landed any better. As a photographer's mate, he had access to KH-11 filmstrips, which would have been of inestimable value to the KGB in determining US satellite imaging capabilities.[19] To make matters worse, Souther had virtually unlimited access to other offices and documents at FICEURLANT on weekends, when most of the staff was absent. There were no bag checks or body searches for employees entering or leaving the compound. Souther was disappointed to learn that his application for Officer Candidate School had been turned down, but that minor setback mattered less to him now that he had hit the mother lode of access at FICEURLANT. He was getting closer, also, to his Russian degree at Old Dominion, which would open other exciting doors for him. His Russian masters would be pleased.

John Walker's arrest in May 1985 resulted in worldwide publicity of the US Navy's penetration by the KGB. Also, the movie *The Falcon and the Snowman* came out in 1985 and told the story of how two young Americans, Christopher Boyce and Daulton Lee, had been swept up in Russian espionage. The similarities did not escape the attention of Lieutenant Smallwood, who had been told three years earlier by Patrizia that Souther was a spy, or of Souther's erstwhile girlfriend, who had accompanied him to Italy and observed his suspicious behavior. After a lot of soul-searching, the girlfriend made a half-hearted effort to convey her suspicions to the FBI but gave up when she found it hard to make contact. Lieutenant Smallwood, however, followed through and went back to NIS in September 1985 to urge that Souther be investigated. Since Souther was no longer on active duty in the Navy, jurisdiction for the case and responsibility for any follow up were passed to the FBI office in Norfolk.

The FBI assumed that the allegations against Souther in Italy in 1983 had been investigated and found groundless, which, of course, was not the case. In any event, the FBI put the NIS report on the back burner and did not interview Souther until May 21, 1986, eight months after the report came in. There was no preliminary investigation; Patrizia was not contacted for her story again. The interview was more informational than confrontational, but the mention of a possible polygraph spooked Souther and sent him into paranoid overdrive. His friends commented on his strange, almost manic, behavior in the days after the interview. Souther purchased a round-trip ticket to Italy and told his friends that he was going to visit his son. Instead, he fled to Russia. His mother, brother, fiancée (he was engaged to be married in July), and friends knew nothing of his whereabouts. He had vanished.

It was not until two years later, in July 1988, that Souther surfaced. The Russian government announced that he had been granted political asylum and Soviet citizenship. A few days later, Souther appeared on Russian TV to denounce US nuclear weapon policies, to profess his love for Russia and Russian literature, and to berate the FBI. He said the FBI had harassed him and "blocked his future." It was obvious that Souther was fully on board to be used for whatever propaganda purposes the Soviets desired. Souther's mother, relieved to learn that her son was alive and well, visited him in Moscow in September 1988. She learned that Souther had been given a Russian name (Mikhail Yevgenyevich Orlov), had married a Russian woman, and had a baby daughter. Souther appeared totally committed to making a new life for himself as a Russian.

The reality of life in the Soviet Union was not, however, the workers' paradise Souther had expected it to be. He missed the comforts and pleasures he had known in the United States. He became increasingly lonely, depressed, and homesick. In June 1989 Souther committed suicide by asphyxiating himself in his garage. He was thirty-two years old. He left a carefully written suicide note in excellent Russian in which he said he had found a "second home" in the Soviet Union and was "living his dreams." He gave no explicit reason for his decision to kill himself. His last wish was to be buried in the uniform of a KGB major, the rank the Soviet government later confirmed he had been awarded. "Major Orlov" was glorified in the Soviet press and eulogized by Vladimir Kryuchkov, the chairman of the KGB, who said that Souther's death was a "huge loss" and that he had played a "vital role." Souther was buried with full military honors wearing, as requested, a KGB uniform.

The high honors, the Russian name, and the KGB rank quickly led to speculation in the United States that Souther was more than he seemed. Could he have been a Soviet illegal "planted" in the US when he was a teenager? Were his American parents really his parents? These theories were rapidly debunked. The truth is that Souther was a confused young American who became disillusioned with his country and who was skillfully manipulated by the KGB into committing treason. The Soviets' extravagant praise of him may have been intended to embarrass the US for its major counterintelligence failure, to gloat over the KGB's success, or to raise doubts about what had happened. My personal assessment is that the KGB's gloating was merited. I believe Glenn Michael Souther, during his eighteen months at FICEURLANT, did more damage to US national security than we acknowledged.

LESSONS LEARNED

- Take tips seriously. NIS was negligent in not following up on Patrizia Di Palma's comments to her brother-in-law at the New Year's party in 1982. What would it have taken for an NIS officer to interview her when she was sober? At a minimum the serious allegation should have been made a matter of official record.
- Do better background investigations. The investigation of Souther in 1983 and 1984 was seriously deficient. If digging more deeply requires that OPM and other investigative agencies have more resources, then so be it.
- Require polygraphs for all SCI clearances. Full-lifestyle polygraphs should be administered to anyone seeking a clearance at that level. Polygraphs are a strong deterrent. I know enough about Souther to conclude that he would most likely have been a "reactor." He would not have passed a polygraph exam. A massive increase in polygraphs, as proposed here, would be expensive, but still cheap CI in the long run.
- Investigate before interviewing. The FBI should have done a discreet investigation of Souther before interviewing him. When a person is alleged to have committed a serious crime, like espionage, it is a mistake to tip off the subject that he or she is under suspicion as the first step in an investigation. The risks are destruction of evidence, a coverup, and flight, as in the case of Souther.
- Implement bag and body searches when employees at highly classified facilities exit the building. Searches are unpopular and slow down close-of-business departures, but most employees accept this measure as justifiable counterintelligence. The searches could be random, but they would have to be frequent enough and thorough enough to deter misconduct.
- Take advantage of foreign services' willingness to recruit Americans as futures by sending them doubles. Do not forget the First Commandment of Counterintelligence: Be offensive. There is little or no cost in feed material if an opposition service is willing to recruit an American who does not have immediate access. Even at this early stage, the double can provide useful information on the service's personnel, requirements, and modus operandi. How can we pass up that opportunity? I very much like the idea of putting foreign intelligence services on notice that their next American

future recruit could be under the control of US counterintelligence. The Russian and Chinese intelligence services, among others, have a predilection for recruiting futures. They are making our CI job easy for us, so let's oblige them by stinging them with doubles.

Jonathan Pollard

> The United States and its "English-speaking cousins"—Britain, Australia, and Canada—enjoy a close intelligence partnership and do not spy on one another. Beyond that, all bets are off.
>
> —Mark M. Lowenthal, *Intelligence*

It should not be shocking to learn that friends spy on friends. The case of Jonathan Pollard is one of the most striking examples of how a close ally of the United States, in this case Israel, ran the political risk of running an American agent. Pollard's case is extremely instructive for counterintelligence professionals in that it encompasses deplorable and inexcusable workplace counterintelligence but also effective CI investigative work to bring a US traitor to justice. My bottom line on Pollard is that his espionage should never have happened in the first place, but my hat is off to Ron Olive and his colleagues at NCIS for some of the finest CI work I have seen.[20] What they did was textbook.

Jonathan Pollard was born in Galveston, Texas, in 1954 to an upper-middle-class Jewish family. He was the youngest of three children. His father, a prominent microbiologist, moved the family to South Bend, Indiana, in 1961, when he was offered a faculty position at Notre Dame University. Jonathan graduated from high school in South Bend in 1972. He was an excellent student and made top grades but was considered "geeky" by his classmates and was picked on repeatedly. By all accounts his childhood was an unhappy one. Some of the taunts he experienced may have been anti-Semitic in nature, but others were simply due to his nerdy appearance and awkward social skills.

Pollard's passion for Israel began at an early age. His parents spoke to him frequently of the Holocaust; many of their relatives had been killed in the concentration camps. Young Jonathan was an avid reader and had several books in his room on Israel and the Jewish experience. A thirteen-year-old boy at the time, he was terrified that Israel might be annihilated during the Six-Day War in 1967, and from then on, he considered Israel's security precarious. A year later, in 1968, Jonathan traveled with his parents to Europe, where a visit to Dachau made shockingly real to him the horrors that until then he had only heard and read about. The result was a growing pride in his Jewish faith and an obsession with Israel. He informed his parents that he dreamed of living in Israel and, if necessary, defending it against its enemies. Finally, in the summer of 1972, Jonathan, for the first time, had the opportunity to visit Israel as part of a high school study program. He came back more convinced than ever that Israel was central to his life and would one day be his home.

Pollard enrolled at Stanford University in the fall of 1972 and graduated with a degree in political science in 1976. He showed flashes of academic excellence but was for the most part an erratic student who spent too much time playing strategy board games and smoking marijuana. His classmates remember him particularly as an ardent Zionist who bragged openly about his ties to the Mossad and the CIA. He hinted that he was an Israeli agent and that the Mossad was paying his tuition. It is clear now, of course, that Pollard was living in a fantasy world and was trying to impress his friends with how mysterious and significant he was. Perhaps he thought that even though he had been bullied his whole life, he was now someone who should not be trifled with.

When Pollard left Stanford, he had no clear idea what he wanted to do next. He tried law school at Notre Dame but dropped out after less than a semester. He was still conflicted about immigrating to Israel (which his parents strongly opposed) or somehow getting himself into the exciting spy world he had so long fantasized about. The key to the latter was to make himself more competitive by earning a relevant advanced degree. In the fall of 1977, Pollard began a two-year master's program in international affairs at the Fletcher School of Law and Diplomacy at Tufts University in Boston. This was a good choice, but Pollard failed to apply himself and left at the end of his second year without a degree. Just as at Stanford, he continued to lie about his supposed connections to the CIA and the Mossad. His classmates referred to him as the "Colonel," a nickname he probably encouraged. Pollard was still harboring the dream of being a player in international intrigue, and now, with Stanford and the Fletcher School on his résumé, he was ready to make his move.

In the early summer of 1979, Pollard applied to the CIA. He got through the preliminary interviews and was advanced to the next round, which included a full-lifestyle polygraph exam. That was game over. Pollard failed miserably on the issue of drugs and was disqualified.[21] He was crushed because the CIA had always been his first choice for employment, but he still thought he could have a career in intelligence somewhere else.

On September 19, 1979, Pollard was hired by the Navy Field Operational Intelligence Office in Suitland, Maryland, as an intelligence analyst on the Soviet Union. His position required a TS-SCI clearance, which would give him access to highly sensitive intelligence information. The navy at the time required a background investigation as part of the clearance process but did not conduct polygraph exams of prospective employees. As a result, Pollard was able to lie his way through the process without getting caught. His major falsehoods were that he had never used drugs, his father worked for the CIA, and he had finished his master's degree at Tufts. The background investigation failed to expose any of these lies or any other significant derogatory information. In other words, the background investigation conducted by the Defense Investigative Service was an utter failure. The investigators apparently did not talk to any of the countless students or faculty members who knew about Pollard's bizarre claims, drug use, or Israel obsession. Nor did they verify his educational credentials.[22] Pollard was granted a full TS-SCI clearance and had broad access to some of the most closely guarded secrets of the US intelligence community.

Now, at last, Pollard was in the real world of spying. Granted, he was just a low-level drudge of an analyst, but he was convinced that he could parlay his sensitive access into some kind of secret agent role. He began fishing around for ways to get into the game. Only a few months into his naval intelligence job, he contacted the South African embassy in Washington with the half-baked idea that he could somehow run an operation against the South Africans. When he proudly shared his clever scheme with his supervisor, the latter was appropriately appalled and recommended that Pollard be fired. His recommendation was strengthened by Pollard's miserable performance on a special issue polygraph exam. Pollard was belligerent and uncooperative throughout the process. The examiner's call was "inconclusive," not "deception indicated," because the excitable Pollard was essentially unreadable as a polygraph subject. Shame on the navy for not firing him then and there. Instead, Pollard's clearance was reduced to secret, and he was reassigned to another unit. This is a classic example of the all-too-common phenomenon in the US government of "passing the trash."

The disputatious Pollard challenged his loss of high-level access and threatened to file suit. While his security reinstatement appeal was pending, he continued his outlandish spy-wannabe activity around Washington. He shared with his friends and anyone willing to listen secret information that he learned on the job. His motive was to make himself out to be an important and mysterious personage worthy of awe and admiration. He passed secret information to the Australians, apparently in the misguided hope of working with Australian intelligence. There is evidence also that Pollard gave classified information to private investors and tried to use his insider knowledge to broker arms deals with shady middlemen. Jonathan Pollard was out of control.

In his frenzy of intelligence peddling, Pollard revealed himself to be not only politically motivated but also mercenary. The classified documents at his disposal offered him an enticing opportunity for extra income. Pollard must have been ecstatic over his good fortune. He could not only cash in on his access with illicit business deals but also indulge his fantasies by adding intrigue to his life. At least initially, Pollard was not particularly discriminating about who his customers or patrons would be. It is clear, however, that his heart was always with Israel. In 1981 Pollard applied for a job with the American Israel Public Affairs Committee (AIPAC), the largest and most influential pro-Israel lobbying group in the United States. What he proposed to the Israelis is not publicly known, but most likely he tried to impress them with his intelligence access and his unwavering support for Israel. He may have thought that his approach to AIPAC was in effect a dangling of himself to the Mossad, which would not have been too far from the truth.[23] In any event the Israelis wanted no part of it. They assessed Pollard as flaky and rejected his application. He was not to be deterred, however; he would find another way to combine Zionism with profit.

The navy, as part of its review of Pollard's suitability, sent the analyst for a psychiatric evaluation. The psychiatrist found no signs of mental illness, and in January 1982 Pollard's TS-SCI clearance was restored. He returned to full naval intelligence duties. In June 1984 Pollard was assigned to the Anti-Terrorism Alert Center (ATAC) of the Naval Investigative Center, where he would have wide-ranging access to US Navy, DIA, NSA, and CIA documents and databases. Compartmentation at ATAC was nonexistent. There were no controls on who accessed what or who took what out of the office. The sloppy counterintelligence procedures at ATAC did not escape Pollard's attention; they were a dream come true for a would-be spy.

All Pollard needed was a connection, and it came almost immediately. Through a family friend, Pollard was introduced to Aviem Sella, an Israeli Air Force colonel and decorated war hero who was doing graduate study in New York. Over lunch with Sella in Washington, Pollard volunteered his services as a spy and bragged about the high-level access he had that would be of incredible value to Israel. Sella communicated this offer to Yosef Yagur, an Israeli intelligence officer working undercover as the scientific counselor at the Israeli consulate in New York. Yagur was a member of a small scientific intelligence organization known as Lishka Lekishrey Mada (LAKAM, or Bureau for Scientific Relations), which was headed by the veteran spy Rafael Eitan. Despite the risk and the categorical refusal of the Mossad to become involved, Eitan authorized Yagur and Sella to proceed.

In July 1984 Pollard made his first delivery of TS-SCI documents to the LAKAM operatives in a suburb of Washington, DC. Sella incorporated clandestine tradecraft into the operation from the beginning, which, of course, was exactly what Pollard had been seeking all along. The operation was electric for him—and so easy. He carried the documents out of his office, drove to a safe house, turned over the documents to the Israeli spies, and then returned them to the files once they had been copied. The Israelis were delighted by the "samples" Pollard provided and saw no reason to question his bona fides.

Sella directed Pollard to travel to Paris with his live-in girlfriend, Anne Henderson, in November 1984 for a meeting with Eitan, Yagur, and Sella. In Paris the Israelis lavished gifts of jewelry and money, probably amounting to more than $20,000, on Pollard and Anne. Pollard's salary was set at $1,500 a month. In the spring of 1985, Pollard asked that his salary be increased to $2,500 a month in recognition of the huge risks he was taking. Later, the Israelis promised Pollard Israeli citizenship and announced that an escrow account in his name had been established to prepare for his eventual comfortable resettlement in Israel. Anne was fully aware of and supportive of these arrangements. Jonathan and Anne were married in Venice in August 1985. Back in the States, their lifestyle changed dramatically, thanks to the generous financial infusions they were receiving from the Israelis.

This could have gone on forever. Pollard's outside tradecraft with the Israelis was adequate; his signaling system, brush passes, safe house meetings, and copying operations were all fine. The Israelis were pros; they knew what they were doing. The navy, however, had done everything wrong up to that point. It had completely ignored the tenets of good workplace counterintelligence. Thank goodness, however, that an alert coworker at ATAC saw Pollard carrying what appeared to be an SCI-marked envelope into the parking lot and reported it to his supervisor.

From that point on, NIS and the FBI ran a professional and successful CI investigation that deserves high marks. A discreet search of Pollard's cubicle showed that top-secret documents he had checked out from the control center were not there. Moreover, he had a stash of sensitive documents under his desk that did not relate to his ATAC duties. Something was definitely wrong. NIS installed a concealed pinhole camera in Pollard's work space and observed further suspicious activity.

On November 18, 1985, Pollard was stopped in the NIS parking lot by NIS and FBI agents as he was getting into his car. He had in his possession classified documents, which he asserted were the object of an authorized courier delivery he was making to another intelligence agency. Pollard agreed to return to the building for a fuller explanation. He was questioned in detail about his actions, but he left later that night without making any admissions or being charged with any crime. Still, he was panicky, and with Anne's help, he tried to conceal or destroy the large quantity of classified documents he had in his apartment. The FBI put the Pollards under surveillance. The next day Pollard dodged a request for a polygraph and continued to deny any wrongdoing, but the pressure on him was reaching the breaking point. He tried desperately to reach his Israeli case officers for an escape plan or for protection but could not.

On November 21 the brilliant master spy packed up his and Anne's personal documents and prized keepsakes and, under FBI surveillance, drove into the Israeli embassy compound in Washington and requested asylum. On political grounds there was obviously no chance asylum would be granted. The Israelis must have been horrified, in fact, to find the supersensitive American spy on their doorstep with a flotilla of FBI vehicles waiting outside. Jonathan was arrested as soon as he left the embassy; Anne, claiming illness, was allowed to go home but was arrested the next day.

The Pollard case was a sensation in both the United States and Israel. The Israeli government initially claimed that it was a rogue operation by a handful of overzealous intelligence officers who did not have the approval of senior government officials. That was a ridiculous defense. Pollard's voluminous intelligence production had to be disseminated widely to the top leaders, and Eitan himself admitted in a 2014 interview that Prime Minister Shimon Peres and Prime Minister Yitzhak Rabin were both aware of Pollard's activities. Pollard portrayed himself as a Jew of conscience whose only objective was to help an American ally. The Israeli government, press, and public rallied to the Pollards' cause and repeatedly pleaded for leniency or a pardon. The US government made the case that even close allies are not entitled to certain categories of US intelligence, particularly those that involve sensitive sources and methods. It was unacceptable, the prosecutors said, for intelligence of this kind to be out of US control in any foreign hands. Jonathan pleaded guilty to espionage and was sentenced to life in prison; Anne was sentenced to five years in prison for her role. Anne was released in April 1990. She and Jonathan are now divorced; she is considered a heroine in Israel, where she currently resides with financial support from the Israeli government. Jonathan was granted parole in July 2015 and released from prison in November 2015. Under the terms of his parole agreement, he cannot give press interviews or leave the US for the next five years. Pollard married one of his strong supporters, Elaine "Esther" Zeitz, in 1993.

LESSONS LEARNED

- Don't trust anyone. Controlled paranoia in counterintelligence officers is a virtue, not a vice.
- US government background investigations must be improved. Doing them right is labor-intensive and expensive, but doing them as we do now—on the cheap and perfunctorily—is false economy. The Pollard background investigation was laughably incompetent. He should never have been hired. The first principle of workplace CI—careful selection of personnel—failed.
- Don't coddle problem employees. Pollard was a loose cannon, and everyone knew it. The South African incident alone should have been grounds for his dismissal. Security clearances are not a right that goes on indefinitely without review. If you are a supervisor, a security officer, or a counterintelligence officer and your gut tells you that one of your employees is no longer deserving of your full trust, act decisively. Any doubts as to an employee's suitability should be resolved in favor of the government. The available options are to fire the employee, rescind or reduce the clearance, or reassign the employee to a position with benign access. Every organization should have a turkey farm where problem employees can still be watched and kept away from sensitive information.
- Polygraph all applicants, without exception. The polygraph should be a full-lifestyle polygraph, not just a so-called CI-only polygraph. The latter will leave untouched too many suitability issues, such as drugs, theft, cheating, alcohol, and credit abuse. It is rare that

an applicant will already have had contact with a foreign intelligence service or have engaged in other CI-relevant activity, so he or she can sail through a preemployment polygraph that does not cover significant lifestyle issues. NIS did not polygraph applicants. I doubt seriously that Pollard could have gotten away with lies about his education and drugs if NIS had given him a thorough and aggressive polygraph up front.

- Agencies must share polygraph and background information, particularly derogatory information, with other agencies. In the past, agencies did not share this information. This problem has been corrected to some extent, but applicants can still conceal the fact that they were rejected for employment somewhere else. At a minimum the ODNI should maintain a searchable database for all applicants to its seventeen constituent agencies who were denied employment for cause. It was inexcusable that NIS had no knowledge that the CIA rejected Pollard.
- Ethnicity and religion should not be ignored as potential counterintelligence risk factors. Profiling is anathema to almost everyone, but in the CI world, it is essential. Applicants with strong family, ethnic, religious, or business ties to a foreign government or foreign nationals should be scrutinized closely to ensure their loyalties are not clouded. Particularly worrisome are romantic relationships and other emotional attachments. Pollard should have been flagged early on, not because he was Jewish but because he was so outspokenly enamored of Israel. Foreign intelligence services seek American targets who share their ethnicity, are coreligionists, or have family ties in their countries. Extended residence in a foreign country may also produce cultural identification and local sympathies that can be exploited by opposition services.
- Every office dealing in classified information should enforce compartmentation on a strict need-to-know basis. That is hard to do because employees work in close proximity to one another and barriers to access impede efficiency, but it is reckless to give any employee unrestricted access to all files and databases. At a minimum every organization must have a registry or some other form of monitoring to follow who accesses what and when. Pollard's office had no compartmentation.
- The Pollard case illustrates the importance of the Sixth Commandment of Counterintelligence: Do not be parochial. Pollard's

suspicious activity was observed at the close of business on a Friday. His supervisor conducted discreet preliminary investigative work over the weekend. On Monday the supervisor notified his command superiors of what he knew and obtained their administrative and operational guidance. On Tuesday the NIS team met with the FBI to coordinate the surveillance and other aspects of the CI investigation. This sharing of information was exemplary, as was the subsequent cooperation. NIS got it right.

- Tighten physical security. Copiers, flash drives, downloads, and cell phones should be excluded from sensitive spaces or strictly controlled. Briefcases, bags, sacks, and purses should be subject to random, but frequent, search. Scanners similar to the devices used for airport screening might even be considered as part of the random checks. Bag checks at ATAC might have deterred Pollard from his bulk deliveries of documents or decreased their frequency. The cavalier security environment at Pollard's office was an invitation to carelessness and intentional wrongdoing.
- If you see something, say something. The Pollard case was broken by an alert coworker who observed suspicious activity and reported it to his superior. Who knows how long Pollard's espionage would have gone on undetected without this acceptance of professional responsibility by the coworker? The third principle of workplace counterintelligence—reporting suspicious behaviors—may be the most important of all.

Edward Lee Howard

> A recurring nightmare . . . was that I would come into the office one morning and learn that someone in the Agency had been recruited by the KGB.
>
> —Richard Helms, *A Look over My Shoulder*

This one really hurt. Edward Lee Howard is the only CIA officer ever to have defected to Russia. And what is especially frustrating is that his defection could have and should have been prevented. The CI lapses in this case were disastrous, and US counterintelligence can never let anything like this happen again.

Edward Lee Howard was born in New Mexico on October 27, 1951. His father was a sergeant in the US Air Force, so the family moved from base to base as Eddie was growing up. In the 1960s the family was in Germany, where Eddie attended school, learned some German, and was active in scouting. His parents were Catholic, and Eddie served as an altar boy at the base church. When Eddie's father was transferred to England in 1969, Eddie returned to the United States and enrolled at the University of Texas in Austin that fall. He participated in army ROTC but dropped out when he was assigned a high lottery number and was no longer at serious risk of being drafted. In May 1972 Eddie graduated with honors from the University of Texas with a degree in international business.

As a new college graduate, Eddie was eager to move on to an exciting overseas adventure. The idea of applying to the CIA crossed his mind, but he was too young and inexperienced to be a competitive candidate. Instead, he applied for and was accepted for service in the Peace Corps. He went to Costa Rica for orientation and Spanish-language training and was then sent by the Peace Corps to Colombia in February 1973. In June 1973 Eddie met the newly arrived Peace Corps volunteer Mary Cedarleaf, whom he would marry in St. Paul, Minnesota, in 1976.

Eddie had been a casual user of marijuana during his college years but graduated to heavier and more frequent drug use while he was in Colombia. Cocaine was cheap and readily available. Eddie partied his way through his Peace Corps assignment. He left Colombia in August 1974 but continued to do Peace Corps work in the States until he enrolled in the MBA program at American University in Washington, DC, in January 1975. He received his MBA degree in November 1976. To all appearances, Eddie was an ambitious yuppie with a bright future.

Next for Eddie was a position with the Agency for International Development (AID). In February 1977 the twenty-five-year-old Eddie and his bride moved to Peru, where Eddie worked as a loan officer serving Peruvian farmers and small-business owners. With his fluent Spanish, Latin American experience, and MBA degree, he was well-qualified for the job and apparently did well. It is not known how extensively Eddie used drugs in Peru, but they were easily obtainable there, and I think it is unlikely, given his subsequent behavior, that he abstained. Eddie could probably have made a successful career at AID, but he aspired to bigger things and was restless to move on. Mary, moreover, missed her family in Minnesota and wanted to return to the States. Eddie left AID in March 1979 and began looking for a job in the US. It did not take him long to find one with a consulting firm in Chicago. He started in June 1979 but left less than a year later for what he thought was a better opportunity with an environmental research company in Chicago. He started there in May 1980. His new job did not turn out as he had hoped, so he reverted to his on-and-off dream of working for the CIA. He submitted his application in the summer of 1980. Even though he had served in the Peace Corps, he was eligible to apply; the rule was that the CIA could hire Peace Corps volunteers after a five-year cooling-off period. Eddie had been out almost six years.

Eddie appeared to be an excellent candidate for the CIA, but in fact he was seriously flawed in his personal life. He had continued using drugs in Chicago and, in addition, had developed a noticeable drinking problem. By the time Eddie applied to the CIA, he had a lengthy and uninterrupted drug history, going back to his college years, that included marijuana, cocaine, hash, LSD, and quaaludes. By no stretch of the imagination could he be characterized as a casual or recreational user.

In October 1980 Eddie began his formal processing for employment at the CIA. The process consists of aptitude testing, a medical examination, psychological screening, and a polygraph. For most mentally and physically healthy candidates, like Eddie, the number one hurdle is the polygraph. The polygraph session is designed to be aggressive, confrontational, and intrusive. As I've mentioned before, the polygraph is not infallible, but I am a strong believer in its effectiveness as a counterintelligence tool. In my experience, if the result is "deception indicated," there is a 95 percent probability that the subject is lying. Yes, candidates who are hypersensitive to right and wrong, overly conscientious, and judgmental about themselves can sometimes trigger false positives by exaggerating the significance of their peccadilloes (we all have them) or simply reacting physiologically to any mention of illicit behaviors. But a skilled examiner can usually cut through the ambient nervousness and hypersensitivity. Occasionally a good candidate is disqualified because he or she is unable to produce clean charts. That is a shame, but the government properly resolves any ambiguity in polygraph results by rejecting the applicant. To do otherwise would be poor counterintelligence.

Somehow Eddie passed the polygraph. I believe he had an inexpert examiner and was able to sail through with smooth talking, sangfroid, and partial admissions. He admitted his drug use but understated the frequency, circumstances, and hard-core nature of the drugs in his history. He convinced the examiner that his drug use was ancient history and nothing more than youthful experimentation and partying. The examiner failed to zero in on Eddie's more recent marijuana smoking in Chicago or his burgeoning alcohol problem. After the polygraph Eddie still had to get through the background investigation, but as already noted, most such investigations are superficial, and they rarely turn up significant pejorative information, particularly from overseas locations. Eddie survived the process and reported for duty at the CIA in January 1981.

As a clandestine service trainee, Eddie spent the first few months in orientation, headquarters-area training, and interim assignments. Then, in August 1981, he began his specialized and intensive operational training at the Farm. The curriculum at the Farm for fledgling case officers is hard work but a lot of fun: surveillance detection, dead drops, brush passes, secret writing, clandestine photography, taps, bugs, flaps and seals, the recruitment cycle, agent handling, double agents, and all the other arcane arts of the profession.[24]

Mary Howard was hired by the CIA in the fall of 1981, initially as a secretary but later as an operational support assistant. Eddie and Mary looked like a promising team. Eddie did well at the Farm and graduated at the end of 1981 with strong training evaluations and performance appraisal reports. His on-the-street skills were exceptional, especially his ability to detect, manipulate, and defeat hostile surveillance. The next decision point was where Eddie would be assigned.

Case officers have a lot of voice in where they go. The CIA knows that people will perform best if they are where they want to be. As trainees at the Farm are completing their time there, they are courted by various headquarters components seeking new staff. Teams from headquarters go to the Farm to extol the virtues of their directorates, offices, or centers. For example, when I was at headquarters, I often went to the Farm to try to recruit soon-to-be case officers for the component where I worked, the Soviet East European Division (SE). Recruitment is a competitive process. Everyone wants the top graduates. The trainees submit their wish list of where they would like to serve, and usually they get one of their top choices.

Eddie ended up on the East German desk. That was a good, "sexy" assignment for him because the East Germans were causing US counterintelligence fits, and the Stasi was as tough an adversary as we had ever faced. The job appealed to Eddie, the thrill seeker, but he wanted something even better. In April 1982 he applied and was accepted into the pipeline for Moscow.[25] He and Mary would be trained as a team. To qualify, they had to go through another round of psychiatric evaluation to ensure that they could live and work successfully in the pressure cooker environment of Moscow and, perhaps most important, that their marriage could survive the stresses of constant surveillance and no privacy, even in their apartment. Eddie and Mary passed. Eddie's past drug use and alcohol problem came up, of course, and Eddie was referred for further evaluation by a counselor concerning his drinking, but the decision was that his problem was under control and not disqualifying. Eddie and Mary had the green light for their Moscow assignment.

First, however, the Howards had to complete a specialized training cycle on how to operate successfully in the police-state conditions of Moscow. The key ingredients of the cycle are countersurveillance, clandestine tradecraft, and husband-wife teamwork.[26] Eddie and Mary looked very good on the street together. SE Division thought it had a winning team. This positive impression was reinforced when Eddie excelled at learning Russian, an essential part of his preparation for agent handling in Moscow.

The plan was to send Eddie to Moscow under deep cover in the hope that he would receive less attention from the KGB than officers with track records from previous CIA assignments. Eddie was "clean" in that he was a first-tour officer with nothing in his history to suggest a CIA affiliation. If he received light or sporadic surveillance from the KGB—or hopefully none—he would be an invaluable asset to the station. By 1982 the CIA station in Moscow had developed a healthy inventory of Russian agents who needed handling, and since most case officers in Moscow were smothered by KGB surveillance, having one who was not would be a real luxury.

The decision on which Moscow station officer would service a given agent was largely dependent on who could "get black," that is, who had no surveillance or could evade it. Since the hope was that Eddie would be in that category, he had to be prepared to handle or service any Russian agent at any time. That meant that he would have to be read in on every agent case. He was also briefed on our technical operations in Moscow because they too sometimes required servicing. Eddie had the keys to the kingdom. This lack of compartmentation was terrible counterintelligence, of course, but frankly unavoidable in the special circumstances of Moscow Station. Everyone on the bench had to be ready to go in at any time.

Eddie and Mary were scheduled to go to Moscow in June 1983. It was a happy time for them. Their son, Lee, was born in March, and they were headed for a dream assignment on the home turf of our country's number one adversary. For a CIA clandestine service officer, it does not get any better than that. But the end came quickly. In April Eddie was directed to take a predeparture polygraph. This was not standard procedure, and Eddie had not expected it, but he was not overly concerned. Why should he be? He had beaten it before; he could beat it again. He was wrong. He bombed it.

In four polygraph sessions in April and May, Eddie admitted to stealing forty dollars from a woman's purse on an airplane. The woman's baby was fussy and prevented Eddie from napping, so when the woman went to the restroom, he paid her back by stealing her money. His action was petty, illegal, and vindictive. That was bad, but even more troubling were his responses to the drug and alcohol questions. The polygraph examiner was convinced that Eddie had used drugs during his CIA employment and was abusing alcohol. He was no longer considered suitable for the Moscow assignment—or for employment anywhere at the CIA. The Office of Security and the Office of Personnel asked Eddie to resign, which he did on May 2, 1983. He had no recourse. His badge was taken away. He had to turn in the keys to his CIA car and was escorted to the exit. To add insult to injury, he had to take a bus to get home. Eddie's world had come crashing down. Everything he and Mary had worked so hard for and had dreamed about for so long was gone. At age thirty-one and with a new baby at home, Eddie was out of work.

The family moved to New Mexico, where Eddie got a job as an economist with the state government in Santa Fe. He did the work, but mostly he brooded, drank heavily, and seethed with resentment at the agency that had so unfairly, he believed, ruined his life. He made drunken calls to the US embassy in Moscow and left messages for CIA officers serving under cover there. His purpose was unclear, but it is possible he wanted to let the KGB know via these intercepted calls that he was angry and on the market. Treason was certainly on his mind because he admitted later that he went to Washington in October 1983 and sat outside the Russian embassy debating whether to walk in or not. In February 1984 Eddie got into a drunken brawl in Santa Fe, threatened his tormentors with a .44 Magnum, lost a fistfight, was arrested, and was charged with aggravated assault. The CIA, alerted to Eddie's erratic behavior, sent a senior officer to New Mexico to meet with him and to arrange for him to receive psychiatric care. It was not enough. Eddie wanted revenge.

What happened next is the subject of a question I pose to my counterintelligence students at the Bush School. I try to teach them to think like a spy so they can better anticipate and foil the actions of real spies. Here is the question: If you are an American government official with access to classified information and you want to sell that information to the Russians, how do you safely make the initial contact? The students explore several scenarios for mail, electronic, phone, or walk-in approaches inside the United States but eventually reject them as too risky because of FBI surveillance.[27] Their consensus is that it would be safer to make the first contact at a Russian embassy outside the country. Howard apparently disagreed or was too impatient. He made a successful approach to the Soviet consulate in Washington (eluding FBI surveillance if it was there) and was given money for a safer and lengthier meeting in Europe. In September 1984 Eddie took Mary and their son on a driving tour of Switzerland, Italy, and Austria. The evidence is clear that Eddie contacted the Russians during this trip, but the location of their meeting is unknown. My best guess is Bern, where we know he spent some time. In any event the operation was off and running and would continue with meetings in Vienna in April and August 1985. What Eddie gave to the Russians is hard to reconstruct because the other CIA spy, Aldrich Ames, was also active in this period and had access that overlapped with Howard's. I am convinced, however, at a minimum, that it was Eddie who betrayed Adolf Tolkachev and a sensitive CIA cable-tapping operation outside Moscow.[28]

Howard's payday from the KGB was relatively modest. His information was valuable, but he had no continuing access and his longevity as an agent was limited. He purchased a Rolex watch and some gold coins. He also opened a secret Swiss bank account, which the FBI later determined had a balance of $150,000. This was meager compensation for destroying his life.

On August 1, 1985, KGB officer Vitaly Yurchenko defected to the CIA in Rome. In his debriefings in Washington, Yurchenko reported that a former CIA officer, code-named "Robert," had volunteered his services to the KGB in the fall of 1984. Yurchenko did not know the true name of the agent, but the circumstances fit no one but Howard.[29] The CIA, now for the first time and very belatedly, had to come clean to the FBI about its troubled ex-employee, who was a clear CI risk. The CIA's decision to keep its dirty laundry in house for over a year was inexcusable.

The FBI put Eddie under surveillance in Santa Fe and obtained approval for a wiretap of his home phone. The bureau apparently failed to take seriously the CIA's warnings about how skilled Eddie was in surveillance detection thanks to his CIA training. As it turned out, it was child's play for Eddie to make the clumsy surveillance the FBI put on him. What ensued was a surreal standoff; Eddie knew he was under surveillance, and the

FBI had to bide its time because it did not have enough evidence to arrest him. The FBI finally decided to confront Eddie in the hope that he would confess or incriminate himself. He did not make any admissions at the first meeting but agreed to a follow-up meeting for further discussion. He had bought himself enough time to put together his escape plan. Eddie knew the hammer was about to drop, and he had to run for it.

On September 21, 1985, Eddie and Mary drove to a restaurant for dinner. On the way home, Mary, who was driving (not unusual because of Eddie's drinking), slowed down at a curve so Eddie could roll out of the car and hide in some nearby bushes. In his place an improvised dummy popped up in the passenger seat to give trailing FBI surveillance the impression that the seat was still occupied.[30] This escape plan was brilliantly executed but, as it turned out, totally unnecessary because the FBI did not even know the Howards had left home.[31] Mary completed the ruse once back in the house by phoning Eddie's psychiatrist to confirm an appointment. Since it was after hours and Mary knew the psychiatrist's answering machine would be on, she left a message that Eddie had prerecorded to fool the listening FBI into thinking he was at home. By the time the FBI figured out Eddie was gone, he was well on his way to Moscow via New York and Helsinki. Howard later claimed that he wandered around Europe for eight months before approaching the Hungarians in Budapest for help. For me, that story does not add up; it is far more likely that he went directly to the USSR through Helsinki.

The KGB received Eddie warmly, gave him an apartment in Moscow and a dacha outside the city, and arranged for him to have a nominal job as an economist. In August 1986 he was granted political asylum. Eddie gave a press conference in Moscow in September 1986 to thank the Russian people (in good Russian) for their "kindness" to him. Mary and their son, Lee, visited Eddie in Moscow, but Mary did not want to live there. She had admitted to the FBI that she had helped Eddie escape and was aware of some of the money he had received from the Russians, but she denied any direct knowledge of his espionage activity. She was never charged with a crime.

Mary knew that Eddie's dacha and other benefits in Moscow had been paid for by treason, perhaps even blood money, and she wanted no part of that. The KGB allowed Eddie to move to friendly communist Hungary, where the lifestyle was somewhat better than it was in Moscow. Mary and Lee joined him there. Lee attended the American School in Budapest. The American writer David Wise interviewed Howard in Budapest in 1987 and wrote an excellent book on the case.[32] Mary and Lee moved back to Minnesota after less than a year, and Eddie returned to Moscow. He settled into a lonely, drab, and alcohol-fueled lifestyle. Nothing much was heard from Eddie until 1990, when Americans in Moscow reported seeing a drunken American in a dollar bar, accompanied by burly looking bodyguards, making a nuisance of himself, offering to buy them drinks, trying to talk about American football, and basically acting like the pathetic slob that he was. Later that year Howard gave an interview to Diane Sawyer on ABC's *Primetime Live*. He tried to put the best face he could on his living conditions in Moscow, but the emptiness and desperation of his solitary existence were apparent.

I used to predict to my students that Edward Lee Howard, the contemptible CIA traitor, would die one day in a shabby Moscow hospital of some awful alcohol-related disease. I was not far wrong. The Russian news agency reported that Howard died on July 12, 2002, by falling down the stairs of his dacha. It is possible, I suppose, that he fell down the stairs drunk and broke his neck, but I am not buying it. Either he committed suicide and the Russians covered it up to avoid bad publicity, or President Putin simply got tired of supporting this pitiable American spy and wanted the apartment and dacha back.

LESSONS LEARNED

- The first principle of workplace counterintelligence was violated. Howard's preemployment screening, specifically his psychological assessment, polygraph, and background investigation, failed. His resentment of authority, vindictiveness, and susceptibility to alcohol and drug abuse should have been picked up by CIA security personnel and taken more seriously.
- The permissiveness concerning drug use that has crept into the screening process should be revisited. The current policy of "no drug use in the previous year" is too easy and opens the door for candidates to play the system by staying clean long enough to get in despite significant earlier drug use. The risk that the candidate will return to drugs after employment is too high. I do not advocate a return to the zero standard of the past, but I believe we have been too lenient in assessing the risk of past drug use. The same applies to alcohol. Howard was deceitful regarding drugs and drinking in

his application and on the polygraph, but he beat the screeners by providing slick half answers. The background investigation was flawed. Many of Howard's acquaintances and colleagues who knew him well could have given the investigators an earful about Howard's carousing, but they were apparently not contacted.

- Own the street (the Third Commandment of Counterintelligence) can lead to disastrous results if not observed. The FBI's surveillance of Howard in Santa Fe was sloppy in the extreme. I will concede that Howard's quiet residential neighborhood made discreet surveillance difficult, but that does not excuse how obvious the surveillance was or how ineffective it was in preventing Howard's escape. The FBI did not own the street; Eddie owned the street.
- There was a total breakdown in personal responsibility by Howard's CIA classmates and colleagues. Everyone around Howard saw that he was drinking too much, including when he was at the Farm and when he was in the pipeline. No one spoke up. Even worse is that Howard confided to a friend, a former CIA case officer, that he was considering walking in to the Russians in Mexico. The friend was no longer a CIA employee and had no professional obligation to step forward, but he had a moral and civic responsibility to do so, which he ignored.
- Do not be parochial (the Sixth Commandment of Counterintelligence) is an essential element of good CI. The CIA sat on its knowledge of a serious CI risk in its ranks for at least eighteen months before it informed the FBI, even though the FBI had clear primacy for CI matters inside the United States. It was only the defection of Yurchenko in August 1985 and his report of a mole inside the CIA that forced the CIA to come forward. I do not know what the FBI would have done with the information, but at a minimum it could have put a travel watch on Howard and monitored his erratic behavior.
- The CIA's firing of Howard in May 1983 was unnecessarily abrupt and demeaning. There was no reason to treat him with such disrespect. It is obvious Howard's behavior disqualified him from the sensitive Moscow assignment, but his access was such that counseling and reassignment to a nonsensitive job would have been better CI.

Larry Wu-Tai Chin

> Levity and passion have destroyed me. Pray for me. I pay with my life for my sins.
>
> —Alfred Redl, suicide note

There are many things about the Larry Wu-Tai Chin case that do not add up. First, how much damage did he really do to US national security? Second, why did the Chinese pay him so much for so many years when his access to sensitive classified information was marginal? Third, how was he convicted of several counts of espionage when the government failed to link him to the passage of any specific classified documents relating to national defense? And fourth, what motivated this quintessential American capitalist to betray for thirty-three years the country that had given him and his children so much?[33]

It was a typical Chinese operation—slow, cautious, and steady. Espionage is never boring, but this one came close. There was no flash, snazzy tradecraft, or historic breakthrough. The protagonist was thin, professorial, and totally unassuming in appearance. The operation just plodded along with little in the way of drama. Larry Wu-Tai Chin was born in Beijing on August 17, 1922. His well-educated father was successful enough to offer his family a comfortable lifestyle. Larry entered Yenching University in Beijing in 1940. He learned English while he was there and may have picked up some notions of Christianity. He later described himself as a Quaker, although there is no indication that he ever practiced a faith. Chin interrupted his studies to work briefly for the British military in 1943 and the US Army in 1944. Already he was capitalizing on his superior Chinese and English linguistic skills to make a name for himself as a translator. In 1947 Chin graduated from Yenching with degrees in journalism and economics.

It is not conclusive, but there are indications that Chin was soft-recruited by Chinese communist intelligence as early as 1948. At a minimum he was in contact with communist friends and perhaps even mentors. Chin never seemed to be a dedicated communist, but he may have opportunistically decided that the communists would win the civil war and that it would be to his benefit to show them friendship. We do not know if Chin applied for his job with the US consulate in Shanghai at the behest of an intelligence officer, but he was certainly positioning himself well for a future intelligence role when he started work at the consulate in October 1948. Chin moved with the US consulate to Hong Kong in April 1949, just ahead of the People's Liberation Army's takeover of Shanghai in May 1949.

Chin continued his job of translating articles from the Chinese press. He impressed his supervisors with his work ethic, the quality of his translations, and of course, his strongly professed anticommunist political views. Larry the Chameleon was already on full display. In 1949 Chin married his first wife, Doris, with whom he had three children before their divorce in 1959.

In 1951 the US government had an urgent need for Chinese interpreters to go to Korea to assist in the debriefings of captured Chinese prisoners. Although Chin had never been vetted and did not have a security clearance, he was considered reliable enough to participate in the program. He went to Pusan, Korea, in July 1951 and stayed for six months. In his work there, he learned where Chinese prisoners were held, what they were saying, and which ones were cooperating with American interrogators. Chin knew his Chinese communist friends would be interested in this kind of information.

It did not take long after his return to the US consulate in Hong Kong at the end of 1951 for Chin to act on this knowledge. He knew how to get back in touch with his soft recruiter from before, and now he had something more interesting than press translations to offer communist intelligence. Chin was paid $2,000 for his information on the Chinese prisoners in Korea. His appetite for money for secrets had been whetted. Chin's motivation for spying throughout his espionage career was primarily money, with the added benefit of a heightened sense of importance. He was somebody in the eyes of his Chinese handlers—and they paid well. Chin paid lip service to his support of the communist cause, but there will be ample indications later that ideology was never a major motivational factor for him.

It is curious that from the beginning Chin's intelligence association was with the Ministry of Public Security, the domestic law enforcement agency, rather than with the Ministry of State Security, the external intelligence collection agency. The explanation is probably as simple as the fact that Chin's first contacts were MPS officers who were not about to give up their promising source to the rival MSS. His intelligence value was reinforced when Chin parlayed his good evaluations at the US consulate into employment with the Foreign Broadcast Information Service (FBIS), a division of the Central Intelligence Agency, in May 1952. Chin worked as a translator for FBIS in Okinawa for the next nine years. One can only imagine the MPS's excitement at having a source inside the CIA, even though

Chin's work was essentially overt, that is, translating mainland Chinese newspapers, journals, and radio broadcasts. I have no doubt that the MPS exaggerated the importance of its penetration of the supersecret CIA to enhance its own prestige.

I suppose it would be of some value to Chinese intelligence to know the selection criteria used by FBIS in assigning articles and broadcasts to its employees for translation. The work, however, was unclassified; FBIS translations, which were of high quality and not easily obtainable from any other source, were made available to a wide range of US government customers.[34] Chin traveled to Hong Kong from Okinawa from time to time to see his family and to report to his MPS case officer. As was evident later, Chin was not above embellishing or even fabricating his reporting to excite the interest of his handlers and, presumably, to cajole more money from them. Chin's handling was upgraded in 1956, when Qiming Ou became his new case officer. Ou would be Chin's exclusive case officer until the operation ended in 1985.

This is how matters stood until late 1960, when Chin visited Hong Kong and informed Ou of an amazing new development: he was being transferred by FBIS from Okinawa to its office in Santa Rosa, California. For a relatively pedestrian intelligence service like the MPS, which had only limited experience in foreign espionage operations, this was a blockbuster. The MPS would have a human source in the homeland of the enemy and, not only that, inside one of its holy of holies, the CIA. In one fell swoop, Qiming Ou became a superstar case officer, and Larry Chin became a superstar agent. They both downplayed the fact that Chin would not have access to classified information in Santa Rosa, but they also realized that by moving to America, Chin would be on the path to US citizenship and eventually a security clearance. This process would take time, but the potential payoff made it an exciting prospect.

In January 1961 Chin moved to Santa Rosa and began his FBIS translation job. His three children by his first wife, Doris, joined him there. The Chin children, two sons and a daughter, were raised and educated in the United States; all three became doctors. In Okinawa, Chin had entered a relationship with a Chinese woman named Cathy who worked at the US Army base. Cathy moved to Santa Rosa in 1962, and she and Chin were married in 1963. It was a troubled marriage from the beginning. Chin was an abusive, sometimes violent, husband who had several affairs. Cathy was a submissive stay-at-home wife who was aware of his affairs but so dependent on him that she was afraid to break away.

The MPS chose not to handle Chin inside the United States. For one thing it had no expertise in sophisticated clandestine tradecraft. Moreover, it was standard modus operandi for the Chinese intelligence services to keep their agents within the bounds of explainable behaviors, that is, personal and business associations and travel that would appear normal to outsiders or investigators. Only rarely did the Chinese run the risk of conducting personal meetings in the United States, using dead drops and cache sites, or issuing agents compromising spy gear like one-time pads or secret-writing carbons. They feared FBI surveillance. Chin's handling by the MPS was true to this form. He maintained contact with his case officer by making regular trips back to Hong Kong and, on a few occasions, to Vancouver, Canada, or to Macao. In the meantime his clock was ticking as a permanent resident alien.

Chin became a naturalized US citizen in January 1965. Naturalized US citizens are generally, as a rule, eligible for US government security clearances after five years of citizenship. This was perfect timing for Chin. The FBIS closed its Santa Rosa office in 1970. As a valued US-citizen employee, Chin was transferred to FBIS headquarters in Rosslyn, Virginia, in the spring of 1970 and was granted a top-secret clearance. This was standard practice for the CIA; with virtually no exceptions, staff employees of the CIA are required to be cleared at the top-secret level. In Chin's case this sounds worse than it was. Even at its headquarters, the FBIS was not a repository of high-level state secrets or operational information. Its mission of translating overt foreign media remained central.

Chin passed a full-lifestyle CIA polygraph examination as part of his clearance process, even though he had been an active Chinese spy for approximately twenty years.[35] He had done something that presumably no other Chinese spy had ever done before: acquire US citizenship, obtain a security clearance, and work inside an organization of mythical proportions in Chinese eyes. Chin had access to some classified analytical reports on China that were made available to FBIS translators for background information. He was briefed on collection priorities. He occasionally interacted with analysts from other components who also worked on China. On at least one occasion, he may have assisted the CIA's clandestine service in translating into Chinese the instructions on how to operate spy gear. He was alleged to have passed vulnerability information on one of his CIA colleagues to Chinese intelligence, which may or may not have acted on it. But in the greater scheme of espionage, none of this amounted to much. Larry Wu-Tai Chin was no superspy.

Still, the documents that Chin stole, photographed, and passed to Chinese intelligence carried CIA markings and were technically classified. They could be easily portrayed to Chinese government recipients as juicy. After Chin's arrest, however, his investigators and prosecutors had difficulty identifying anything in the way of damaging classified defense-related information that he had compromised. In fact, one of the few linchpins of the government's case against Chin was his passage of information to the Chinese on the interrogations of Chinese prisoners of war in Korea over thirty years earlier.

Chin could easily take documents out of FBIS headquarters and photograph them in the comfort and security of his home. There were no controls. The challenge of delivering his spy products to the Chinese did, however, become more difficult. Now that Chin was an American citizen working for a sensitive agency, his travel outside the country was scrutinized more closely. The solution was for Chin to make regular trips to Toronto, where he passed his film to a Chinese courier. He first traveled to a US city near the Canadian border and then crossed the border unobtrusively as part of the large and routine daily stream of US visitors to Canada.

Chin's espionage settled into this easy, relatively safe, pattern for the next several years until his retirement from FBIS in 1981. Chin was considered a model employee and was given a CIA medal in 1980 for his long and dedicated service. Throughout this period, however, he was enjoying a comfortable vice-filled lifestyle thanks to the lavish payments he was receiving from his Chinese masters. He had a series of affairs, engaged in phone sex, gambled compulsively, and continued to abuse his wife. He financed his huge gambling debts in Atlantic City and Las Vegas by transferring money from his MPS-fed bank account in Hong Kong to the US casinos. Chin reportedly lost $96,000 in one trip to Las Vegas alone. Not all his lucre was lost on the gambling tables; he purchased twenty-nine rental properties with a book value of close to $1 million in the Washington, DC, and Baltimore areas. One prosecutor later referred to Chin as a "slumlord." Another outlet for Chin's illegal and entrepreneurial profits was to pay for the expensive American educations of his three children. Larry was leading an extravagant good life—and no one seemed to notice. He made occasional references to his friends and colleagues about apocryphal gambling winnings, but no one paid much attention. Even after his retirement, Chin tried to convince the MPS that he still had access to valuable information and pleaded for a continuation of his salary. Greed was one of his most consistent and salient personal traits.

Chin most likely would never have been caught if it had not been for good offensive counterintelligence: the CIA recruited a penetration of the MPS. As is often the case, the source's access was indirect; he could not identify the US spy by name. What he reported to the CIA in early 1982 was that the spy was a male of Chinese ethnicity employed inside the US intelligence community. The CIA scrubbed its own employees but found no one who fit the bill. It may have overlooked Chin because he had retired the year before. In October 1982 the CIA passed the source's information to the FBI, which immediately opened an investigation.

It was tough sledding. The US intelligence community is huge and contains many Chinese-American employees. The FBI's CI investigation was going nowhere until the CIA's penetration provided a tantalizing new tidbit in late 1982. The Chinese-American spy had traveled to China on a Pan Am flight on February 6, 1982, and had returned to the US on February 27, 1982. The FBI's CI analysts had to fight through some misleading information gaps and discrepancies but stuck with it and finally made a breakthrough. Even though the airline manifests for that period were no longer available, the US Customs declaration forms for San Francisco Airport, the port of entry for the flight from China, were. I would love to have been in the room when the FBI team combing through the forms found an American citizen with a Chinese name—and quickly verified that he had been employed by the CIA. It was Larry Wu-Tai Chin! These are unforgettable moments for any counterintelligence officer.

But it was still not game over. Chin's espionage career was dormant. The FBI could find no contemporaneous evidence that a crime had been committed. It put a tap on Chin's phone in April 1983, carried out physical surveillance of his movements, and examined his financial records. There were anomalies, of course, in his finances because of his outside income, but there was no smoking gun. Chin's wealth was far beyond what a mid-level employee of the federal government should have been able to accumulate, but the FBI was unable to link it to espionage activity. Moreover, the FBI was constrained in its investigation by two factors that are common in CI cases of this kind. First, the investigation must be conducted in a way that the target remains unaware that he or she is under suspicion. A tipped-off suspect can flee, cease all illegal activity, or destroy all compromising materials, including spy gear. Second, the source of any CI lead, in this case a penetration, is extremely vulnerable. If the Chinese learned that Chin had been compromised, the CIA's source would have been on a short list of suspects. It is close to a sacred moral obligation for any intelligence service to protect its sources, even at the cost of letting a guilty party stay in place until the source is out of harm's way.[36]

From January 1983, when the FBI matched Chin's travel to the then-unidentified spy, until November 1985, when the FBI finally decided to confront him, US counterintelligence was convinced that Chin was a traitor but could not make a prosecutable case. In its frustration the FBI considered luring Chin back to government employment with a contract with FBIS or some other agency that would require a clearance and a polygraph. Perhaps that would trip him up. But Chin wanted no part of that deal. There is no indication that he knew he was under suspicion, but in his mind, he was home free after a long and lucrative spying career. Why tempt fate? He could live comfortably on his US government pension and the MPS money he had stashed away and invested. He had pulled it off.

The FBI was down to its last resort: an interview of Chin. This was essentially an all-or-nothing gamble. The only way the FBI could conceivably make a case against Chin was if he incriminated himself or if a search warrant uncovered evidence of espionage. On November 22, 1985, the FBI knocked on Chin's door and, under the guise of requesting his help on a security matter concerning someone else at FBIS, got him to start talking. Chin seemed open and cooperative at first but soon realized to his shock and dismay that *he* was the target of the investigation. The FBI had to walk a fine line. If Chin refused to talk or, even worse, demanded a lawyer, the government's chances of gaining a conviction were probably nil. It was touch and go, but the FBI skillfully peeled off what it knew, specifically the details of Chin's trip to China in February 1982 to meet with his case officer, Qiming Ou. Chin reacted just the way the FBI had hoped, that is, by assuming that Ou had either defected to the US or been recruited by US intelligence. Chin knew that if Ou had betrayed him, he was a goner. His only hope was to make the best deal he could with the FBI through some form of limited cooperation. He did not want to alienate his FBI visitors by throwing them out. Maybe he could save himself by becoming a double agent or by convincing the FBI that he was sincerely trying to improve US-China relations. He talked on. Chin revealed the details of his initial recruitment, his reporting on the Chinese prisoners in Korea, and his passage of classified documents to the MPS. His story amounted to a voluntary confession of espionage against the United States. At the end of the interview, the FBI placed Chin under arrest.

A search of Chin's apartment turned up nothing of great significance. He had kept some copies of his performance appraisal reports, which were technically classified, and some low-level official documents, but there was no treasure lode of highly classified defense-related material. The FBI found the camera that Chin had used to photograph documents, his diary, and financial records that were incriminating, but the totality of the evidence was thin. Chin's confession was the critical piece of evidence.

On February 7, 1986, Chin was found guilty of seventeen counts of espionage, filing false tax returns, and failing to disclose foreign bank accounts. His sentencing was set for March 17, 1986. On February 21, 1986, while awaiting sentencing in the Prince William County Jail in Manassas, Virginia, Chin took a plastic garbage bag from the day room of the jail. When he returned to his cell, he removed his shoelaces, lay down on his bunk, tied the garbage bag over his head, and suffocated himself. He was sixty-three years old. Chin left no note, so the mystery remains as to why he killed himself. Was it shame for what he had done? Was it despair at the idea of spending the rest of his life in prison? Was it a sense of honor for having failed his Chinese masters? We will never know. What we do know, however, is that it takes incredible dedication and discipline to lie quietly in a bed and to suffocate oneself.

LESSONS LEARNED

- The Larry Wu-Tai Chin case had a successful outcome because of the First Commandment of Counterintelligence: Be offensive. If the CIA had not recruited the penetration of the MPS, Chin would probably never have been identified. Note to all case officers: in setting your recruitment priorities, put opposition intelligence officers at the top of your target list.
- The Fifth Commandment of Counterintelligence was critical in the Chin case: Do not ignore analysis. The FBI had the analytical expertise, patience, and discipline to grab the already stale lead of Chin's travel to China several months earlier, to correlate it to phone tap information, and to track down the one person who fit the available data. The Chin case was a showcase of painstaking and professional counterintelligence analysis.
- The Tenth Commandment of Counterintelligence proved essential: Never give up. When the CIA passed the source information to the FBI in late 1982, the counterintelligence task was like looking for a needle in a haystack. The CIA had already struck out in its own internal CI investigation. The travel information in early 1983

was a breakthrough, but the FBI still came up empty when it tried to prove that Chin was the spy inside the intelligence community. It poured a tremendous amount of resources into the investigation over the course of the next twenty-one months, with little to show for it. It would have been easy for the FBI to say, "It's just not there. Let's spend our time and resources on something better." But that would have been totally unprofessional counterintelligence. Never give up.

- Workplace counterintelligence failed miserably. Chin was never vetted properly. Even though he came from a CI criteria country, he was hired with virtually no background checks. His loyalty was assumed owing to his faithful service as a translator. His polygraph exam during his security clearance processing was bungled. Chin's heavy gambling was known to his FBIS colleagues, and his ownership of rental properties was public knowledge, but no one came forward to raise security concerns. Chin had no requirement to submit financial disclosure forms to the CIA. There were no exit controls at FBIS headquarters; anyone could walk out with anything, as Chin routinely did. FBIS may have considered itself a relatively nonsensitive facility, but that did not excuse it for its egregious workplace counterintelligence.
- Confrontational interviews have their place in counterintelligence but should be used as a last resort only. The risks are high. We have already seen how the FBI interviews of Souther and Howard backfired. In the Chin case, there may have been no choice, but I wonder if the FBI even considered a false flag alternative.[37] What is most important is that if the decision is made to confront, the confrontation must be meticulously planned and gamed out in advance to prepare for any possible twists that might arise. A psychologist knowledgeable of the Chinese psyche would provide valuable input in this planning process. The FBI's confrontation of Chin had some tense moments, to be sure, but in the end, it was expertly done and achieved its objectives.

Conclusion

> There is no traitor like him whose domestic treason plants the poniard within the breast that trusted to his truth.
>
> —Lord Byron

What still torments me and that should torment every currently serving US counterintelligence officer is that traitors are still out there. We have not caught them all. Who would not want to be part of such an important, challenging, and exciting profession? So, I say to all you men and women of the counterintelligence community, "Go get them. Right now." In the words of the immortal Sherlock Holmes, "Come, Watson, come. The game is afoot."[1]

Counterintelligence is an art. We start with an empty canvas and use the CI tools on our palette to paint our picture. Our tools are penetrations, surveillance, analysis, training, persistence, cooperation, and double agents. Our adversaries are smart and redoubtable, but we can beat them. And when we do, we bring to justice a despicable human being, a traitor to our country.

It is fitting, I think, that in Dante's *Inferno* the ninth and deepest circle of hell, Cocytus, is reserved for traitors. In Dante's vision traitors are locked in ice. Their heads are above the ice, but they cannot move their necks. They suffer unspeakably for their betrayals. I am no friend of traitors, but sending them to the ninth circle of hell might be extreme. Imprisonment in a supermax prison will be enough.[2]

There seems to be universal agreement that betrayal of one's country is an especially accursed crime and deserves merciless punishment. Joseph Addison's condemnation of traitors in *Cato, A Tragedy* is memorable in this regard:

Is there not some chosen curse,
Some hidden thunder in the stores of heaven,
Red with uncommon wrath, to blast the man
Who owes his greatness to his country's ruin?

A nation's well-being requires good counterintelligence. Too many Americans are sadly willing to betray us by selling out or by playing fast and loose with our security. They are doing grave damage, sometimes irreparable damage, to our country. They must be stopped. Counterintelligence professionals are dedicating their lives and careers to stopping them. Spy catching is love of country personified.

Appendix

The Counterintelligence Officer's Bookshelf

In the interest of promoting what I believe should be an essential home-study program for any current or future counterintelligence practitioner, I would like to offer my nominations for a professional reading list. Anyone who has read the following twenty-five books will, in my opinion, be counterintelligence literate and able to hold his or her own in any discussion of a CI topic.

1. Thomas Mangold, *Cold Warrior: James Jesus Angleton, the CIA's Master Spy Hunter*

No one has done a better job of elucidating the labyrinthine CI world that Angleton created than Mangold. This was the book I urged all my junior officers in the Counterintelligence Center to read, and I do the same now for my advanced intelligence students at the Bush School. It is a cautionary tale of how not to do counterintelligence.

2. J. C. Masterman, *Double-Cross System: The Incredible Story of How Nazi Spies Were Turned into Double Agents*

This is the classic account of Britain's brilliant double-agent operation during World War II. Every spy the Germans dispatched to England was captured and then either executed or doubled. The disinformation radioed back to Germany by these controlled spies played a decisive role in deceiving the Germans about the location of the D-Day landing site and other key strategic decisions. There is no need to look any further than Masterman for the definitive manual on how to conduct double-agent operations.

3. David C. Martin, *Wilderness of Mirrors*

Martin wrote the first serious analysis of Angleton and the conspiracy theories that he and his disciples hatched. The section on legendary CIA officer William Harvey is fascinating reading, but the real value of the book is its inside look at Angleton's misguided Counterintelligence Staff during a critical period of the Cold War.

4. Bill Gertz, *Enemies: How America's Foes Steal Our Vital Secrets—and How We Let It Happen*

I consider Bill Gertz the best US journalist writing today on the counterintelligence threats our country faces. His still relevant book is a wake-up call for Americans who have no idea what the Chinese, Russian, Cuban, North Korean, and even so-called friendly intelligence services are doing to us. He paints a gloomy picture of the state of US counterintelligence—and I am afraid he has it right.

5. Oleg Kalugin, *Spymaster: My 32 Years in Intelligence and Espionage against the West*

US counterintelligence can learn a lot by studying the memoirs of foreign intelligence officers who worked against us. Kalugin is surprisingly forthcoming in describing his many successes recruiting and handling American spies. I find his book the most reliable and readable of the many books written by former KGB officers. US spy catchers need to know how the other side thinks and operates. Thank you, Oleg, for your contribution to our CI literature.

6. Markus Wolf, *Man without a Face: The Autobiography of Communism's Greatest Spymaster*

Markus Wolf, who headed East German intelligence from 1953 to 1986, was perhaps the world's greatest spymaster ever. In my CIA career, I worked against many formidable adversaries; Wolf's Hauptverwaltung Aufklarung (HVA, Main Intelligence Administration) was the best. Wolf pulls no punches and makes no apologies in this well-written book. His account of his "Romeo spies" and the HVA's other sex operations is worth the price of the book alone.

7. Christopher Andrew and Oleg Gordievsky, *KGB: The Inside Story of Its Foreign Operations from Lenin to Gorbachev*

If there is a single book that can be called the bible of the KGB, this is it. British intelligence scholar Christopher Andrew and former KGB officer Oleg Gordievsky collaborated on this comprehensive and carefully researched study of KGB operations against the West for over fifty years. This book is the first place to look for reliable information on the KGB.

8. Christopher Andrew and Vasily Mitrokhin, *The Sword and the Shield: The Mitrokhin Archive and the Secret History of the KGB*

When Vasily Mitrokhin, a former KGB archivist, defected to the British in 1991, he brought with him 25,000 pages of secret KGB documents. When the British decided to allow selective publication of the material, the intelligence historian Christopher Andrew was the obvious choice to join forces with Mitrokhin for an explosive exposé. This is the often-shocking story of KGB domestic and foreign espionage operations, straight from the official files.

9. Allen Weinstein and Alexander Vassiliev, *The Haunted Wood: Soviet Espionage in America—The Stalin Era*

When Allen Weinstein died in 2015, the US lost one of its best intelligence historians. Weinstein and Alexander Vassiliev, a former KGB officer and writer, wrote a carefully researched and well-sourced overview of Russian intelligence operations in the United States in the 1920s, 1930s, 1940s, and 1950s. Any serious student of US counterintelligence should be conversant with these multifarious penetrations of the American government.

10. David Wise, *Molehunt: The Secret Search for Traitors That Shattered the CIA*

I am a big fan of American journalist David Wise, the author of numerous books on intelligence. In *Molehunt* he provides a savvy account of James Jesus Angleton's destructive search for a mole inside the CIA. Few nonprofessionals have the kind of astute feel for counterintelligence that Wise shows in this book.

11. Milt Bearden and James Risen, *The Main Enemy: The Inside Story of the CIA's Final Showdown with the KGB*

US counterintelligence met its Waterloo in 1985. Those of us who were there will never forget the anguish we felt as we lost one Soviet agent and technical operation after another. It was devastating. Milt Bearden of the CIA had a front-row seat for these horrible events and teamed up with journalist James Risen to describe what happened day by day.

12. Peter Wright, *Spycatcher: The Candid Autobiography of a Senior Intelligence Officer*

Wright served in MI5, the British counterintelligence and security agency, from 1954 to 1976, eventually reaching the rank of assistant director. His book caused a sensation when it first appeared in 1987. Although some of Wright's accusations are Angletonian in their paranoia and outlandishness,

I still recommend this book as a highly readable inside look at one of our country's major counterintelligence partners.

13. Stuart A. Herrington, *Traitors among Us: Inside the Spy Catcher's World*

We should never forget that the US military is a key counterintelligence player and stakeholder. No book I know of does a better job of illustrating this than Colonel Herrington's account of two major counterintelligence cases that he personally oversaw: Clyde Lee Conrad and James Hall. I am in awe of the professionalism, creativity, and meticulous attention to detail shown by Herrington and his team of CI specialists in these lengthy and complex investigations.

14. John Barron, *Operation Solo: The FBI's Man in the Kremlin*

For thirty years Morris Childs and his brother, Jack, were double agents for the FBI. This is an amazing story of how two American communists working for Soviet intelligence as couriers became disillusioned with communism and shifted their allegiance to the United States. Morris was so trusted by his Soviet masters that they welcomed him into their inner leadership circle as a valued confidante. With this kind of access, Morris became one of the best sources US intelligence had on Kremlin politics. The FBI's handling of this history-making double-agent case was masterful.

15. David Wise, *Cassidy's Run: The Secret Spy War over Nerve Gas*

The FBI, with the full support of US Army counterintelligence, pulled off a sensational double-agent operation by dangling an army sergeant, Joe Cassidy, to a Soviet GRU officer at a volleyball game at the YMCA in Washington, DC. The Russians took the bait and thus began a twenty-year deception designed to pass disinformation to the Soviets on US nerve gas research. In the course of the operation, the GRU exposed ten of its officers and three Soviet illegals. This was a textbook double-agent operation from beginning to end. The disinformation objectives were not fully met, but the planning and execution were nearly flawless.

16. Ronald J. Olive, *Capturing Jonathan Pollard: How One of the Most Notorious Spies in American History Was Brought to Justice*

I have included Olive's book on the list lest we forget that even close friends cannot be taken for granted when it comes to espionage. The decision by Israeli intelligence to recruit Jonathan Pollard, a loose cannon in every way, as a penetration of US Navy intelligence was shocking in its recklessness. Ron Olive headed up the Naval Investigative Service team that uncovered Pollard's spying and gathered the necessary evidence. His book takes the reader into the very heart of an incredibly challenging CI investigation.

17. Howard Blum, *I Pledge Allegiance: The True Story of the Walkers: An American Spy Family*

There are several books on the John Walker espionage case, but this is the one I like best. Walker was a US Navy warrant officer who passed communications key lists and other sensitive data to the KGB from 1968 to 1985. He was one of the most damaging American spies in our history. Blum does a superb job of analyzing the psychological makeup of Walker and his victimized family. He uses an innovative novelized approach to tell his story, but he stays scrupulously faithful to the facts.

18. Scott W. Carmichael, *True Believer: Inside the Investigation and Capture of Ana Montes, Cuba's Master Spy*

This book is the best example I can come up with of how good counterintelligence must be patient and tenacious. Ana Montes was the senior analyst on Cuba for the Defense Intelligence Agency—and also a spy for the Cuban DGI. Scott Carmichael led the DIA's investigative team, which overcame countless delays and roadblocks to get the job done and eventually caught her. This was US counterintelligence at its best.

19. Peter Earley, *Confessions of a Spy: The Real Story of Aldrich Ames*

This book is based on extensive interviews that Earley conducted with former CIA officer Rick Ames in prison. Earley allows Ames to reveal his sociopathic personality and to indict himself in his own words. I have known Rick for many years and can attest to the fact that Earley unmasks him. No CI education is complete without an in-depth understanding of this infamous case.

20. David Wise, *The Spy Who Got Away: The True Story of the Only CIA Agent to Defect to the Soviet Union*

The story of Edward Lee Howard, the CIA traitor who got away, is a case study of counterintelligence ineptitude. The CIA and the FBI both dropped the ball badly and bungled a case that should never have happened in the first place. I teach this case in my counterintelligence classes because it is so rich in teaching points. Wise, once again, gets it right.

21. Bryan Denson, *The Spy's Son: The True Story of the Highest-Ranking CIA Officer Ever Convicted of Espionage and the Son He Trained to Spy for Russia*

I was riveted by this account of how Harold James Nicholson, a CIA clandestine service colleague, let his personal problems and amorality get the better of him. Selling out to the Russians was certainly not the right answer for him, nor was dragging his son into spying. Denson has written a compelling counterintelligence treatise.

22. Robert Lindsey, *The Falcon and the Snowman: A True Story of Friendship and Espionage*

This book about the spies Christopher Boyce and Daulton Lee belongs on the list because it highlights the importance of tight security at US firms doing classified work for the US government. A twenty-two-year-old college dropout, Boyce got a job in California with the firm TRW, where he had access to top-secret information on CIA satellites and eavesdropping programs. He and his drug-dealing buddy Daulton Lee were soon in the business of selling this information to the KGB. It was incredibly easy for Boyce to bypass the lax security at TRW. My students and I find this book to be a gripping story of college-age espionage.

23. Ronald Kessler, *The Spy in the Russian Club: How Glenn Souther Stole America's Nuclear War Plans and Escaped to Moscow*

This is the sad saga of how a young Navy enlisted man, Glenn Michael Souther, became a spy for the KGB, did grave damage to US national security, and then escaped to the USSR. A key lesson from this case is that Russian intelligence does not hesitate to recruit futures, that is, young Americans with no immediate access to valuable information but with possibilities for the future. The Souther case was an embarrassment for US counterintelligence. I am sure both the Navy and the FBI would like a do-over, but there are none in counterintelligence.

24. David Wise, *Spy: The Inside Story of How the FBI's Robert Hanssen Betrayed America*

This is another must-read book. I am amazed that Robert Hanssen survived as a KGB and SVR spy at the heart of FBI counterintelligence for as long as he did without getting caught. Wise does an excellent job of analyzing the many facets of Hanssen's psyche, describing the tradecraft involved, and critiquing the investigation.

25. David Wise, *Tiger Trap: America's Spy War with China*

The counterintelligence literature on Chinese espionage in the United States has not kept up with the magnitude of the danger. One exception is Wise's *Tiger Trap*, a good starting point for anyone interested in learning more about America's number one counterintelligence threat. The focus of the book is on older cases, many from the 1980s, but the targets and tradecraft of Chinese intelligence have not changed.

* * *

That completes my recommendations for the Counterintelligence Officer's Bookshelf. My compliments in advance to future readers. If you read these twenty-five books, you will know your history and have earned the equivalent of a master's degree in strategic counterintelligence.

NOTES

Introduction

1. Kendall Myers, a former State Department official, and his wife, Gwendolyn, were arrested by the FBI in 2009 and charged with spying for Cuba for thirty years.

2. James M. Olson, "The Ten Commandments of Counterintelligence," *Studies in Intelligence*, no. 11 (Fall/Winter 2001): 81–87.

3. I have BA and JD degrees from the University of Iowa.

4. James M. Olson, *Fair Play: The Moral Dilemmas of Spying* (Washington, DC: Potomac Books, 2006).

Chapter 1: China

1. A co-optee in intelligence parlance is an individual who agrees to collaborate with his or her country's intelligence service and to perform services as directed. Co-optees are usually unpaid. The French intelligence service DGSE refers to its co-optees by the quaint term *honorables correspondants*.

2. Chi Mak is the subject of a case study in chapter 8.

3. Bill Gertz, "Cyber-attack on U.S. Firms, Google Traced to Chinese," *Washington Times*, March 24, 2010.

Chapter 2: Russia

1. KGB stands for Komitet Gosudarstvenoy Bezopastnosti; it was the Soviet external intelligence service from 1954 to 1991.

2. Oleg Kalugin, born in Leningrad in 1934, served as a KGB officer in the US under student, journalistic, and diplomatic covers. In 1974 he was named chief of counterintelligence for the KGB. He became an outspoken critic of Russian intelligence, moved to the United States in 1995, and became a US citizen in 2003. He is the author of the surprisingly candid memoir *Spymaster*, published in 2008.

3. Nicholas Shadrin, born Nikolai Fedorovich Artamonov, was a Soviet naval officer who defected to the United States in 1959. In the United States, he did valuable work for the Office of Naval Intelligence and the Defense Intelligence Agency. In 1966 he was approached by the KGB and recruited as a spy. Actually, he was a double agent for US counterintelligence for the next nine years. The KGB eventually suspected Shadrin's treachery, lured him to a meeting in Vienna in 1975, and killed him. Oleg Kalugin managed the assassination. Georgi Markov was a Bulgarian writer and political dissident who defected to the British in 1969. In England he worked as a journalist and broadcaster—continuing his harsh criticisms of the Bulgarian regime and Chairman Todor Zhivkov. The Bulgarian intelligence service, the DS, appealed to the KGB for help in silencing Markov. Oleg Kalugin was the KGB intermediary. In 1978 Markov was assassinated in London with a device supplied by the KGB, an umbrella modified to fire a deadly ricin pellet into Markov's leg.

4. FSB stands for Federal'naya Sluzhba Bezopasnosti; SVR is Sluzhba Vneshney Razvedki.

5. The Russian press reported in September 2016 that Putin intended to merge the SVR and FSB into a super intelligence service modeled after the former KGB. If that happens, it would be a massive consolidation of security functions into a single agency—presumably under Putin's direct control. That cannot be good news for the West.

6. GRU stands for Glavnoye Razvedyvatel'noye Upravleniye.

7. Forty armed Chechen militants stormed the Dubrovka Theater in Moscow on October 23, 2002, and took about 850 members of the audience hostage. They demanded Russian military withdrawal from Chechnya and an end to the war. On the morning of October 26, Russian special forces (Spetsnaz) attacked the theater in force, killing all forty militants but also many hostages from the effects of the gas pumped into the building before the attack.

8. There is no question that Berezovsky would have been at risk of assassination if he had remained in Russia. He was a prominent and vocal critic of Putin. Berezovsky fled to the United Kingdom in 2000 to avoid prosecution (or worse) for alleged financial crimes. The UK refused to extradite Berezovsky to Russia, despite repeated requests from Putin's government. There were unsubstantiated reports that hitmen had been dispatched from Russia to murder Berezovsky in London. He died of hanging in 2013—apparently a suicide, but under suspicious circumstances.

9. A *mokroye delo*, or "wet affair," is Russian intelligence slang for assassination.

10. Serious students of Russian intelligence operations should not fail to read Christopher Andrew's two excellent books based on the Mitrokhin material: *The Sword and the Shield: The Mitrokhin Archive and the Secret History of the KGB* (1999); and *The World Was Going Our Way: The KGB and the Battle for the Third World—Newly Revealed Secrets from the Mitrokhin Archive* (2005). Vasili Mitrokhin died in London in 2004 at the age of eighty-one.

11. Edward Lee Howard joined the CIA in 1981 and was selected for an undercover assignment in Moscow. Just before his departure for Moscow in 1983, he failed a polygraph test, which revealed recent drug use, alcohol abuse, and a disturbing incident of petty theft. Not only was Howard's assignment to Moscow canceled, but he was also abruptly fired by the CIA. In a rage of resentment, Howard contacted the KGB and began passing information on the CIA's operations in Moscow. In 1985 the Soviet KGB defector Vitaly Yurchenko identified Howard as a Russian spy. Using his CIA training, Howard evaded FBI surveillance and escaped to the USSR in September 1985. The KGB put him up in style in a dacha outside Moscow, where he died under mysterious circumstances in 2002 at the age of fifty. Was it an accident, as the Russians claimed, or did Putin get tired of supporting this now-worthless, drunken American spy? The Howard case is examined in more detail in a case study in chapter 8.

12. The exact amount of money Ames received from the KGB and SVR is hard to determine, but it is most likely \$3–\$4 million. One reason for the uncertainty is that Ames's Colombian-born wife, Rosario, who loved the high life and was a conspirator in Rick's treason, may have secretly deposited some of the money in Colombian or offshore accounts.

13. Nicholson was paid about \$300,000 by the SVR.

14. For a more extensive counterintelligence analysis of the Nicholson case, see a case study in chapter 8.

15. Canny intelligence and law enforcement organizations sometimes "misrepresent" themselves to gain a tactical advantage over a target. In the trade this misrepresentation is called a "false flag" operation. An operator, for example, might pose as a representative of another service, a criminal enterprise, a company, a private organization, or whatever else the circumstances require. Good services have specialists who have the right appearance, language skills, and acting ability to be convincing in their assumed roles. Nobody does false flag operations better than the FBI does.

16. Earl Edwin Pitts is the subject of a case study in chapter 8.

17. The KGB exercised tight control over the Russian Orthodox Church, and many priests and bishops actively supported the KGB as informants and operators.

18. For readers who want to know more about the Hanssen case, I recommend David Wise's book *Spy*, published by Random House in 2003. Very worthwhile also is the movie *Breach* (2007). The actor Chris Cooper brilliantly portrays Bob Hanssen, especially the latter's arrogance and dour personality. The Bonnie character is underdeveloped, and the role of the young FBI surveillant is exaggerated, but the movie does a commendable job of capturing the complexities, pace, and excitement of an actual CI investigation.

19. Illegals are buried inside a foreign country and have carefully concocted false identities and cover stories. They generally try to live and work inconspicuously in the target country, often posing as ordinary citizens of that country. Their intelligence missions include handling sensitive penetrations, spotting and

assessing recruitment targets, and eliciting whatever information they can from their circle of contacts. Illegals do not have diplomatic immunity and are subject to the full force of the law if they are caught.

20. The Russian illegals arrested in 2010 are the basis for the FX television series *The Americans,* the story of a Russian husband-and-wife spy team with two children posing as a typical American family. The creator and executive producer of the series is my former colleague and friend at the CIA, Joe Weisberg. The sixth and final season of *The Americans* is scheduled for broadcast in 2018. If you enjoy the spy genre, you will not be disappointed by tuning in. Be sure to start with season 1.

21. Edward Snowden is a highly controversial figure. He has limited formal education but is a self-taught computer genius. He worked for the CIA from 2006 to 2009 as a cybersecurity specialist. Beginning in 2009 he did contract work for NSA on behalf of his new employers, Dell and, briefly, Booz Allen Hamilton. Snowden had virtually unlimited access to information on NSA worldwide electronic eavesdropping programs. In June 2013 he began releasing to US and foreign journalists large quantities of classified NSA documents he had illegally downloaded from NSA databases. The Department of Justice charged Snowden with espionage on June 21, 2013, but he escaped to Russia two days later and was granted political asylum. The hundreds of thousands of documents that he made public caused irreparable damage to US intelligence capabilities and severely strained US bilateral relationships with numerous allies. Snowden is lionized by many Americans and non-Americans as a hero and courageous whistleblower. That is not my view. As of this writing, Snowden is still in Moscow, which I hope, short of eventual prosecution and punishment in the US, will turn out to be a prison of his own making.

Chapter 3: Cuba

1. DI stands for Dirección de Inteligencia. Until 1989 the official name of the main Cuban intelligence service was the Dirección General de Inteligencia, and many CI professionals continue to call it by that name today.

2. All intelligence services, including the CIA, benefit from individuals who come forward to volunteer their services as spies. These volunteers typically come in the form of walk-ins to an embassy or another official installation. Intelligence officers who receive walk-ins are trained to separate the wheat from the chaff and, if appropriate, to arrange for secure follow-up. The Russians call their walk-ins *dobrovoltsy*, or "goodwillers."

3. This gap in US law was corrected in 1982 with the passage of the Intelligence Identities Protection Act, which criminalized such disclosures. The act was passed in response to Agee's revelations.

4. Ana Montes is the subject of a case study in chapter 8.

5. One-way-voice-link (OWVL) radio messages are a staple of many of the

world's top intelligence services. The DGI is no exception. A radio station in Cuba transmits coded messages in five-digit number groups to agents in the United States. All an agent requires for this reliable method of communication is a short-wave radio receiver and onetime pads (OTPs) to decrypt the messages. The agent has assigned broadcast times and usually more than one frequency to account for atmospheric disturbances. Anyone who goes to South Florida today and knows where to look on the short-wave dial can hear a computer-generated female Cuban voice reading off long lists of numbers. OWVL messages are completely unbreakable if the OTPs are protected and used properly. The so-called number stations operated by the DGI and other intelligence services fascinate many amateur radio operators and would-be codebreakers. I hope they are having fun, because they are wasting their time trying to break the unbreakable.

6. The bible on DGI espionage and covert action is the comprehensive and authoritative study by my former CIA colleague and friend Brian Latell: *Cuban Intelligence, the CIA, and the Assassination of John F. Kennedy* (2012).

Chapter 4: The Ten Commandments of Counterintelligence

1. Iran has two intelligence services: the civilian Ministry of Intelligence and Security (MOIS), or VEVAK, its acronym in Farsi, and the intelligence branch of the Islamic Revolutionary Guard Corps (IRGC). Both VEVAK and IRGC operate inside and outside Iran using a variety of diplomatic, commercial, airline, banking, and student covers. VEVAK has over 30,000 employees and is known for its sophisticated and ruthless operations, including support for international terrorism. IRGC is much smaller, probably fewer than 5,000 employees, but it still competes effectively with VEVAK in human and technical intelligence operations.

2. Human intelligence is the bread and butter of any intelligence service. HUMINT officers have as their primary mission the spotting, assessing, developing, and recruiting of foreigners with access to secrets that our country needs. The epitome of a HUMINT success is the recruitment of an intelligence officer from a hostile country who can identify the Americans working as spies for that service.

3. Ronald Pelton was a former National Security Agency analyst who called in to the Russian embassy in Washington, DC, in 1980 and offered to sell classified information to the KGB. He worked for the KGB until 1985. He was convicted of espionage in 1986 and sentenced to life in prison, but he was released in 2015.

4. Larry Wu-Tai Chin immigrated to the US from China in 1961 and became a US citizen in 1965. He worked as a translator for the CIA, where he had access to classified information on US-China relations. Chin was recruited by Chinese intelligence while he was still in China and was paid well by the Chinese for his espionage services. He was convicted of tax evasion and espionage in 1986 but committed suicide in his cell before sentencing. Larry Wu-Tai Chin is the subject of a case study in chapter 8.

5. The ABC surveillance method was for many years the basic three-person

configuration taught by intelligence services, the military, and police departments. A is directly behind the target; B is farther back on the same side of the street; and C is across the street roughly parallel to B. A, B, and C rotate their positions frequently to mix things up.

6. Margarita Tairova was a well-trained GRU illegal designated for assignment to New York in 1957. US intelligence knew her identity thanks to an in-place penetration of the GRU, Pyotr Popov. When Tairova picked up US surveillance, she and her illegal husband fled New York and returned to safety in the Soviet Union. Popov came under suspicion and was eventually arrested. Edward Lee Howard, the former CIA officer, easily detected inexpert FBI surveillance on him in New Mexico in 1985 and escaped to Russia before he could be arrested and prosecuted.

7. Thomas Mangold, *Cold Warrior: James Jesus Angleton—The CIA's Master Spy Hunter* (New York: Simon & Schuster, 1991); David C. Martin, *Wilderness of Mirrors* (New York: HarperCollins, 1980).

8. Yuriy Loginov was a KGB illegal who walked into the US embassy in Helsinki in 1961 and agreed to work in place for the CIA, which he did for the next six years. Angleton was convinced that Loginov was a KGB plant and arranged for him to be arrested by the South Africans in 1967, interrogated, and then forcibly returned to the Soviet Union in 1969. Loginov's fate is unclear, but it could not have been good—particularly after the KGB became aware of his cooperation with the CIA. In a 1979 report, the CIA concluded that Loginov had been a bona fide KGB defector from the beginning. I consider Angleton's betrayal of Loginov one of the most shameful episodes in US counterintelligence history.

9. HONETOL was the frenzied and highly secret operation begun by Angleton in 1964 to find the mole inside the CIA that he was certain existed. Several loyal CIA officers had their reputations and careers destroyed by false suspicions and allegations. No mole was found. MHCHAOS was a CIA operation from 1967 to 1974 to uncover possible links between foreign governments and domestic unrest in the United States, particularly in the anti-Vietnam War movement. In his zeal to prove that these ties existed, Angleton authorized the CIA to carry out eavesdropping and other surveillance activities against US citizens inside the United States in clear violation of the CIA's charter. A similar program at the FBI was called COINTELPRO. Yuri Nosenko was a KGB officer who defected to the US in 1964. He was considered a fake defector by Angleton and was subjected to harsh interrogation and solitary confinement in an effort to break him. The CIA eventually recognized Nosenko as a legitimate defector, apologized to him for his abusive treatment, and compensated him financially for his ordeal. Most veteran CIA counterintelligence officers today, but not all, agree that Nosenko was bona fide. His case remains highly controversial. I am firmly in the camp of those who believed in Nosenko. I am appalled at what happened to him. He died in 2008.

10. Bryan Denson, *The Spy's Son: The True Story of the Highest-Ranking CIA Officer Ever Convicted of Espionage and the Son He Trained to Spy for Russia* (New York: Atlantic Monthly Press, 2015); David E. Hoffman, *The Billion Dollar Spy* (New York: Doubleday, 2015).

11. This is a good time to get the terminology straight. A clandestine service officer is correctly called an operations officer, an operator, a spy, or best of all, a case officer. We are never, ever, ever agents. Agents are the foreigners recruited by the CIA as human sources. I tell my students at the Bush School that it is a flunkable offense to call me or my operational colleagues at the CIA agents. This can be confusing because the FBI, DEA, and other government agencies call their staff officers agents, but this is not the case in our spy world. We are case officers and proud of it. When I die, I would be very happy if my simple epitaph were "Jim Olson—Case Officer."

12. Anatoly Golitsyn was a KGB major who defected to the United States in 1961. He initially provided some valuable CI information on Soviet intelligence penetrations of the West but then assumed the role of feeding Angleton the conspiracy theories and unproven allegations Angleton wanted to hear. Among Golitsyn's claims was that the KGB would send other defectors to discredit him. Angleton bought into everything Golitsyn said. When Nosenko defected in 1964, Angleton was certain he had been dispatched by the KGB, as Golitsyn had predicted. Golitsyn wrote *New Lies for Old* in 1984, a compilation of his conspiracy delusions. If you read Golitsyn's later rantings, you will learn that perestroika was a complete sham, a diabolical communist plot to deceive the West. Golitsyn died in 2008, but some of his adherents are still out there. One annoying "Golitsyn-ite" in San Antonio periodically harangues me for being blind to the Angleton-Golitsyn truth.

13. The fundamentalists were the tight-knit group of CI officers that Angleton handpicked as his closest collaborators. They became known in the CI literature as "fundamentalists" because of their hard-core views, extremist ideology, and unwavering loyalty to Angleton.

14. Once recruited, the dangle becomes a double agent.

15. The term "black hatter" probably originated in Western movies, in which the heroes wear white hats and the villains black hats. In the counterintelligence world, the term was adapted to describe CI officers who see everything in a bad light. If, for example, a complex CI question has two possible interpretations, one benign and the other malevolent, the black hatter will instinctively go with the latter. This usage became permanently embedded in the CI lexicon when it was noted that James Jesus Angleton was rarely seen outside without his trademark black fedora. Angleton was a classic "black hatter," literally and figuratively.

16. After CIA case officers have graduated from their operational training, they are assigned "a home base," i.e., a geographic division or center that will be responsible for managing their careers. It is commonplace for case officers to do "rotational" assignments in other areas, but their home bases will oversee their assignments, additional training, and promotions. Officers who reach Senior Intelligence Service status no longer have a home base; their careers are managed at the directorate level.

17. The Russian foreign intelligence service has had several different names. From 1934 to 1953, it was called the Narodnyy Komissariat Vnutrennikh Del. In

1953 it became the KGB, the name that lasted until the breakup of the Soviet Union in 1991.

18. Leopold Trepper, a Polish Jew and ardent communist, ran the clandestine espionage network Rote Kapelle for the Soviet GRU in Belgium and France from 1938 to 1942. He was arrested by the Gestapo in Paris in 1942 but escaped in 1943. After the war he was imprisoned in Russia (falsely accused of having collaborated with the Germans). He was released in 1955 and returned to his native Poland. He immigrated to Israel in 1975 and died there in 1982. Trepper's autobiography, *The Great Game*, appeared in 1975. I consider Trepper one of the greatest spies of all time.

19. Professional intelligence officers from all countries are trained to defeat hostile surveillance. The standard procedure is to conduct what is called a surveillance detection run (SDR) to determine the presence or absence of surveillance. An SDR consists of a succession of movements and stops around the city that are consistent with a normal daily pattern. If these routine activities do not identify surveillance, the officer pushes his or her actions into more provocative moves designed to flush out surveillance if it is present. Only after lengthy maneuvers of this sort—sometimes over two to four hours or more—will the officer declare himself or herself "black," i.e., free of surveillance, and proceed to the operational act. It is a life-or-death determination. There is no such thing as being *mostly* black. If there is any doubt whatsoever about being black, the officer is professionally and morally bound to abort the operation. Intelligence officers often speak about the exhilaration they feel when they know they are black and have an operational act to perform. Black is beautiful.

20. The KGB's misdirection ploy backfired. It was so artless that it reinforced in our minds the conviction that our problem *was* human—not technical.

21. The Foreign Intelligence Surveillance Act (FISA) of 1978 requires that the requesting agency, e.g., the FBI, provide probable cause to the FISA Court that the target of the proposed physical or technical surveillance is an agent of a foreign power. Mere suspicion or access to compromised information is insufficient.

22. In 1991 I tasked some of the Counterintelligence Center's junior officers with driving periodically around the CIA's parking lot to jot down the license plate numbers of luxury vehicles. The center then used Department of Motor Vehicles (DMV) records to identify the vehicle owners and to do a low-key investigation to determine if the owners had explainable income to justify such a purchase. The center's lawyers told me to knock it off because driving a certain kind of car was not considered sufficient probable cause for an investigation. When Rick Ames was arrested in 1994, I was bemused to learn that he had been driving a Jaguar XJ6 to work since 1991.

23. The Venona Project was a brilliant and highly sensitive program by the US Army's Signal Intelligence Service and the National Security Agency to decrypt intercepted Soviet intelligence communications. Most of the messages were from the period 1942–45. Venona revealed that approximately 200 American citizens were engaged in espionage on behalf of the Soviet intelligence services.

Chapter 5: Workplace Counterintelligence

1. A good intelligence service protects its operations and case officers by establishing a protective perimeter around key operational acts to identify hostile surveillance if it is present. These countersurveillance measures may include an observation post in the vicinity, technical monitoring to pick up opposition radio traffic, and most notably, additional personnel on the street to ensure the area is clear before the case officer arrives on the scene.

2. Jonathan Pollard is the subject of a case study in chapter 8.

3. Sharon Scranage was a CIA clerk assigned to the CIA station in Accra, Ghana. She became romantically involved with a local Ghanaian, a member of the local intelligence service, who pressured her to provide him with information on the CIA's activities in Ghana. Her unreported liaison with the Ghanaian and her spying on his behalf came to light only when she failed a routine reinvestigation polygraph in 1985. Scranage was sentenced to five years in prison. She and Harold James Nicholson are the subjects of case studies in chapter 8.

4. Lonetree is the subject of a case study in chapter 8.

5. Honey traps, sometimes called honey pots, are sexual entrapment operations. They have been used successfully by the Russians, Chinese, East Germans, and numerous other intelligence services to lure vulnerable targets into an illicit sexual relationship. In some cases the target develops an emotional attachment to the seducer. In others it is a brief fling. In both cases the target is manipulated or blackmailed into providing classified information. The CIA, alone among major intelligence services, chooses not to use sex in its recruitment operations. This is not because honey traps do not work—they do—but because the CIA considers them immoral. Some of our Western liaison friends find it curious, to say the least, that the CIA can approve targeted killings as morally acceptable but not seduction.

6. It is hard to apportion blame for the CIA's 1985 losses among Howard, Ames, and Hanssen because parts of their access overlapped and they were active during the same period. Still, I have no doubt that Howard compromised some of our most sensitive human and technical operations in the Soviet Union.

7. One of my officers told me that his one-night stand with a foreign woman did not require reporting because the relationship would not be "continuing." Nice try. Some US government employees and applicants are unsure if their social media contacts are reportable. That is harder, but I tell them that when in doubt, they should report the relationship. Otherwise, I say, they risk running into problems on the polygraph if they have not reported it.

Chapter 6: Double-Agent Operations

1. "Double Agent," *The Week*, August 12, 2016, 9.

2. Ben Macintyre, *Agent Zigzag: A True Story of Nazi Espionage, Love and*

Betrayal (New York: Broadway Books, 2007). Agent Zigzag was Eddie Chapman, a low-level criminal and scoundrel who was recruited as a spy by the German Abwehr but who shifted his loyalty to the British and became a double agent.

3. From 1935 to 1944, the Abwehr was headed by Adm. Wilhelm Canaris, who was executed in 1945 for his alleged involvement in the July 20, 1944, plot to kill Hitler. The Abwehr had many intelligence successes but was characterized by weak leadership and poor tradecraft. The SD (or Sicherheitsdienst) was the intelligence arm of the SS (Schutzstaffel; Protection Squadron) and the Nazi Party. The SD was headed first by Reinhard Heydrich, who was killed by Czech resistance fighters in Prague in 1942, and then by Ernst Kaltenbrunner, who was sentenced to death at the Nuremberg Tribunals and hanged in 1946. The SD, especially under Heydrich, was known for its barbarity and ruthlessness. Britain's success breaking the German codes encrypted on the Enigma machine was one of the greatest achievements in cryptanalytic history. The British codebreakers at Bletchley Park were led by Alan Turing and could not have done what they did without crucial help from Polish cryptographers who had broken an earlier version of the Enigma. The British success in breaking the German codes became known as "Ultra," one of the most closely guarded secrets of World War II.

4. Many intelligence services choose to have their first contact with an agent at an ICP. The case officer and the agent meet briefly at the ICP and then proceed separately or together to the meeting location (e.g., a safe house or a nearby café). Sometimes, particularly at night, they walk around the neighborhood together and conduct their business in that manner. A common variant is for the case officer to pick up the agent at the ICP in a vehicle and then carry out a "car meeting." ICPs are not chosen randomly. The service running the operation wants a location that is easily described and unmistakably precise so that the agent will not show up at the wrong place. Also, a good ICP will provide cover for the countersurveillance team. Ideally, an ICP will have countersurveillance support so that the case officer will not appear at the ICP until an all-clear signal is given. A typical ICP might be a statue, a theater, a church, a post office, a street corner, a clearly marked doorway, and so on. It is crucial that the agent and the case officer show up on time (i.e., "hit their window"), usually a matter of a few minutes. It is poor security and potentially suspicious for either the agent or the case officer to stand at the ICP alone for a lengthy period.

5. I am using the Russian term "residency" to describe the operational center of an intelligence service in a given country. The actual Russian word is *rezidentura*. The corresponding term for a CIA operational center overseas is a "station." The senior officer in charge of a residency is the *rezident*. The senior officer in charge of a CIA station is the chief of station (COS).

6. See David Wise, *Cassidy's Run: The Secret Spy War over Nerve Gas* (New York: Random House, 2000).

7. It is a common practice for intelligence services to recruit individuals who have natural access to target communities that are hard or impossible for the service's case officers to reach. These so-called access agents do not usually

have the means to provide hard intelligence information on their own, but by circulating socially or semiprofessionally among valid targets they can provide useful biographical and assessment information. The CIA, for example, might recruit a low-level Latin American diplomat to socialize with the local Cuban community. The FBI might recruit a bartender who works in a Washington, DC, bar frequented by Russian diplomats. The access agents pass on whatever they learn about the targets' personality, patterns, associates, attitudes, and vulnerabilities.

8. Erickson is the subject of Alexander Klein's book *The Counterfeit Traitor*, published in 1958, and the movie of the same name, starring William Holden, released in 1962. A quicker read is Stephan Talty, *The Secret Agent: In Search of America's Greatest World War II Spy* (Seattle: Amazon Digital Services, 2014) (Kindle). Erickson died in 1983 at the age of ninety-two.

9. This exquisite FBI double-agent operation is the subject of John Barron's *Operation Solo: The FBI's Man in the Kremlin* (Washington, DC: Regnery, 1996). It is required reading for every counterintelligence professional.

Chapter 7: Managing Double-Agent Operations

1. John Walker was a US Navy communications specialist who spied for the Soviet KGB from 1968 to 1985. He gave the Russians the US Navy cryptographic key cards that enabled them to read all or most of the classified navy message traffic during that period. Walker died in prison in 2014.

2. Ronald Kessler, *The Spy in the Russian Club* (New York: Charles Scribner's Sons, 1990). Souther is the subject of a case study in chapter 8.

3. When I served in Vienna in the 1980s, I felt a shudder whenever I walked or drove by the Votivkirche—because that was where a brave and dedicated American double agent met a horrible fate.

Chapter 8: Counterintelligence Case Studies

1. The best book on the Lonetree case is Rodney Barker, *Dancing with the Devil: Sex, Espionage, and the U.S. Marines* (New York: Ivy Books, 1996). My only problem with Barker's otherwise excellent work is that in his account of the ambassador's Christmas party he refers to me as "a tweedy professorial type." I object.

2. I do not know what the numbers are today, but when I served in Moscow many years ago, the US embassy employed over three hundred Russians. Many of them were attractive young women.

3. I am indebted to my friend and former colleague Col. Stuart Herrington, who wrote the definitive account of the Conrad case: *Traitors among Us: Inside the Spy Catcher's World* (Novato, CA: Presidio Press, 1999). Much of this case study is based on this book. Stu assumed command of FCA in January 1988 and built

on the superb work of his predecessor, Col. Bob Lunt, and the entire FCA staff to successfully manage the complex end game of the Conrad operation.

4. The Naval Investigative Service (NIS) was renamed the Naval Criminal Investigative Service (NCIS) in 1992.

5. Surreptitious entries or "black bag jobs," as the FBI calls them, are works of art. They require meticulous planning, surveillance, locksmiths, expert searchers, photographers, safecrackers, alarm technicians, and computer specialists. It is the height of counterintelligence rapture to be standing in a target's home or office in the middle of the night with the safes, desks, drawers, and computers open and within reach. Obviously, nothing can be left out of place; there can be no trace that anyone was there. I recall that a surreptitious entry against a US installation overseas was compromised when the Americans who entered the office the next morning detected a lingering, pungent body odor. The opposition team should have showered before it entered.

6. Scott W. Carmichael, *True Believer: Inside the Investigation and Capture of Ana Montes, Cuba's Master Spy* (Annapolis, MD: Naval Institute Press, 2007).

7. Oliver "Buck" Revell and Dwight Williams, *A G-man's Journal: A Legendary Career in the FBI—From the Kennedy Assassination to the Oklahoma City Bombing* (New York: Simon & Schuster, 1998).

8. I think this is a spurious suggestion, but it is a fact that both the FBI and the CIA have a large number of Latter-Day Saint (LDS) employees. LDS applicants have fared well in the application process for national security jobs because of clearable backgrounds, overseas experience as missionaries, and foreign language ability.

9. It is not uncommon for Russian and American intelligence officers to meet in the field, sometimes under the guise of their respective covers, sometimes without even the pretense of being anything other than spies. These meetings can be an awkward pas de deux, in which both parties are blatantly probing the other for vulnerabilities that could lead to a possible pitch.

10. My instructors at the Farm were first-rate. How could I ever forget, for example, the many hours in the student lounge at night listening to the legendary CIA case officer George Kisevalter regale us trainees with accounts of his handling of the Russian spies Pyotr Popov and Oleg Penkovsky? Intelligence training does not get any better than that.

11. Ames was probably paid close to $4 million. Some of the money may have been stashed in Colombia, the native country of his wife, Rosario.

12. For years reinvestigation polygraphs of CIA employees were scheduled every five years. That interval proved to be too predictable for would-be spies, so a new policy of "random" polygraphs was established. Conceivably, an employee's number could come up for a reinvestigation polygraph at any time. This change was obviously a boon for counterintelligence investigators, who could manipulate "randomness" to get a polygraph of a subject of CI interest at any time without revealing an investigative purpose.

13. I am appalled. Did he even do an SDR before mailing the letters? I feel sorry

for Nicholson's trainees at the Farm if this was the kind of tradecraft he taught them.

14. Bryan Denson's *The Spy's Son* (New York: Atlantic Monthly Press, 2015) is the definitive and meticulously researched story of the Nicholson case, on which much of this summary is based, along with press reporting and court records. Denson focuses particularly on the pathetic sequel to Nicholson's arrest, that is, his recruitment from prison of his son to carry on his espionage activity with the SVR.

15. Sec. 215. Access to Certain Business Records for Foreign Intelligence and International Terrorism Investigations. (a)(1) The Director of the Federal Bureau of Investigation or a designee of the Director (whose rank shall be no lower than Assistant Special Agent in Charge) may make an application for an order requiring the production of any tangible things (including books, records, papers, documents, and other items) for an investigation to protect against international terrorism or clandestine intelligence activities.

16. I am indebted to one of my favorite intelligence writers, Ronald Kessler, for his definitive account of the Souther case: *The Spy in the Russian Club* (New York: Scribner, 1991).

17. OTPs are small pieces of paper that contain random numbers, usually in four- or five-digit groups. An agent uses OTPs to decipher encrypted OWVL messages. An OTP encryption system is absolutely unbreakable if the following three conditions are met: (1) the numbers are perfectly random (not a trivial mathematical challenge); (2) the OTPs have not fallen into the wrong hands and been copied; and (3) the same OTP has not been used to encipher more than one message. OTPs must be carefully concealed by the agent; possession of OTPs is prima facie evidence of espionage.

18. DIS is now known as the Defense Security Service (DSS). In 2004 personnel security investigations for federal employees, including for the Department of Defense, were consolidated under the Office of Personnel Management. DSS remains responsible for security at DOD contractor firms and for security awareness programs.

19. The KH-11 went into service in 1976 and was the first US satellite to use digital real-time imagery.

20. Ron Olive, a consummate CI pro, wrote the definitive account of the Pollard investigation: *Capturing Jonathan Pollard: How One of the Most Notorious Spies in American History Was Brought to Justice* (Annapolis, MD: Naval Institute Press, 2006).

21. The CIA's policy on drug use has evolved in keeping with changes in societal norms. Up until the early 1970s any use of a controlled substance was considered disqualifying. By the late 1970s, however, exceptions were being made. A candidate's drug history was evaluated in terms of which drugs he or she had used, how recently, how often, and whether any dealing was involved. Pollard was disqualified because of his heavy drug use over an extended period. Today, no applicant will be considered who has used drugs in the past year, but many current employees have been cleared despite significant drug histories.

22. To be fair, the US government has an impossible task in conducting thorough background investigations of the 3.1 million employees and 900,000 contractors who hold security clearances. Consequently, many, if not most, of background investigations today are superficial.

23. In 2005 Lawrence Franklin, an analyst at the Department of Defense, was convicted of passing classified information to two AIPAC officials.

24. "Flaps and seals" is the handy skill of opening letters and packages without leaving a trace. It is particularly useful for parents of teenaged children—just kidding (maybe).

25. My wife, Meredith, and I went through the Moscow pipeline just a few years earlier. The pipeline is a tough but intensely exhilarating experience.

26. The staples of clandestine tradecraft, as practiced by the major intelligence services of the world, are discreet personal meetings, car pickups, dead drops, brush passes, caches, signal sites, and electronic exchanges. The pipeliners already know the basics of these techniques because of their time at the Farm, but they are taken to a new level of expertise for their denied area assignment.

27. However, several American spies made successful, undetected contact with Russians in the US. Some that immediately come to mind are Aldrich Ames, Robert Hanssen, Richard Miller, Ronald Pelton, and John Walker.

28. Adolf Tolkachev was a Soviet avionics expert who worked for the CIA in Moscow from 1979 to 1985. He provided incredibly valuable intelligence on Soviet military aircraft radar systems. He was arrested in 1985 and executed in 1986. Tolkachev is the subject of David Hoffman's book *The Billion Dollar Spy* (New York: Doubleday, 2015). The cable-tapping operation in Moscow, code-named CKTAW, involved CIA officers (including myself) gaining access to the cable by going down a manhole on the outskirts of Moscow and installing a tap. CKTAW ran for five years before it was compromised in 1985.

29. I will never forget the day in August 1985 when Burton Gerber, chief of the Soviet East European Division, came to my office and said simply, "It's Eddie." We did not know yet about Ames's treachery, but thanks to Yurchenko, we had at least a partial explanation for our losses in Moscow. It was devastating.

30. This technique, called a jack-in-the-box (JIB), was part of the training Eddie and Mary received in preparation for their assignment to Moscow.

31. The FBI admitted later that losing Eddie the night of his escape was "human error."

32. David Wise, *The Spy Who Got Away* (New York: Random House, 1988). Wise, as always, gets it right.

33. The definitive account and analysis of the Chin case has been provided by the Canadian writer and former intelligence officer Tod Hoffman: *The Spy Within: Larry Chin and China's Penetration of the CIA* (Hanover, NH: Steerforth Press, 2008). I assign this book to my counterintelligence students because of its operational and psychological insights into how Chinese intelligence services operate.

34. FBIS was rolled into the Open Source Center under the director of national intelligence in 2005. Its headquarters is in Reston, Virginia. In my career I found

FBIS translations extremely helpful as an aid in following foreign news outlets in areas of interest to me.

35. I do not believe the MPS trained Chin in counterpolygraph measures. For one thing neither Ou nor anyone else in the MPS would have had the expertise to do that; for another, countermeasures do not work anyway. A skilled operator will easily see through them. Chin beat the machine, in my opinion, because of operator failure, an impassive personality that flattened his affect and made him a poor reactor, a language barrier, or some combination of the above. He was tested in English, a language he knew well, but one with nuances of meaning that might not have affected him physiologically the way they would a native speaker.

36. The CIA's penetration was Zhensan Yu, chief of the Foreign Affairs Bureau of the MPS. The FBI was punctilious about source protection throughout the investigation. In fact, it did not move against Chin until the CIA's source had safely defected to the US in 1985.

37. It would have been interesting to see how Chin would have reacted if a native Mandarin speaker had shown up at his door with an envelope full of cash and the following message: "I come from Ou Qiming with urgent instructions from him that we reactivate you."

Conclusion

1. Sir Arthur Conan Doyle, *The Adventure of the Abbey Grange.*

2. Supermax (super-maximum security) prisons are the harshest regime in the US penitentiary system. They typically house the most heinous and dangerous criminals. Supermax inmates are in solitary confinement and have virtually no contact with other inmates or guards. They are fed through a slot in their cell door and are allowed out only one hour a day for solitary exercise in a small windowless room. The best known of the supermax prisons is Florence ADX in Colorado.

INDEX